# From Baddeck to the Yalu
## Stories of Canada's Airmen at War

### By Norm Shannon

ESPRIT DE CORPS BOOKS
OTTAWA, CANADA

## ABOUT THE AUTHOR

Norm Shannon flew 52 operations with #180 Mitchell Squadron during WWII and has since retained an interest in the impressive role of Canadians in aerial warfare. Some 20 years as the Royal Canadian Legion's public relations director also gave him grassroots insights into the contribution of army veterans. He produced seven films on military history and has authoured hundreds of published articles. It is his hope that this somewhat informal approach to history will provide a bridge with our past in the Year of the Veteran.

**1ST PRINTING – OCTOBER 2005**

**NATIONAL LIBRARY OF CANADA CATALOGUING IN PUBLICATION DATA**
Shannon, Norman, 1921 -
From Baddeck to the Yalu : stories of Canada's airmen at war / Norm Shannon
Includes index.
ISBN 1-895896-30-4
1. World War, 1939-1945--Aerial operations, Canadian--History--Anecdotes. 2. World War, 1914-1918--Aerial operations, Canadian--History--Anecdotes. 3. Korean War, 1950-1953--Aerial operations, Canadian--History--Anecdotes. 4. Canada. Royal Canadian Air Force--Airmen--History--Anecdotes. 5. Canada. Royal Canadian Air Force--Biography--Anecdotes.   I. Title.

UG635.C2S533 2005          358.4'00971'0904          C2005-906613-X

Printed and bound in Canada
***Esprit de Corps Books***
1066 Somerset Street West, Suite 204
Ottawa, Ontario, K1Y 4T3
1-800-361-2791
www.espritdecorps.ca / espritdecorp@idirect.com
From outside Canada
Tel: (613) 725-5060 / Fax: (613) 725-1019

# From Baddeck to the Yalu
## Stories of Canada's Airmen at War

On the day the war ended in 1918, Redford Mulock was on a somewhat bizarre assignment. While final negotiations were underway and troops on either side of the line were on stand-down, Lt-Col Mulock's newly formed bomber group was on standby. If the peace talks failed, Mulock's bombers would strike Berlin, in the German capital in the first raid of the war. The fact that the task was assigned to the Winnipegger was a tribute to all Canadians who had served with dignity but without recognition in the British Flying Services.

Although half of the top 10 British aces were Canadian, they were literally aces without an air force. Prime Minister Robert Borden has the distinction of being the only leader in history to wait until after a war to form an air service. He briefly pulled two squadrons of outstanding airmen together late in 1918, but they lacked a defined mission and were disbanded when the British asked Canada to pay costs.

During WWII, the Canadian government took a more aggressive approach in establishing a Canadian identity even though hundreds of individual Canadian airmen were in action from day one. The British Commonwealth Air Training Plan provided 131,500 Commonwealth aircrew, over half of them Canadian. Although a Canadian Bomber Group was formed in the RAF, more Canadians flew as individuals with RAF squadrons.

They were the first and the last, and their exploits have been virtually lost to Canadian history. Albert Prince was killed in action five days before his country declared war. Hammy Gray was shot down in a daring attack six days before the end of the Pacific War. That afternoon Lt Gerald Anderson of Trenton died trying to land a crippled aircraft on Gray's carrier. The personal side of history can be a throat-grabber.

# DEDICATION

Dedicated to the thousands of young Canadians who flew for freedom and the men and women who kept them flying. Although the clouds of yesterday mourn their passing, may their devotion to duty inspire our uncertain future.

# ACKNOWLEDGEMENTS

The author wishes to recognize the work of Ron Dodds, Syd Wise and Les Allison in tracing our aviation heritage. For further reading on this subject, I recommend *The Brave Young Wings* by the late Mr. Dodds, Canadian Airmen in the First World War by Mr. Wise and Mr. Allison's Canadians in the RAF.

As a former airman with the 2nd TAF, I have the highest respect for Bomber Command crews. Although some portions of this book question early Bomber Command efforts, I am talking organization, training and equipment. In spite of early deficiencies, crews were magnificent from the first day of the war.

My special thanks to Katherine Taylor, Julie Simoneau and the staff at *Esprit de Corps*, including Bill Twatio, Diana Rank, Darcy Knoll, Sheila Muxlow, for their work in giving life to the ramblings of an old vet.

**ABOVE:**  *The only man with any flying experience in the Aviation Corps was Frederick Sharpe, who was later killed after he transferred to the Royal Flying Corps after Canada's Aviation Corps was abandoned.* (DND/PL-39933)

**OPPOSITE PAGE**: *Although Casey Baldwin had flown almost a year before, John McCurdy made the first flight in Canada with the Silver Dart at Baddeck, Nova Scotia, in February 1909. It climaxed two years later in which a few Canadians made significant inroads into world aviation, but failed to gain government support.* (NAC/PA-61741)

# ✍ OUR BRIEF AVIATION CAMELOT

*AFTER CENTURIES OF EXPERIMENTING* with kites and balloons, man bounced and spluttered into the air under powered flight at Kitty Hawk, North Carolina, on a blustery day in December 1903. Orville Wright climbed onto the wing of the Wright Flyer while his brother, Wilbur, steadied the wing. The machine trembled on skids at the top of a 150-foot track. When Orville dropped a weight from a derrick, the Flyer lurched down the track. Brother Wilbur ran alongside as the machine flirted with the air at 8 m.p.h. Then it rose to six feet and Wilbur snapped a stopwatch, which started the clock on powered flight.

Their achievement and subsequent flights, although secretive, set off a flurry of intrigue in France's elegant Aéro-Club some two years later. The club was awash with money and nationalism as members recoiled in shock at the thought of some American developing the first successful aircraft. Ernest Archdeacon, a Britisher, became a leading promoter of French aviation. In March 1904, he created the Grand Prix d'Aviation and matched French oil magnate Henry Deutsch de la Meurthe by putting up half of the $10,000 prize for the person who would be the first to fly a kilometre. Apparently, the Wright brothers did not subscribe to Paris newspapers because it took four years for someone to claim the prize and by then Orville and Wilbur Wright were flying 28 miles. The Wright brothers were, however, trying to sell their machine to the U.S. government and they had no intention of exposing secrets to the competition. Although Wilbur eventually went to France where he stunned aviation circles, he was hardly the Lee Iacocca of aviation and refused to be rushed into public flights.

On January 13, 1908, Henry Farman covered one kilometre, won the Grand Prix d'Aviation, and introduced powered flight to Europe. What isn't generally recognized is how close two Canadians were to world-class aviation at the time. Two months after Farman's first European flight, on March 12, Toronto native Frederick "Casey" Baldwin flew the Red Wing off frozen Lake Keuka in New York state to become the first person in the British Empire to fly under power. Although Baldwin's flight was only 319 feet, Glenn Curtiss flew the Red Wing a measured mile that summer.

The Red Wing was the first product of the Aerial Experiment Association (AEA), a group founded in 1907 by Alexander Graham Bell in Baddeck, N. S. The group included two recent engineering graduates from the University of Toronto, John McCurdy and Casey Baldwin, and two Americans, Glenn Curtiss and Lieutenant Thomas Selfridge of the U.S. army. After a period of experimentation at Baddeck, they moved to Hammondsport, New York, where Curtiss had an engine repair shop.

For a brief moment the engineering and flying skills of the AEA challenged the Wright brothers. Although Orville and Wilbur had never been very outgoing, at one point they had presumably given Selfridge design information which they later regretted. When Curtiss sold an AEA "experimental" machine, a dispute over patents would occupy lawyers for a decade.

Events took a bizarre twist on September 17, 1908 when Selfridge, a member of the aeronautical board that was appraising a Wright machine in U.S. army acceptance trials, was killed. Selfridge had joined Orville on a test flight of the Wright Flyer, but difficulties with the plane's propeller proved deadly when the Flyer nose-dived into the ground. Orville survived but was hospitalized for three months. Selfridge, however, died within hours of the crash, earning him the dubious distinction of being the first man to die in powered flight.


## AIRBORNE AT BADDECK, GROUNDED AT PETAWAWA

Following Bell's initial designs, the Silver Dart, a gasoline-powered biplane, was built by the AEA. Hauled out onto the ice with John McCurdy at the controls, the Silver Dart rose into the air and flew three quarters of a mile on February 23, 1909. It was the first flight in Canada. The Aerial Experiment Association was disbanded in the spring of 1909. That same year, McCurdy and Baldwin set up their own partnership, the Canadian Aerodrome Company, in Baddeck. The Canadian Aerodrome Company produced two more aerodromes whose flights attracted international attention. (For some reason an "aerodrome" was then what you landed and not *where* you landed.) As for Glenn Curtiss, he formed his own company. While the French had made great strides in aviation, it was Curtiss who won a major international race, the Gordon Bennett trophy, at Rheims in 1909. With an average speed of 46.5 m.p.h., his Golden Flyer was clocked at 50 m.p.h. in local trails.

While the Silver Dart may not have been the most efficient aircraft of its day, it was world-class. And based on its success, McCurdy tried to interest politicians in an arrangement whereby he would train pilots for each aircraft purchased. Colonel W. Rutherford eventually convinced the military council to arrange for demonstration flights by McCurdy and Baldwin at Petawawa. But even before the event, there were strange hints as to the outcome. The night before the demonstration, the deputy minister of militia and defence told the *Ottawa Citizen*: "We must wait a great many years yet and experiment much more before the true use of these machines can be demonstrated." At Petawawa, the army provided lumber for a shed, but little was done to improve the condition of the field, which was spotted with sandy knolls.

In fairness to the assembled politicians, what followed in the demonstration was not impressive. McCurdy got off the ground four times and did a brief circuit, but on the final landing the nose wheel hit a mound and the machine was wrecked. The aviators unpacked a second machine that had never been flown. McCurdy took off on another brief yet unimpressive flight, which ended in switch failure. Most of the official party hurried back to the joys of Ottawa while the airmen spent the night repairing the switch. McCurdy's flight the next morning was brief, ending in another crash. It was a defining moment for Canadian aviation as politicians dismissed McCurdy's original proposal.

Sir Frederick Borden, the minister of Militia and Defence from 1896 to 1911, explained that the British War Office would be guiding the Canadian government in aviation matters. Due to a lack of government support, McCurdy and Baldwin were forced to close the doors at Baddeck in 1910. The lack of vision and political will brought an end to Canada's aviation Camelot and the country lost a skilled design and flying team — a process that would be repeated 48 years later when myopic politicians scrapped the Avro Arrow.

## SAM'S AIR FORCE INVADES CANADA

As for the British War Office guiding Canada's aviation destiny, when war came in 1914 it got off to a slow start according to Canada's then Militia and Defence Minister Sir Sam Hughes, whose patience with the mother country was exhausted by the time Britain went to war. Hughes' secretary entered the office the day prior to the ultimatum to Germany to find his boss abusing a folded copy of the *Ottawa Citizen* while complaining, "They're going to skunk it!"[1] Hughes ordered that the Union Jack be lowered from his headquarters, and when the military council met for a critical meeting, stunned members were fascinated by the offending flag folded on his desk.

"Complex" is a charitable word in describing Sam Hughes; Governor General Lord Connaught allegedly considered him insane. Elected to Parliament in 1892, Hughes needled Sir Wilfrid Laurier into sending troops to South Africa during the Boer War in 1899. Somehow, he worked his way to South Africa where he was soon under a cloud for his public criticism of senior British commanders. Upon his return to Canada, he complained that he was never awarded the two Victoria Crosses he felt he won on the battlefield.

Canada declared war on August 4, 1914. As minister of Militia and Defence from 1911 to 1916, Hughes littered Canada's war effort with disasters like the Ross rifle fiasco, yet achieved a few notable successes. And his meddling in the war effort started at an early date. National defence had a mobilization plan that called for troops to assemble at Petawawa where a military training camp had been established in 1905. Hughes figured Petawawa was too far from the ocean and sent 226 night telegrams to militia commanders telling them to report to Valcartier instead, a place 16 miles northwest of Quebec City where nothing existed. He then got in touch with his old friend, lumber baron Sir William Price, and asked him to build a camp that would accommodate over 30,000 men. Within six weeks, 35,000 men were under canvas at Valcartier, which had undergone a remarkable transformation.

An incredible volume of natural confusion surrounded the arrival of so many untrained men plucked from all corners of the Dominion which then had a population slightly in excess of 7.2 million, and Hughes' daily presence and his "come one come all" invitation added black-comedy twists to the confusion. Units came as they were, which meant that one reported with 11 officers, 14 other ranks and one horse. Some units were loaded with colonels but had no captains. A daily monopoly game developed where organizers offered three colonels for a captain, or two captains for a good horse.

About three weeks before the contingent was due to sail a smooth-talking gent from Galt, Ont., came into Hughes' tent with a proposal to form an air force. Ernest Janney probably had never seen an aircraft, but Hughes made him an instant captain and provisional head of the Canadian Aviation Corps and authorized Janney to spend $5,000 on an aircraft. Amazingly, Janney happened to know just where one was available at that sticker price and he rushed off to Marblehead, Massachusetts.

Starling Burgess would later recall a day late in September 1914 when a young man in civilian dress rushed into his office at Marblehead, put a loaded six-shooter and a fat wallet on his desk, and ordered an aircraft. "I didn't know which one he was going to use first," wrote Burgess.[2] Janney peeled off $5,000 and demanded that a machine be hauled out of the water, dismantled, and shipped out that night. Burgess shipped the aircraft by train that night to Hero, a point near the Canadian border on Lake Champlain. Janney went ahead to prepare for its arrival and the task force was soon assembling Canada's first warplane, the Burgess-Dunne, on Isle La Motte, Vermont.

People around nearby St. Albans traditionally measured strange occurrences by a day in October 1864 when a patrol of Confederate horse soldiers suddenly appeared on the main street, robbed a couple of banks, and started a few fires. But what the Vermonters saw that day as Burgess's work party and pilot Cliff Webster assembled the aircraft gave new meaning to strange occurrences for the locals. According to Burgess, by noon a thousand people had gathered to watch the secret operation. Then "a curious little man with black moustache, seemingly like a villain in a play, approached us, threw back his coat to show his sheriff's badge and told us ... we were all under arrest."[3] They were driven to the railroad station and tried as German spies about to bomb Canada. After Burgess managed to get the judge on a telephone line with the Aero Club of America, the judge was finally satisfied that the party was not a group of German spies.

The Burgess-Dunne, designed by British aeronautical pioneer J.W. Dunne and built by American boat builder Starling Burgess, was a two-seater tailless swept-wing pusher floatplane. After Cliff Webster and Ernest Janney took off from the glass-like surface of Lake Champlain, they soon ran into strong headwinds. It took two hours and all their fuel for the 100-h.p. Curtiss engine to cover the 80 miles to Sorrel, Que. It would appear as though many Vermonters had phoned ahead to warn their Canadian cousins that the Germans were coming, for when the Burgess-Dunne taxied up to the wharf its was met by a large crowd along with the sheriff who arrested Webster and Janney as spies. The commander of Canada's Aviation Corps and his companion were hustled to the local jail.

Janney's bluster didn't cut it with the sheriff nor did his first phone call to Ottawa. Sam Hughes had formed the air service on the back of an envelope without consulting his military. Janney's first phone calls reached personnel at military headquarters who had never heard of an air service. Finally, the deputy minister remembered a mysterious telegram he had received from Hughes which had asked him to provide any assistance to Ernest Janney. It did not explain Janney's status, but the exasperated deputy minister finally recommended that Janney be set free.

Once released, Janney was seized with the urgency of the situation. Every day's delay was a day closer to failure. The First Contingent was shipping out within days and the Burgess-Dunne had to be part of it. Janney had been conscious of the urgency before leaving Marblehead and insisted on departing without a company inspection of the aircraft, a well-used demonstration model. An inspection was again on Webster's mind when the engine seized up out of Sorrel and they came down.

The pilot suspected trouble with bearings, but the commander of Canada's Aviation Corps was still in no mood for frills like engine inspections. He insisted they move onward and upward. This time the flight lasted 15 minutes. The machine lost height as the engine shrieked and seized. They were picked up by a group of happy woodsmen who towed the machine to Deschaillons, Que., with such gusto that two holes were punched in the hull of the main float. A crew with knowledge of hull repair was brought up from Marblehead with spare parts for the engine. Delays ate into eight precious days and by the time Webster put the Burgess-Dunne down at Quebec City, the ships were loading. A cheer went up from the *Athenia* as Canada's first warplane settled onto the water like a pregnant duck.

During Janney's absence, Sam Hughes had added to the Aviation Corps by assigning Lt Frederick Sharpe of Ottawa, who had some flying experience, and Staff Sgt. Harry Farr, who knew engines and was hired as a mechanic. The three men and the aircraft became part of Canada's answer to the motherland as the contingent sailed for England. Few in Canada knew the Aviation Corps had left and none in England knew it was coming, or cared. Janney wandered around the English countryside for a few months looking at aircraft factories while Canada's answer to the air war languished for all time in its crate.

On January 23, 1915, Janney was struck off strength as militia headquarters informed the 1st Contingent "to sever Lieutenant [sic] Janney's connection with the (Canadian Expeditionary Force)."[4] He later resurfaced as a civilian operating a flying school in Canada and served with the Royal Canadian Navy Volunteer Reserve. Unfortunately, Sharpe was killed in a flying accident during his first solo flight on February 4, 1915, after transferring to the Royal Flying Corps and was the first Canadian air casualty. Farr was discharged in May of that year "in consequence of the Flying Corps being disbanded."[5] The Canadian Aviation Corps didn't even make it to file 13 at the British War Office, which was soon fully engaged in a massive retreat from Mons. It did not take long for the traditions of the stuffy War Office to be tweaked by something called the Royal Flying Corps.

**TOP:** *This Burgess-Dunne seaplane was Canada's first war plane, but residents in Sorel, Quebec, saw it as an enemy bomber and arrested the pilot and the head of Canada's Aviation Corps.* (PAINTING BY ROBERT BRADFORD, NATIONAL AVIATION MUSEUM)

**ABOVE:** *The Aerial Experimental Association, formed by bearded Alexander Graham Bell brought together Glen Curtiss, John McCurdy and Casey Baldwin. Not shown is Lt. Thomas Selfridge.* (NATIONAL LIBRARY, C-28213)

**ABOVE:** *Frederic Wanklyn was with the RFC when war broke out and was soon flying the first "legitimately" armed RFC aircraft in France. Wanklyn later commanded #4 and #5 Squadrons and was the first of some 5,400 Canadians to transfer to a flying service. (DND/AH-535)*

**OPPOSITE PAGE:** *The Vickers Gun Bus was the first RFC aircraft to mount a gun. Wanklyn was chosen to fly the prototype in France and he distinguished himself in the Ypres sector in the spring of 1915. (IWM)*

# 👒 FIRST TO WAR:
# THE ROYAL FLYING CORPS

*THE GREAT DEBATES OF* the summer of 1914 were finally over. At the British War Office these had centred on Germany's previously announced Schlieffen Plan to invade Belgium and France. The British army scenario for meeting such activity was to confront the invaders, but the navy had plans to invade 10 miles of beach in northern Prussia. Although the Royal Flying Corps was two years old (it was formed in May 1912), it entered few of the strategy discussions that summer. In fact, few people ever mentioned the young service in serious conversation, except to grumble about it being a haven for idiots who flew around frightening horses. And crusty General Sir Ian Hamilton once prophetically observed that the only thing the cavalry could do in the face of entrenched machine guns was to cook rice for the infantry. But when war came, the RFC moved with amazing swiftness. Eight days after the outbreak of hostilities, three squadrons assembled at Dover for a mass flight of 36 assorted machines across the English Channel.

One machine crashed that morning at Netheravon, killing the pilot and mechanic. James McCudden cradled his friend's body at the crash site wondering "if war was going to be like this always."[6] For McCudden, it was. Although he became Britain's fourth-ranking ace with 57 victories, he would die in a similar accident on July 9, 1918. The machines that landed at Dover were crude, underpowered, and unreliable; this was to be expected since it had only been five years since Louis Blériot first flew the English Channel.

The young men up on the downs at Dover were in high spirits as they prepared to challenge the Channel. Lieutenant D. Harvey-Kelly was the first to brave the cliffs and head for France. He ignored orders to land at Cap Griz Nez and flew to Amiens. Another pilot was forced down and immediately arrested. While he languished in jail, the others were guests at an instant party that broke out at the Hotel du Rhin in Amiens. Curious civilians overflowed the lobby with gifts of flowers, wine, and civility. The airmen were told that Roland Garros, the premier French aviator, had died ramming a Zeppelin. Although Garros was alive and well, the French civilians seemed to have better insights into aviation than the British general staff did.

The RFC's first job was to seek out the British Expeditionary Force, which was still en route, and locate other ground forces. In the confusion of the German advance, this was not as simple as it may sound because soldiers of any nation had a tendency to fire at anything in the air. The German advance through Belgium was so swift that nobody had an accurate picture of the deployment of even Allied troops.

The first reconnaissance on August 19th was not an unqualified success. One pilot got lost over a large city, later identified as Brussels. Another crew landed to ask two gendarmes where the Belgian army was. The stunned gendarmes shook their heads, studied the strange machine, and suggested the pilot try Belgian army headquarters at Louvain. They reasoned that a headquarters should know where its army was.

Operating from Maubeuge, France, the squadrons flew into the Battle of Mons, which soon became a retreat in haste. They evacuated 10 airfields in two weeks but remained operational throughout. The RFC reported that the Germans had turned east which prevented the encirclement and possible annihilation of the British land forces. Later, at the gates of Paris, air observation discovered a gap between the German armies, which the Allies exploited in a counterattack that became the decisive Battle of the Marne (September 6-10, 1914).

By mid-October the static lines ran up past Ypres to the Channel and, with the rains of November, the lines extended to Switzerland. The stage was set for disaster. Millions of young men would die, but the lines would not change more than a few miles for four years. In fact, some four years later, Canadian troops would initiate the drive that would end in victory by breaking out of Amiens — where it all began for the RFC. Ron Dodds' magnificent *The Brave Young Wings* traces the arrival of Canadian airmen by the fall of 1914.

Major Frederick Wanklyn of Montreal had trained several of the first RFC pilots to fly to France. He was in France himself in November as acting flight commander. He then went on to #5 Squadron where he flew the first Vickers FB5 "Gun Bus" in France. It was a pusher with tail booms, and the observer in the front cockpit had a Lewis gun with an unobstructed field of fire forward. Wanklyn flew escort to an unarmed Avro 504 in the Ypres sector on artillery spotting missions at the time of the German gas attack and was awarded the Military Cross for his work. The first of some 4,500 Canadians who would transfer to the British flying services, Wanklyn commanded #9 Squadron on the Somme. He established many notable firsts and the influx of Canadians became a trickle not long after he took the Gun Bus aloft at Abeele, Belgium.

Malcolm "Mickey" Bell-Irving was a young man in a hurry. When war broke out, he was working at a mine in Alaska and phoned home to Vancouver to find out who was fighting whom. Satisfied at the outcome, the son of a prominent Vancouver family that saw six sons and two of four daughters in the service, went overseas at his own expense the month war was declared. He then learned to fly in nine days, also at his own expense, and presented himself to the Royal Flying Corps where he was accepted. He was the first of 5,300 Canadians to join the British flying services by direct entry; an additional 2,300 or more would enlist in the RFC training plan in Canada.

Bell-Irving was sent to France with #1 Squadron in March 1915 and soon became noted for his aggressiveness as some of his exploits took on the character of legend, having been nurtured by frequent tales over squadron bars. While flying a Martinsyde Scout and armed with only a pistol, he engaged a German single-seater. Flying over the enemy, he got off a few shots when the pistol jammed. He then furiously threw it at the other pilot. Some versions have him hitting the confused enemy on the head. (Apparently, there was a direct ratio between the accuracy of Bell-Irving's aim and the number of drinks consumed in the telling of the story.)

When the RFC developed squadron reports in April 1915, some of the earliest included the adventures of Mickey Bell-Irving. One has to read between the lines to deduce that the frustrated Canadian took the matter of poor armament to his commanding officer. Shortly after the pistol-throwing incident, Bell-Irving's CO sent up a memo complaining of the lack of machine guns. Major-General Geoffrey Salmond noted that the squadron had only three machine guns while home squadrons were better armed.

In one afternoon, armed with two pistols, Bell-Irving engaged nine aircraft in four different encounters. Although he scored no victories on that occasion, he drove off all hostiles, which was all that was asked of a pilot at that stage of the war. However, pilots began to consider merely driving off an enemy aircraft a make-work project because they would be back the next day. Consequently, during the spring and summer of 1915, pilots worked harder at getting a gun aloft than most senior commanders. Some, like Lt Louis Strange, had been trying since before the war.

## THE GUN GROWS WINGS

Louis Strange was a day late in joining his squadron when it flew to France because he had to pick up a new aircraft at Central Flying School. En route from CFS, he was mysteriously forced to land in a pasture at Upper Wallop where a farm lady fed him and then helped him with his machine while complaining about her useless son who went traipsing off to war leaving her with the farm chores. Strange was somewhat vague about the "repair" work done on his machine, but when he caught up with his squadron at Amiens, a Lewis gun hung from the front cockpit of his Farman like an indolent toothpick. Not only was it the only gun in the RFC, it was definitely forbidden.

Strange had been given a passenger in England — a fat, drunken sod with a talent for producing whisky bottles out of thin air. Strange had thrown him in the brig at Dover, hoping a night in the cooler would be a sobering influence, but the fat man escaped and before Louis and the service police could round him up, he was again adrift in a sea of intoxication. To make matters worse, when Strange touched down at Amiens, the RFC was staging an open day for the citizens. As he taxied up the crowded runway, his passenger led the crowd in songs while waving an empty bottle like the Pope dispensing holy water.

A week later, six enemy machines appeared over the field at Maubeuge and Strange in his Farman was among the six RFC aircraft to fly the first scramble. But with the gun and observer aboard, Strange couldn't get the Farman an inch above 3,500 feet while the Germans cruised insolently above. One version of the story has Strange's observer suddenly firing at the sky. The noise and vibration so startled Strange that he pushed the yoke forward and the observer was tossed out, clinging to the rim of the front cockpit without a parachute. The machine went into a disgraceful series of gyrations as Strange reached for his observer, finally recovering him like a fisherman reeling in a prized salmon. When he landed, Louis Strange had the option of getting rid of the gun or transferring back to the Devonshire Yeomanry.

Predictably, he transferred to another squadron within a few months. Here he and Maj Lanoe Hawker spent hours in the sheds and Strange came up with putting a Lewis gun on the top wing of a sensitive Martinsyde Scout. One morning while engaging the enemy, Strange exhausted a drum of ammunition; he stood to replace it with the stick between his knees. He reached up, the nose dropped and he was thrown out. Grasping the ammunition drum, which normally would have been released from a slight tug, he whirled out in space as the plane fell into a flat spin. The German pilot watched the twisting, kicking figure trying to find a haven for his body as the plane plunged a mile and a half. Strange kicked his way back into the cockpit at treetop height, took control of the aircraft, and scurried home. He would meet the German pilot some 20 years later.

Major Lanoe Hawker's early experiments were more successful. He mounted a Lewis gun at an angle to the fuselage in order to avoid hitting the propeller, and became so adept at flying crabwise that he shot down three machines in one engagement in July 1915.

In the French sector, Lt Roland Garros mounted a Hotchkiss machine gun on his Morane-Saulnier. A clip of 25 bullets fed it but only 17 passed through the propeller arc without hitting it. While slowly shooting off his own propeller, Garros scored five victories in three weeks before being forced down behind enemy lines. The Germans examined the gun and turned it over to Anthony Fokker, a Dutch designer who worked for them. Fokker made clucking sounds as he examined the crude synchronization. He borrowed from a patent by a Swiss engineer to develop a synchronized gun and ran off a quick copy of the French Morane-Saulnier. The result was the Fokker Eindecker: the first aircraft to successfully fire a machine gun through the propeller arc without destroying the propeller. While the Eindecker's performance was not outstanding, the fact that all the pilot had to do was aim it at his target made it revolutionary.

By the spring of 1915, more Canadians were flying on the Western Front. Lieutenant Edmund Tempest, of Perdue, Sask., arrived in May, as did Lt William Ewart Gladstone Murray of Vancouver. Murray turned up at St. Omer, France, as an observer, having transferred from the Highland Light Infantry. He flew reconnaissance and bombing missions for two months until he was wounded, later returning as a pilot. Lt Kenneth Kennedy of Sherbrooke, Que., followed a similar route and a similar fate. He served with the Canadian Field Artillery at Ypres and transferred to the RFC as an observer. Then, after being wounded, he re-mustered to become a pilot. Another transfer from the army, Second Lieutenant John Parker from Edmonton was the first Canadian killed due to enemy action when he failed to return from a reconnaissance over Baupame, France, in July. After his death, a German plane dropped a tribute: "The German pilots have the highest praise for their opponent who died in an honourable fight."[7]

The new Fokkers were distributed to German units in limited numbers, and during the late summer and fall of 1915, the upgraded aircraft inflicted heavy losses on the modest RFC forces. Lieutenant William Reid of Port Arthur, Ont., had transferred from the army and was attacked by a Fokker when flying an un-armed bomber over enemy territory in late July. He was alone because the machine would not carry both an observer and a bomb. The Fokker riddled Reid's machine, smashing his arm, but he managed to land behind the lines. The Fokker landed beside him and Max Immelmann climbed down. Immelmann would become Germany's premier ace and the unarmed Canadian was among his first victims.

Lieutenant John Williams of Toronto flew a photo mission in a BE2c over

Lille, France in October. Lille was near the base of Section 62, which had two active Fokkers flown by Immelmann and Oswald Boelcke. A Fokker dived on William's aircraft, wounding his observer in the hand. On a second pass, the Fokker hit Williams in the arm and leg and he passed out. His observer, Lieutenant T.D. Hallam of Toronto, climbed into the rear cockpit as the British had not yet come to grips with the logic of putting the pilot in the front cockpit. The observer managed to switch off and guide the riddled machine to a rough landing behind Allied lines.

Many of the original Canadian pilots or observers were transfers from the army. Lieutenant Stan Caws, a 36-year-old Boer War veteran and a former Mountie, transferred from the Alberta Dragoons. He turned up as a pilot on #10 Squadron and flew throughout the summer on BE2cs. He and his observer were jumped by fighters in September and fought until ammunition ran out. Caws was killed by enemy machine gun fire. His observer, Sudgen-Wilson, was wounded in the leg and taken prisoner after gliding the plane down behind enemy lines.

By December 1915, there were two Bell-Irvings in the RFC. Malcom's older brother Duncan flew as an observer with #7 Squadron until he was wounded. Duncan went on to become a pilot, scoring seven victories and being shot down four times. Although he was the first Canadian RFC pilot, Malcolm was five days too late for the title of the first Canadian to bring down an enemy machine. That honour goes to F/S/L Arthur Strachan Ince, the first graduate of the Curtiss Flying School John McCurdy had set up in Toronto. Ince brought down an enemy while flying with the Royal Naval Air Service (RNAS). On December 19th, flying a Morane Scout, Malcolm took on three enemies and shot one down. Two withdrew but he was later attacked by three more fighters and was closing in on one when hit by British anti-aircraft fire. Although he survived, Malcolm's operational career was over. He won the first Distinguished Service Order awarded to a Canadian in the RFC.

As the winter of 1915-16 closed over the Western Front, some 21 Canadians were serving in the RFC. Although their performance was strong and the first of the Curtiss School graduates were overseas, trouble hung like snow clouds over the training program in Toronto.


## *RICH CANADIANS "LEARN AEROPLANE"*

When the RFC set up a recruiting program in Canada during the winter of 1915, personnel were as lonely as Maytag repairmen without promotional abilities. The first recruiting officer begged his superiors "not to leave me to languish here forever." His successor liked the job even less and had a low opinion of potential candidates on social grounds. Lt/Col C.J. Burke proudly reported to associates in London that he had "saved" the RFC by turning down two undesirable characters, one who had been a common farm labourer in England two years previously while the other operated a newspaper stand in Regina.

Early in the war, Sam Hughes had enthusiastically suggested to the British that there were many potential pilots in Canada. But the Catch-22 was that neither the RFC nor the RNAS would accept a candidate without a pilot's license. When Hughes made the statement eight Canadians had pilot's licenses and two of them were abroad. The rationale for demanding a pilot's certificate was difficult to understand in view of the fact that a man could transfer from the army or navy to a flying service without any previous flight experience. But in the spring of 1915 any civilian who wanted to serve his country in the air had to first learn to fly at his own dollar. Including living expenses, the cost almost matched a year's wages in the manufacturing sector. Some elected to go to England, others to schools in the United States, but most enrolled at the Curtiss Flying School in Toronto.

John McCurdy offered training in three Curtiss flying boats at Centre Island and more advanced training in four JN-3 biplanes at nearby Long Branch. The school soon became the victim of success as response outstripped facilities and too many students were left chasing too few aircraft. Early in July, Arthur Strachan Ince and Homer Smith took off from Long Branch, did a figure eight and returned to earth. The Royal Aero Club pronounced them airworthy and they became the school's first graduates. Both were soon sent overseas where, as we have seen, Ince became the first Canadian airman to down an enemy seaplane while flying out of Dunkirk with the RNAS on December 14, 1915.

It cost on average $400 to get the prescribed amount of flying time, and as summer lengthened so did the time required for a student to get another flight. Many had given up jobs or borrowed money to be there and when airtime dwindled with poor fall weather students were in a serious financial bind. When winter brought a halt to flying, 66 had graduated but 285 were stuck in the system with nowhere to go. Although small schools opened and closed in various parts of the country, the Curtiss School was by far the largest. The Aero Club of Vancouver operated an active school for a period but collapsed. Although most of its students did not graduate, many were later absorbed into the air services.

As the pace slowed in Toronto, a number of Canadians went to the Wright School in Dayton or the Stinson operation in Texas. The influx of Canadians in these communities prompted a Dayton newspaper to welcome the 30 wealthy Canadian men who were "being taught aeroplane." More than 200 students received certificates at the American schools where the training was excellent. The town of Carleton Place, near Ottawa, became an icon. With a population of 4,300, it provided 15 pilots to the British flying services — one would be credited with downing Baron Manfred von Richthofen and another would become head of the

RCAF years later. Many from this group ended up across the border, but not all centres of aviation learning were as reputable as the Wright or Stinson schools. Canadians found themselves on expensive detours. Nick Carter and Tom Shearer of Calgary drifted into a school in St. Augustine, Florida, where they paid their $400 and began unloading a Burgess-Dunne. The "mechanic" tried to assemble the engine backwards while the instructor had never been off the ground.

When the Curtiss School closed in November, a delegation of stranded students went to Ottawa for help from Sam Hughes who listened to the spokesman and gently put his hand on the boy's shoulder leading him to the window which overlooked the Gatineau Hills and E.B. Eddy's woodpile. As told in Raymond Collishaw's memoir, Hughes, the man who 15 months earlier had formed the Canadian Aviation Corps, now said: "My dear boy, you and your friends have been indeed led astray and I am sorry for you."[8] Hughes told them to join the infantry because the aeroplane was an instrument of the devil that drew away the best of our young men. He then went on to lecture them on observation: "If I were the commander of a force in the field and I wished to see what the enemy was doing, I should climb a hill. If the hill was not high enough then I should climb a tree on the hill."[9]

While apologists for the government's ignorance in aviation matters fall back on the argument that aviation was in its infancy, the state of infancy had long passed by the winter of 1915-16. Fifteen months earlier, Gen Sir John French commended the work of the RFC during the retreat from Mons and the Battle of the Marne. Even if Hughes hadn't learned of this through official channels, he could hardly miss the communiqué on the front page of the *Ottawa Journal*. Yet the man with the destiny of our armed forces in his hands still preferred trees to aircraft for observation purposes.

**LEFT:** *Malcolm Bell-Irving (left with brother Duncan) was the first Canadian civilian to volunteer for air duties. An estimated 5,300 Canadians would follow, with most of them paying their way to war. (RE19933)*

**OPPOSITE PAGE:** *Kenneth Kennedy later flew a BE2 machine whose deadly appearance belied the effectiveness of its guns. The observer was in the front cockpit and had to shoot through a forest of struts or blow the pilot's head off in an attack from the stern. (DND)*

*When "Boom" Trenchard decided that control
of enemy sky was essential regardless of cost,
the air then became...*

# ✍ A NEW BATTLEGROUND

**WHEN MAJ-GEN SIR DAVID** Henderson, head of the RFC, visited England after the fighting on the Marne in the fall of 1914, he was in a good mood. The fledgling RFC had been singled out for commendation in the first major communiqué of the war. Air observation had been critical in the retreat from Mons and again at the gates of Paris when it spotted a gap in the German forces. An Allied counterattack led to the successful Battle of the Marne. All in all, it had been a difficult but successful three weeks for the fledgling flying corps.

So Henderson was taken aback when Lt.-Col. Sir Hugh Montague Trenchard delivered a tirade and demanded to be sent back to his regiment because he didn't want to associate with an air arm that was not aggressive. Henderson outflanked his old friend and calmly suggested that Trenchard hie himself to France to take over one of three wings then being formed. It was a perfect display of one-upmanship and the most important single posting in the history of the RFC, because Trenchard accepted the challenge and left his aggressive stamp on the air war, as control of enemy sky became the cornerstone of RFC policy.

"Boom" Trenchard had one lung shot out during the Boer War and also lost the use of his legs. He took up bobsledding for therapy and a horrendous crash on Switzerland's Cresta run did what doctor's couldn't – it restored the use of his legs. At the age of 40, Trenchard managed to graduate in the first class at the RFC's Central Flying School which he commanded two years later when war broke out. Early in 1915, he took over command of a wing in France where the

RFC was reorganizing its meagre forces

The war had stagnated with the first Battle of Ypres in November and the reconnaissance function passed over from horses to the remnants of five squadrons of aircraft although many generals had yet to learn of the change. Winter storms destroyed over half of the 72 RFC machines, but operations continued to expand. Air to ground radio gave the RFC a vital new role in directing artillery shoots but transmitters were in short supply and so heavy that the pilot had to fly without an observer. He had to observe, transmit and fly the cranky aircraft without two-way communication to the ground.

Photography became another important aerial function during the early months of 1915. Prior to the Battle of Neuve Chapelle, the RFC provided a complete montage of the enemy sector identifying German gun emplacements. The battle, however, was not a success because the British tried to pour too many troops through a narrow corridor and created a massive traffic jam that was knocked off by German guns. Bombing raids in support of the land action were sporadic. Although Trenchard's particular wing was not involved, the failure impressed upon him the need for concerted air attacks in the land battle. Trenchard was made commander of the RFC in France in August 1915. He inherited 12 squadrons and some 160 line machines, although most were of ancient vintage. He also inherited the Fokker menace as the Germans introduced the synchronized gun that fired through the propeller arc.

Although the RFC lost the first round in technological warfare, Trenchard persisted in taking the war to enemy skies in spite of the cost. Trenchard's immediate answer to the Fokkers was to have observation aircraft escorted by at least three armed machines, a response that greatly cut the effectiveness of his forces. However, the report of one Fokker pilot attested to the success of what became flying in loose formation. The German wrote: "The enemy squadron seemed well practiced against attacks from Fokkers. The aircraft kept close together at slightly different heights ... in this way we were continually under fire from more than one aeroplane ... I obtained the impression that the British were not trying to get out of the way of the Fokkers." [10]

At this same period, the enemy began flying in small groups but for a different reason. Oswald Boelcke, one of the first Fokker pilots and father of the German air force, concluded that the sky was too big for one man to search while occupied with the details of flying. Two pilots sharing the sky could conduct a much more efficient search. Soon fighters were flying in pairs or kettes of three. Boelcke's finger-two formation survived WWII and has been popular ever since.

Throughout the period of Fokker domination and later when the enemy introduced Albatros and Halberstadt Scouts, Trenchard maintained his policy of leaning over enemy territory. He sent fighters or scouts on distant operational patrols looking for trouble behind enemy lines while his ancient machines at the front became easy targets for enemy fighters. The pendulum of air superiority swung briefly in his favour with the arrival of Maj Lanoe G. Hawker's first RFC fighter squadron in February 1916. Second Lt Robert Kerr of Victoria, B.C., was one of the first of the select group whose nimble DH2 single-seaters became a primary weapon in bringing down the Fokker. Hawker's men were in the air or on call 17 hours a day, flying escort missions, or distant offensive patrols and by late June the RFC dominated enemy sky.

## THE SOMME

On July 1, 1916 the Allies zeroed 1,500 guns on 18 miles of territory at the bend of the River Somme. That morning an intense barrage opened the ground attack. Airmen had been warned to stay clear of La Boisselle because sappers had mined the area, but the few pilots who ventured near were awestruck as an island appeared in the sky at 4,000 feet. It hung there briefly then fell away in dust and debris. A second explosion ripped the air and when the dust cleared La Boisselle looked like two poached eggs. But the German positions were intact because the tunnels the mines were planted in didn't reach the enemy lines.

Then 120,000 men shouldered 60-pound packs and went over the top. So intense was the bombardment that they sauntered confidently across no man's land where German machine gun fire then slashed their ranks. The Royal Newfoundland Regiment was wiped out in half an hour with a 91 per cent casualty rate; by dusk 60,000 men were dead or wounded on the barbed wire. It was only the opening scene in a horror drama, which would linger until fall when more than one million men would be dead.

In spite of the disaster on the ground, the first day of the attack called for the most intense use of air power to date. About 80 Canadians were flying at the front that day and the 13 with corps squadrons had the most monotonous and dangerous job of all. They flew back and forth over the battlefield like cops pounding a beat. Their cumbersome machines were fair bait for fighters and fair game for artillery from either side as they monitored and directed artillery fire. By 10 o'clock the RFC had sealed off the battleground. Innes van Nostrand of Toronto was one of four Canadian casualties. George Simpson of Vancouver was killed when he attacked 10 bombers while Ian Macdonnell of Winnipeg, bombed troops trapped in a quarry and later ranged guns on them. Macdonnell was killed the next day. Reginald Carroll's patrol on July 3rd typified the work of the corps squadrons. The pilot from London, Ont., and his observer spotted a German gun battery in action. They flew back to the Allied lines and dropped the position of the enemy guns to a siege battery, which opened up and destroyed the enemy guns and several ammunition wagons.

Although the RFC deprived German aircraft of airspace over the front and provided excellent information for the artillery, it was not so successful in contact patrols or getting information back about the progress of Allied troops through the maze of trenches. The theory was that the troops would wear reflective material on their backs so airmen could identify the point of their advance. Troops were supposed to shoot flares or use ground sheets to identify their location. Presumably nobody had advised the troops that shooting flares or wearing reflective material in a shell hole yards from the enemy was not a good idea. While air support had generally been good, the ground attack failed because men were vulnerable to entrenched machine guns. British Gen Sir Douglas Haig counted heavily on artillery to soften up the enemy who merely went underground and waited. The Somme fighting then became a series of spasmodic attacks at different places, which went on for four and a half months.

For most of the summer the RFC had control of the air. By September, contact patrols had improved and artillery spotting was effective. RFC aircraft also dominated the area behind the front to such an extent that German machines could not monitor their own artillery. This meant that enemy artillery had to shoot blindly without knowing where their shells were landing.

Although the RFC had superiority in the early stages of the battle, resistance stiffened when the enemy brought in the Roland and Halberstadt fighters and transferred air support from the Verdun front. Enemy fighters inflicted serious damage on #60 Squadron which flew the ancient Morane Parasol. The squadron was withdrawn and re-equipped with the Nieuport 17 that mounted a Lewis machine gun on the top wing. It would then claim 320 victories. Alan Duncan Bell-Irving would account for seven and Billy Bishop would later contribute 47 to the squadron total.

But the ultimate success of #60 Squadron was an isolated bright spot in a dismal picture, which developed that fall as Oswald Boelcke brought in a squadron of Albatros fighters with twin machine guns. During the summer, Hawker's #24 Squadron accounted for 70 hostiles and among the Canadians who contributed were Alfred McKay of London, Ont., who scored four of his 10 victories, while Arthur Knight of Toronto, listed eight. Henry Evans of McLeod, Alta., was awarded the Distinguished Service Order for bringing down four machines in two weeks. Evans became an ace on August 9th, but was shot down by a new enemy fighter less than a month later. His death was a grim prelude of what was to come as the summer of 1916 drew to a close.

Oswald Boelcke brought a squadron of new fighters in to face his old adversary Hawker. Although the two men had not met in combat, they were kindred spirits in different uniforms whose leadership qualities and grasp of aerial combat would leave their stamp on generations of fighter pilots. Hawker destroyed an enemy airship in 1915 and shot down three aircraft in one day to win the Victoria Cross. Boelcke was one of the earliest and most successful Fokker pilots and the design of the new Albatros incorporated many features that he had recommended. Boelcke's squadron's first sweep on September 17 1916, brought down eight British machines. Within a month, his pilots destroyed 40 while his personal score rose to 35. On a windswept afternoon late in October, Knight and McKay were on intruder patrol over Pozières when they were attacked by six Halberstadts, the other new fighter at the front. As the Canadians fought the Halberstadts to a standstill, Boelcke led his flight off the ground at Lagnicourt. It was his sixth sortie of the day and he had just scored his 40th victory.

Over Pozieres, Boelcke led his flight, which included *Kapitän* Manfred von Richthofen who became known as "The Red Baron" and Lt Werner Voss, down on the Canadians. Knight and McKay were still skidding through enemy formations while snapping off short bursts. Their ammunition drums, although expanded, contained a mere 97 rounds while each enemy Spandau machine gun was capable of firing some 800 rounds a minute. Boelcke closed in on Knight who was high man and Knight kicked left rudder. Boelcke turned sharply and collided with wingmate and old friend Erwin Boehme. The wheels of Boehme's machine barely touched Boelcke's upper wing but the leader's Albatros started a slow spiral. Then the wing peeled off and the machine became a projectile, which carried the father of the German air force to his death.

A month after Boelcke went down, Hawker flew as an observer on a four-man patrol. Two pilots were forced to turn back and the flight leader went down in an attack over the lines. Alone, Hawker turned to face his attackers, one of whom was an eager Baron von Richthofen who had the advantage of speed, armament and wind. Hawker's only advantage was the short turning radius of the DH2, but every turn pushed him deeper into German territory. He used the short turn until he ran out of height and the macabre dance continued down river valleys at tree-top height. Hawker was running out of fuel and ammunition when a burst hit him in the head. Hours later, Richthofen wrote to his mother and told her that the man called the British Boelcke had given him his greatest combat.

Arthur Knight fell to Richthofen a month later. He was one of 65 Canadians who became part of the 583 RFC casualties as the ground war bogged down in the mud and the war of attrition took to the air.

## HOME FRONT: FEAR OF FLYING

While individual Canadians were making their mark on the air war by the fall of 1916, the federal government resolutely pursued a policy based on a fear of flying. When Sam Hughes was minister of Militia and Defence, it was relatively easy to understand Canada's negative and erratic air policy. As we have seen, a few months after the outbreak of war, Sam gave a bicycle repairman $5,000 to buy an aircraft and made him an instant captain. Then he changed his mind and turned his back on aviation, calling the airplane an instrument of the devil.

For two years the government resolutely resisted attempts by individuals and groups to form an air force. Two months after war was declared, Griffith Brewer was in England selling a proposal to senior RFC officers and the secretary of state for war, Lord Kitchener. Brewer's plan was to form a squadron of Canadians in the United States under the cover of exhibition flights. Both Kitchener and the assistant director of aeronautics, Lt/Col Sefton Brancker, liked the idea, but when it was referred to the Canadian government it went missing in action.

Although Sam Hughes was perceived as the opponent of aviation, he exerted little influence on the prime minister. Robert Borden went to Maj-Gen. G.W. Gwatkin, a Britisher, who was chief-of-the-general-staff, for advice and Gwatkin managed to weave a negative spell around Borden and his cabinet. Earlier, when John McCurdy proposed the creation of an aircraft industry with a plan to develop an air corps, the idea was rejected along with his proposal to train pilots in return for the purchase of aircraft. Proposals by the British to form Dominion squadrons in Canada, Australia and New Zealand were also turned down based on the advice from Gwatkin. Although Canada rejected the plan, Australia was quick to accept what became the Australian Flying Corps.

When McCurdy's school in Toronto faltered in the fall of 1915 because of weather and demand on limited resources, a volunteer group of businessmen and patriots known as the Canadian Aviation Fund then began to subsidize students. In an effort to give students more training time than the standard 400 minutes, they challenged the government to match their financial contributions. The government allowed it and had no objections to the plan, but contributed nothing but adjectives.

Disillusioned with the federal government, Col William Hamilton Merritt, founder of the Canadian Aviation Fund, formed a strong network of support with many provincial lieutenant-governors. Merritt was the impetus behind a newspaper campaign to create public support for a Canadian air corps. In March 1916 the newspaper *Toronto World* wrote an article placing Canada behind every other nation in the world in aviation. Perhaps it overstated the case slightly, but its conclusion was accurate enough. It lamented the fact that those in Ottawa with power had no vision while those with vision had no power.

Merritt with the help of A.G.C. Dinnick, a Toronto investment banker, bypassed Ottawa and took a proposal to London that linked a training school to a proposed factory. He was also hopeful that each provincial lieutenant-governor and leading Canadian industrialists would assist with the funding. The private sector had effectively done an end run around Ottawa's inertia, but the gains were short lived. Although the RFC saw virtue in the plan, it turned the matter over to the Imperial Munitions Board (IMB), an agency producing war goods but devoted to maintaining Imperial economic domination.

When the IMB began negotiations with the Canadian government, free enterprise and Merritt's proposal was shuffled into back baskets, but the British still wanted a training plan. The final stages of the Somme brought heavy casualties and the now Maj-Gen Hugh Trenchard was calling for some 50 squadrons in France. Having a factory and a school in Canada would be both an economic advantage and a valuable source of manpower. But after 18 months of frustrating negotiation with Canada, the British were unable to get the Canadian government to take responsibility for training squadrons or the formation of an air service.

**THE BRITISH ARE COMING!**
The RFC's Brig-Gen Sefton Brancker finally decided to act unilaterally and two days before Christmas in 1916, the Canadian high commissioner in London was told that the British were coming. Canada reacted to the foreign invasion by later throwing a $1 million loan at the Imperial Munitions Board to enable it to buy out Curtiss and start a company called Canadian Aeroplanes Ltd.

The man who headed up the plan was a combination of Ollie North and Ross Perot. Lt/Col Cuthbert G. Hoare was an unorthodox ex-cavalry officer who thrived on wheeling and dealing and had the boundless energy to make things work. On January 19th after his ship docked in Saint John, N.B., Hoare went to Ottawa to outline his requirements to Maj-Gen Gwatkin, an immovable force on aviation matters. When Hoare stated that he needed 500 men to get his plan started, the temperature in Ottawa dropped several degrees as Gwatkin said he couldn't raise 500 men in six months. Although the initial meeting between Gwatkin and Hoare was negative, they soon became great friends and Gwatkin was central in supporting the creation of the RFC training camps.

Hoare went to Toronto where a skeleton staff was setting up, and the following day left for Camp Borden by train but became snowbound at Angus. Two hours and five miles behind a team of horses did little to induce enthusiasm and neither did the stumps that protruded through the snow at Borden. Yet in spite of its dismal appearance, Hoare decided this was the place to start. The area had been a military camp and the land belonged to the Canadian government. By the end of the month, with contracts let by the IMB, 400 men had opened the rail line from Angus and stump clearing began. Some 1,700 men worked around the clock under arc lights and the first hangar was up in six weeks. After four months, 57 buildings were erected, 850 acres graded and five miles of asphalt laid. Stunned at the speed and efficiency of construction, Hoare pressed on. Within a month of the Borden construction, stations were springing up at Deseronto, Armour Heights and Leaside. He re-activated the station at Long Branch and by the middle of March, nine candidates of the RFC-Canada plan were undergoing training.

The plant, called Canadian Aeroplanes, went up on a nine-acre plot on Dufferin Street in Toronto and opened up after three months. Within six months the factory turned out 150 Jenny JN4s. By the end of 1917, supply exceeded RFC demand and the plant had sold 1,000 machines to the Americans who were now at war. While the plan went ahead with stunning rapidity, a major problem developed recruiting tradesmen. There were always aircrew volunteers but strong competition came from army recruiting and industry where tradesmen were in high demand and offered good wages.

Competition for aircrew also came from the RNAS as they offered a candidate higher pay as a provisional sub-lieutenant during training. Hoare organized recruiting across Canada and was able to successfully secure 6,000 qualified tradesmen. His success came from his emphasis on recruiting centres and a network of flying clubs. He opened a recruiting centre in New York and his recruitment of Yanks sent shivers through the diplomatic corps. Technically it was against American law and Canadian policy even though the United States was now in the war.

Hoare was not one to quibble with success. He informed the War Office of his activities, but didn't spend much time dealing with Ottawa. By September, half the intake of the RFC were Yanks. Hoare had also worked out a deal in Washington whereby the RFC agreed to train 10 American squadrons in Canada for the use of three American fields during the winter. The exchange had merit but no plan is perfect. The Americans arrived without records and adequate clothing; they were also unpaid and under-officered. The RFC NCOs who took them in hand found them loud-mouthed, ill- mannered, and discourteous with little respect for discipline. On the positive side, the aviation section of the U.S. Signal Corps was able to incorporate RFC training into its own syllabus, thereby gaining years of valuable experience. It may be a slight exaggeration to say that by the time the prime minister became fully aware of what was going on there were more Yanks in Canada than had been present at Queenston Heights, but it does cover the situation. However Canada did have two foreign military forces on its soil with little or no control over either of them. Ironically, these events took place the summer Canada was awash in nationalism set in motion by a brilliant performance on Vimy Ridge.

That fall, five aero squadrons moved to new quarters around Fort Worth, Texas. Three American squadrons were added to the training program in exchange for an extra month's use of the facilities in Texas. Hoare also agreed to train another eight American squadrons, and this had a profound influence on the establishment of the U.S. Air Corps. However by the spring of 1918, Hoare had problems because the agreement did not carry over to the following winter.

The aerial training was moved to Beamsville, a village in the relatively temperate Niagara fruit belt, The community became the site for the School of Aerial Gunnery and three squadrons returning from Texas moved in by April 1918. It became the School of Aerial Fighting and was designed to bring the student as close to combat as aircraft permitted. The evolution of the plan was directly influenced by the lessons learned in England, where for over two years pilots had been going into combat with a very rudimentary knowledge of flying and suffering for it.

Even in 1917 when Lt Tommy Williams of Woodstock, Ont., transferred from the army to the RFC, instructors warned him never to get into a spin. However they never told him how to get out of one, and Tommy concluded they didn't even know how. They also insisted he stay out of cloud because it caused compass malfunction. Williams began spinning his Camel and flying into cloud, deciding that in cloud it was the pilot not the compass that malfunctioned. Students like Williams, who had the drive to seek their own answers, had a chance of survival but the less perceptive often became subjects for a church parade

The RFC-Canada program graduated 3,135 pilots of whom 2,500 went overseas and 137 fully-trained observers . Furthermore, the factory turned out some 3,000 aircraft. In spite of the government's original timidity, Canadians reacted positively to the plan that provided a strong outlet for the grassroots interest in aviation. Most of the students and many of the instructors were Canadian and the bases had a pronounced effect on aviation in Canada in spite of the government's initial fear of flying.

*The Curtiss Flying School in Toronto soon became a victim of its own success. Demand for air time at Toronto Island and Long Branch soon exceeded aircraft available and after one summer the system was gridlocked. (RE-64654)*

**ABOVE:** *One of the few bright spots during the summer of 1917 was the performance of Canadians with the RNAS. Redford Mulock's squadron helped the RFC survive in April and Raymond Collishaw's Black Flight later fought Richthofen to a deadlock.* (PAINTING BY ROBERT BRADFORD, CANADIAN AVIATION MUSEUM)

**OPPOSITE PAGE:** *Raymond Collishaw took command of RNAS Naval Three squadron in early 1918 and was fortunate in having a number of Canadian pilots – such as Art Whealy with 19 kills – as Allied air strength grew.* (PA-2789)

# ❦ THE PENDULUM SWINGS

*FORTUNATELY, BUT IRONICALLY,* the RFC training plan got under way in Canada during Bloody April, the month that almost broke the force's back. As 1916 drew to a dreary close, the British counted 420,000 casualties when the Somme fighting bogged down in November mud. As well, the RFC had almost 600 casualties but nobody at the War Office seemed to care as they sought a way to hit back at the enemy. Sir Douglas Haig was the commander in chief responsible for the high casualties on the Somme. Although public and political sentiment in England was opposed to more Somme-type combat, after King George V made him a field marshal, Haig kept the British forces fighting on the Western Front and the casualties continued to mount. When David Lloyd George became British prime minister in December, he was aware of the public sentiment against Haig's plan and began dabbling in developing military strategies on his own. He originally favoured a vague concept of opening a second front at some unspecified place along the Eastern Front, but considering the unhappy adventure at Gallipoli in 1915, it was an idea whose time had not come again.

While travelling within Europe the prime minister's train made a stop in a Paris station, where he was sweet-talked into another joint venture with the French. Gen Robert Nivelle had a plan for an attack on either side of the Aisne River, which he felt would end the war in 48 hours. According to Nivelle's plan, the British would attack at Arras early in April while the French would move in later further south. The British attack, which involved the Canadian Corps, was to be a diversion for the larger French drive.

The prime minister agreed to Nivelle's plan over the protests of his own commander Field Marshal Haig. As well, the British air commander Maj-Gen Hugh Trenchard had been protesting to anyone who would listen for months. In January, he warned Brig-Gen Sefton Brancker, the RFC's director of air organization, that the RFC would be hopelessly outclassed unless something was done to improve the quality and quantity of aircraft.

Sefton Brancker was Trenchard's link to the aircraft factories. As a pilot with limited experience, Brancker believed that stability in aircraft was a major virtue even at the expense of manoeuvrability. A strong supporter of the Royal Aircraft Factory designs, he stocked the RFC with machines that were too slow to run and too clumsy to fight. Built to replace the BE2, the RE8, was notorious in this respect and was also difficult to land. Yet over 4,000 such machines were produced and shipped out. Trenchard actually refused another aircraft that he considered absolutely unfit for service.

Before Canadian troops went over the top on Easter Monday, Canadian airmen were part of the crews that photographed and plotted 180 of 212 hostile batteries on Vimy Ridge and were central in bringing back detailed information on intricate trench systems. However, the strange attitude of the RE8 aircraft led the RFC to lose 75 aircraft to enemy action and 56 in crashes within five days before the attack.

T.W. McConkey of Bradford, Ont., was an observer in an RE8 of 59 Squadron whose experience gives a personal dimension to what observation crews were up against. He reported: "We were attacked by five Albatros scouts. ... Between us we shot down two of the enemy and drove another down, apparently out of control. My pilot, Capt Pemberton from Victoria, B.C., manoeuvred the machine in a most excellent fashion, evading the fire of Huns as much as possible and giving me every opportunity to bring my Lewis gun into play. He received a spent bullet in the back, necessitating his spending a week in a casualty clearing station. I came off less fortunately with four bullet wounds in the right thigh, one in the shoulder and one in the face."[11]

One of the few bright spots in Trenchard's dreary winter was the assignment of Canadian Squadron Commander Redford Mulock's Naval Three Squadron to the Western Front. The Winnipeg pilot, known for his ability as a leader and organizer, had a predominately Canadian squadron and Trenchard acknowledged it was one of the best on the front.

The pilots with Mulock flew Sopwith Pups, which were agile enough to turn inside enemy fighters, but lacked speed and firepower. Raymond Collishaw of Nanaimo, B.C., was not overly impressed with the single belt-fed Vickers gun that had slow synchronization. He later commented: "We found out that when we got into combat and opened fire there was almost a casual put-put-put sound, almost like a motorcycle about to expire."[12]

Collishaw bitterly remembered flying escort to unarmed BE2c bombers. "In order to carry their standard load of two 112-pound bombs these wretched aircraft had to takeoff without their observers. This left them quite defenseless. The procession seemed to draw every enemy scout that was in the sky, like bees swarming to a bowl of honey. I could never understand the crass stupidity of those people in high places who kept ordering more."[13] Despite this, in four and a half months the squadron destroyed 80 enemy machines, most of which were superior in performance and firepower.

Naval Three went up against Jasta 2, led by the "Red Baron" Manfred von Richthofen and a formidable array of top pilots. It flew offensive patrols and did escort work for bombers on distant penetrations, particularly in the region of Douai. On one patrol, Collishaw's Vickers jammed during combat and, while trying to clear the malfunction he froze his face, and was hospitalized on the eve of the ground attack. Four days before the ground attack, Manfred von Richthofen led a flight down on six new Bristol fighters that were making their operational debut. In a swift, savage battle the Bristols were decimated as their leader, Capt William Leefe-Robinson VC, and three others were shot down while a fourth crashed back at base. It wasn't until pilots like Lt Andrew McKeever of Listowel, Ont., began to fly the machine aggressively that it achieved its potential.

Richthofen and his pilots were celebrating their victory over the Bristols on the night of April 5th when 18 FE2bs from #100 Squadron hit the Baron's base at Douai. At first the German pilots were amused at the sight of the "prehistoric English packing cases," but the FEs sent the Baron's pilots diving for shelter as they bombed for 20 minutes at 200 feet. The bombers departed and the German pilots rushed out to help the ground crew extinguish flames and push aircraft out of hangars. They were still trying to sort out the damage when the FEs returned and resumed bombing, leaving four hangars and several aircraft damaged. The next night the FEs struck again with back to back raids. Richthofen was awakened by anti-aircraft fire and the sound of low flying aircraft. This time he was not amused and wrote: "In my sudden fright, I pulled the blankets over my head."[14]

Billy Bishop of Owen Sound, Ont., joined #60 Squadron in late March. Shortly after his arrival, he had the misfortune to crash a Nieuport at the feet of a visiting general known as "old bum and eyeglass" and was ordered back to training command. His commanding officer, Jack Scott, arranged for a stay of deportation by allowing Bishop to remain on the squadron until a replacement arrived.

Bishop bagged a balloon and brought down six aircraft within 15 days. On April 9th, he was contour flying through an artillery barrage on Vimy Ridge. As

Canadian infantry advanced, German machine gun emplacements occasionally halted progress. Low flying aircraft were used to neutralize the guns but they flew into the teeth of a gale that was like a wall of steel at less than 50 feet. For Bishop it was an exercise in terror: The ground was a mass of bursting shells and, as he described, "hot flames flashing from thousands of muzzles gave the impression of a long ribbon of incandescent light ... several of our machines were hit by shells"[15]

Weather was extremely hostile to both men and aircraft. When #100 Squadron hit the railroad station at Douai in a daylight raid, it destroyed a train loaded with chemicals and derailed a second train, but three of six machines were forced down as ice choked engines and coated wings.

The Canadian Corps ground attack at Vimy was a success and afforded the Allies high ground overlooking the plains of Douai. In view of the French attack which came later, resulting in 200,000 casualties, a mutiny by the troops and the ultimate dismissal of Nivelle, all the Allies got for the victory at Vimy was a view of the slag heaps to the north.

But the air war raged on throughout April. Five days after the Canadians took the ridge, #60 Squadron lost 10 of 18 Nieuports to Richthofen in one weekend. In other action, Naval Three's Lloyd Breadner of Carleton Place, Ont., and J.S. Fall of Hillbank, B.C., each scored three victories in one combat. Later that month, John Malone, Regina, shot down one enemy aircraft and forced a second down but as he turned on the third he ran out of ammunition. Malone flew to a nearby aerodrome where he rearmed and then returned to the battle to drive down a third victim. This exceptional pilot had seven victories when he was killed a week later.

Malone was but one of 39 Canadians among the killed or wounded during Bloody April when the RFC lost 316 aircrew and 151 aircraft. The enemy inflicted a four to one loss ratio on the British through better aircraft, better armament and better tactics. By month's end, the RFC was fighting for its very survival. In addition to poor equipment, Trenchard's edict of controlling enemy sky through distant fighter patrols was seen as a factor in the high losses. Enemy fighters evaded RFC intruder patrols and pounced on lumbering corps machines or unarmed bombers.

Although the first SE5 and Sopwith Triplanes appeared late in April they had not made an impact when Richthofen went on leave on May 1st. He had every reason to believe that complete domination was within their grasp, and had personally brought down 30 aircraft in two months for a total of 52. He left with a great sense of satisfaction and confidence, but was recalled early. By June the RFC was hitting back and this led to a bitter stalemate during the summer of 1917. German raids on London from bases on the coast gave a new urgency to Field Marshal Haig's plans in the Ypres area following the battle at Vimy Ridge.

The well planned, well executed battle of Vimy Ridge was a successful attack in a failed campaign that did little to influence the conduct of the war because of the catastrophe which befell the French further south. Gen Nivelle was dismissed in mid-May and replaced by Gen Henri Pétain who spent a month trying to come to grips with open revolt in the French army. For a period, the British conducted diversionary attacks on the Scarpe to draw enemy strength from the disorganized French, but Field Marshal Haig then reverted to his original plan for 1917 which was to force a passage from Ypres to the coast.

### THE SAVAGE SUMMER:

In early June, nine British divisions moved on Messines Ridge, south of Ypres, and the air war moved north with them. After inflicting critical losses on the RFC in April, Manfred von Richthofen was recalled from leave on June 10th because of increasing German air losses. His first act was to attend the funeral of Karl Schaefer, a close friend and 30-victory ace, who had been shot down by Capt Harold Leslie Satchell and Lt Thomas Lewis in a FE2d from #20 Squadron. It was an occasion fraught with omens. The "prehistoric English packing cases" that had insolently bombed his drome at Douai several nights running in April had carried off his friend. In five weeks the balance of air power began to shift as the RFC began getting new aircraft.

When Lt Andrew McKeever joined #11 Squadron in May, he flew a modified version of the Bristol Fighter which had easily fallen to Richthofen. The pilot used aggressive fighter tactics and soon he and his observer, Lt L.A. Powell, were rolling up an impressive string of victories. At least 13 Canadians flew the two-seater that summer and the Bristol fighter became one of the most effective air-craft of the war.

#56 Squadron with SE5s came to the front that April with Constantinesco synchronization gear enabling a pilot to fire a Vickers through the propeller arc. The new scouts were solid and manoeuvrable and although early models lacked power to stay with the Albatros at heights of 18,000 feet, the new models had a more powerful engine, which turned the SE5 into one of the best fighters of the war. #56 Squadron became home to several aces that grew up on the job, includ-ing Lt Reginald Hoidge. A transfer from the Canadian artillery, the Toronto pilot scored 25 victories during the summer while the entire squadron destroyed 200 aircraft.

Thirteen of Naval Three's pilots resurfaced on Naval Ten, which flew the spec-tacular Sopwith Triplane, a highly agile aircraft that performed extremely well at altitudes up to 20,000 feet. However, similar to the Pup, its armament was indif-ferent and it could not stay with the Albatros D-111 in a dive, but in the hands of

Naval Three it became a major weapon in reversing German ascendancy. Yet the pace of technology was now so rapid that the Sopwith Triplane was virtually obsolete within three months.

Raymond Collishaw led a Naval Ten flight, which brought the first trace of Canadian identity to the Western Front. The fuselage decking from cockpit to nose including the engine cowling and the wheel discs of their Triplanes were painted black. The ominous black theme was carried forward with names stencilled below the cockpit rim. Collishaw chose *Black Maria*. Ellis Reid was *Black Roger*, fellow Torontonian William "Mel" Alexander flew the *Black Prince*, Gerry Nash of Stoney Creek, Ont., was the *Black Sheep* while John Sharman from Oak Lake, Man., was *Black Death*. The official reason for the paint job was that it made the aircraft easier for ground crew to identify the machines as they came in for a landing, but there was a suspicion in the days of brightly coloured enemy aircraft that the Canadians were trying to make a statement.

Naval Ten was posted to Droglandt, France, in mid-May as preparations for the Messines offensive were underway. The day before the Messines attack of June 7th, Collishaw led a full flight of five over Polygon Wood where they encountered 15 Albatros and Halberstadt fighters that were escorting an observation machine. Collishaw got two, which burned, and a third went down out of control with the pilot dead or wounded. Nash got the two-seater and sent an Albatros down, which was last seen diving towards the ground at 500 feet. Reid took down a Halberstadt and John Page got an Albatros. Sharman, Alexander and John Keens of Toronto each sent an Albatros down out of control. The combat lasted 35 minutes during which the flight was credited with five destroyed and five driven down out of control.

The ground attack at Messines started with over 450 tons of explosives erupting from the detonation of 19 mines followed by an intense artillery barrage. Naval Three flew two patrols, accounted for five enemy aircraft and lost John Keenes who was wounded in the lung but got back to the Allied lines.

Richthofen began operating as air commander of four squadrons or Jastas. His original squadron was now based in Belgium at Marcke, directly across from Naval Ten, but he relinquished command of Jasta 2 to become leader of the Jagdgeschwader 1 Hunting Group. Because the squadrons were mobile, the tactic of grouping meant that up to 60 aircraft could be diverted at any time to any spot on the front. Richthofen acted as ringmaster, stacking the squadrons in layers and bringing them into play on demand. It was a tactic that would have deadly efficiency until the last day of the war.

Billy Bishop attacked a German aerodrome on June 1st and was credited with downing four machines. By the end of July, he scored his first victory in a SE5 to bring his total to 37, but shortly afterwards was shot down by anti-aircraft fire at

Monchy-le-Preux. He was attempting to glide home when his engine caught fire and he went into a sideslip to keep the flames away from the cockpit, but they ate their way into the strut. The wing held long enough to enable the machine to cartwheel into trees and Bishop was upside down in the burning plane when he fainted. After a brief rest, he remained on operations until mid-August where his victories rose to 47. He was then marched off to Buckingham Palace where the King presented him with the Victoria Cross, the Distinguished Service Order and the Military Cross.

Karl Allmenroder was a high scoring ace with Jasta 11 who took down *Black Sheep* Gerald Nash. Nash survived the crash, but was taken prisoner as he fell behind enemy lines. A few days later, while in prison, he heard church bells. A guard told him they were ringing for Allmenroder's funeral. Nash later learned that Raymond Collishaw had brought down Allmenroder.

On the morning of July 6th, German fighters jumped six FE's far behind the lines. Pilots from #100 Squadron had developed a milk run to Richthofen's base in April, and the only thing tougher than the machines, which Richthofen scorned as "packing cases," were the men who flew them. July 6th had been a busy day for observer Albert Woodbridge. The six FEs of his flight had fought off 40 enemy fighters and sent four down when Richthofen attacked. Woodbridge opened fire at long range but Richthofen bore in with confidence as he held his fire. Then a bullet hit him in the head and he blindly spiraled downward, enduring the agony of death without its release. The Baron recovered in time to land behind the lines but the experience would haunt him for the rest of his limited days.

As the battle continued, Collishaw, Reid, Alexander and Britisher D. FitzGibbon swept down from above while the FEs tightened their defensive circle. Collishaw got six hostiles while Mel Alexander and Ellis Reid each got two. The FEs accounted for seven and ironically Woodbridge didn't claim the Baron's fall as he was much too busy to watch.

The British preparation for the third Battle of Ypres drew over 1,300 aircraft into a 30-mile corridor between the Lys and the English Channel. About 200 were French, 500 were British while 600 were German. Five of Collishaw's "all-Canadian" Black Flight became aces during this period and those who were not killed ran up impressive totals.

In Collishaw's words, the summer was "strictly a war of attrition and it was simply a question of who was going to give out first. I feel that we were simply being asked to do too much."[16] The pilots were in the air or on call from dawn until dark. About 50 per cent of pilots developed neurosis during their tour and unless a perceptive commanding officer noticed the twitch and diagnosed it early, it was probable that the pilot would experience a nervous breakdown. But the stigma of "coming down with nerves" was so great that many pilots sought death instead. Mel Alexander remembered men crying like babies because they were leaving their comrades in a "tight corner."

British ace Capt Albert Ball's last days left the haunting sound of violin music as he lived apart from the others and spent his last nights pacing back and forth playing the violin. He later flew into a cloud and was never seen again. Another British ace, Capt James McCudden, died in unusual circumstances some months later suggesting that combat fatigue had dulled his excellent flying skills. The engine of McCudden's fighter stalled on takeoff and the 57-victory ace made the rookie mistake of trying to get back to base and died in a crash.

Billy Bishop wrote: "I don't think my nerves will last more than three months. ... They are getting shaky now. I find myself shuddering at chances I didn't think anything of taking six weeks ago."[17] The tension which wound itself around aircrew in that narrow corridor was universal. Richthofen went to hospital for six weeks after Woodbridge's bullet, which had a profound psychological effect on him. After his fall, he no longer felt confident in a German victory and his flying became much more cautious.

Andrew McKeever and his observers posted 31 victories in five months and all but two were Albatros fighters often meeting odds of five to one. In late November, McKeever was flying alone over Cambrai when an enemy patrol of two-seaters and seven fighters suddenly emerged from the cloud. McKeever attacked and brought down the first aircraft with 10 bullets. His observer got two more and McKeever's front gun brought down a fourth. Although Canadians were very effective in helping wipe out German superiority, the cost was high. Of the 13 Canadians who served on McKeever's squadron during this six-month period, six were killed, two were wounded and three became prisoners of war.

At high cost the RFC had fought back from virtual extermination. Some 240 Canadians flew at the front line in July 1917, but by Christmas 200 became casualties. Naval Three was statistically wiped out as 10 pilots were killed, two wounded and three taken prisoners of war. In the mud of November, Canadian troops took the remains of Passchendaele and tanks moved into Cambrai where they were shot like buffalo. Meagre gains in the ground war had cost Haig some 300,000 casualties while total air casualties for the dismal year ran to some 1,900. The RFC had survived Bloody April and made a strong comeback, but history has never measured the depth of resentment towards Trenchard's policy of leaning over enemy sky.

One pilot who went on to senior rank said: "The futility of such wasteful losses was deeper because if the DOP (Distant Offensive Patrol) was weak it was overwhelmed. But if it was strong, the Germans could and frequently did ignore it, leaving us with a debit of forced-landed aeroplanes, wasted engine hours and wasted petrol." [18]

Maj W. Sholto Douglas, who became an air chief marshal in the Second World War, questioned Trenchard's policy that resulted in the loss of 32 of his 35 aircraft in one month. Another pilot recorded: "Our casualties mounted alarmingly ... the aim seemed to be to contrive the greatest number of confrontations of British and German aircraft ... there was no discernible military objective."[19]

Lt Arthur Gould Lee, later a RAF air vice marshal, expressed the fighter pilot's disenchantment with distant offensive patrols. "Had there been a specific purpose to out deep penetrations, such as covering a bombing raid or a photographic reconnaissance, we would have thought nothing of it, but we could see no rational purpose in our coat-tailing DOPs."[20]

The savage summer of 1917 saw the end of the solitary hunter, a breed that began with Roland Garros and flourished with Oswald Boelcke and the other Fokker pilots of his time. In spite of his high score, Manfred von Richthofen hardly qualified as a hunter as he usually had his squadron isolate his victims before he attacked. Werner Voss, on the other hand, epitomized the hunter. After 48 victories, he fell in a classic duel with seven of #56 Squadron's best. Albert Ball became the leading British hunter over the Somme and although later was assigned as a flight commander, he was the happiest when stalking his prey alone. Billy Bishop's career followed a similar path, but the tactics that evolved during the summer of 1917 introduced a new breed of fighter pilot.

Raymond Collishaw and his high-scoring Black Flight showed the discipline and skill necessary to survive the new form of combat. One evening over Polygon Wood in the Ypres sector an air action dramatically pointed out the way to change. An RFC flight intercepted four German observation aircraft reconnoitring British lines at Ypres. They attacked and suddenly groups of fighters spilled out of the clouds from ground level to 17,000 feet. Over 100 machines were drawn into the vortex of a mass dogfight and they fought private battles for half an hour. With ammunition exhausted, both sides withdrew but they were so well matched not a fighter was lost. The battle ended as suddenly as it erupted and then night birds claimed the sky over Flanders for a few hours.

***ABOVE:*** *Louden Watkins was awarded the MC for bringing down the L-48, but he later died of wounds suffered on the Western Front. (AH604)*

***OPPOSITE PAGE:*** *During the attack, Louden Watkins watched the L-48 glow and then burn. Although the Germans lost 53 airships in 40 raids on England, much of the damage was due to accidents and anti-aircraft fire. (PAINTING BY DON CONNOLLY, RE-210H)*

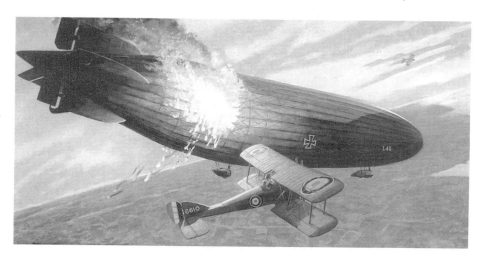

*Peter Strasser was a war ahead of his time. His aim
was to bring Britain to her knees by burning London...*

# ৯ BOMBS AWAY

*KORVETTENKAPITAN PETER STRASSER,* head of the German
navy's airship division, fought doubts and inertia from the outbreak of hostilities.
He also wielded enough influence in the corridors of Berlin to train 25 airship
crews within four months of the outbreak of war. With 3,740 men scattered
around eight bases in Germany and Belgium, Strasser was a leading proponent of
bombing. He saw the airship as a means of bringing England to her knees. Obsessed by a dream of putting 20 airships over London, dropping 6,000 incendiary
bombs and burning the capital into submission, Strasser was a war ahead of his
time. Thankfully Canadian airmen became major factors in denying Strasser his
dream and bringing about his death.

On Christmas day, 1914, a British task force swept into the Heligoland Bight
and lumbering seaplanes bombed the port of Cuxhaven and Strasser's major airship base at Nordholz. One aircraft dropped a bomb in the woods near the site of
a million cubic feet of explosive hydroGen Although little damage was done,
Strasser made the most of the issue by protesting to the Kaiser that Germany's
magnificent weapons should not be destroyed on the ground. The impact of
Strasser's arguments on the Kaiser was never measured, but within three weeks
Strasser got qualified approval to bomb England. Strasser flew the first-ever aerial
bombing mission, against England on January 19, 1915 when one airship struck
Yarmouth and the other hit King's Lynn. The third airship, with Strasser on
board, was forced to turn back because of engine trouble. While the Kaiser had

agreed to the bombing of English ports, London was still off-limits, but Strasser took heart from the fact that he was now one step closer to his goal.

By the end of April, German army airships were also involved. Flight Sub-Lt Redford Mulock, a Canadian with the RNAS, made the first interception after the LZ-38 bombed Ramsgate. At a time when few men had flown at night, Mulock took off in an Avro 504 armed with two petrol bombs and two grenades. Some accounts have him wearing a pistol and others have the machine mounting a Lewis gun that immediately jammed on firing. *Hauptmann* Eric Lennarz, commander of the LZ-38, was able to jettison ballast and the airship out-climbed Mulock and disappeared into the clouds. Two weeks later, Lennarz bombed London but a week after that the LZ-38 was destroyed in a shed at Evere, near Brussels.

On the evening of June 6, 1915, F/S/L Reggie Warneford spotted a LZ-37 off Bruges. He challenged machine gun fire for some time until he had a height advantage at 11,000 feet. Then, through intense fire from the 500-foot target, he dropped the first of his bombs but nothing happened. He dropped his second and third bombs, and as he was turning away in disgust, the tiny Morane Parasol monoplane was suddenly tossed about the sky by a massive explosion, making Warneford the first pilot to destroy a Zeppelin in the air.

Alfred Muhler was at the helm of the LZ-37. "The whole immense hull above me was ablaze, instantly becoming a roaring hissing inferno ... I threw myself flat on the floor of the car. I wondered how long it took to fall 5,000 feet ... at last the gondola struck and everything went black."[21] The gondola crashed through the roof of a convent and Muhler landed in a bed with minor injuries.

The German naval airship division began to dominate the airship war when *Kapitanleutnant* Heinrich Mathy hit London on September 8, 1915. He knew London and used St. Paul's as a reference point, bombing extensively from Queen's Square to Liverpool station. Damage ran to $3 million and 22 people were killed. Mathy became a German national hero and the raid ushered in a year of assaults on the British capital. Strasser was able to get bigger and better airships and the war became a contest between the London defences and the height climbers which could get above the anti-aircraft fire that originally was a more potent defence than aircraft.

Strasser directed raids on other parts of England in order to make the British spread their defences. On January 31, 1916, he won a major psychological victory when eight of his ships prowled the Midlands, bombing at will for hours. Not one airship was intercepted by the RNAS and 11 of the 15 RNAS aircraft sent aloft crashed. The event raised a furor in England and home defence was taken out of the hands of the RNAS.

Strasser still had major critics in Berlin but his boast that his airships were making the British tie up 17,000 men in home defence ensured delivery of new height climbers in the spring of 1916. The LZ-30 series were 650 feet long and 90 feet high. Powered by six Maybach engines, they could reach 62 m.p.h. and climb to 17,400 feet where 10 machine guns laid down a curtain of fire against possible aircraft. Although army crews used parachutes, Strasser issued his men cyanide pills and made up the weight of some 23 parachutes with extra bombs.

Strasser was able to mount his climatic attack on September 2, 1916, with 16 raiders, including four army machines. This gave him the striking power to achieve his dream of destroying London. Four of the army airships dropped out en route, but most of Strasser's force circled London shortly after midnight. When the two remaining army ships reached their rendezvous, *Hauptmann* Willhelm Schramm flashed his navigation lights in recognition and Strasser's dream died with a flick of the switch.

Lt William Leefe-Robinson couldn't believe his luck as he closed in on the blinking navigation lights. But the airship escaped into clouds and the pilot searched for half an hour before finding it. A burst of Brock-Pomeroy bullets found the army airship and the combination of incendiary and tracer bullets set it on fire. It sizzled in the air, then fragments fell into the night like meteors while millions cheered. It was a sight capable of shattering the bravest airship officer. *Kapitän* Ernst Lehmann, who would later die on the Hindenburg, was the only commander to bomb as planned. The others climbed or dove for cover. *Kapitän* Werner Peterson waited for Strasser's orders but none came. He later described the raid as a "disgraceful failure" and added, "I was deeply worried about Strasser's mental state on the trip home. He simply sat and stared ... not saying a word."[22]

But, later that month, Strasser was back over London and so was Peterson. This time Strasser flew with Mathy and once again the night was filled with a hellish glare of a burning airship. Peterson had flown 11 raids and was one of the top commanders. His L-32 broke cloud over London and was immediately coned by searchlights and became a target for anti-aircraft guns. RFC pilot Maj Frederick Sowrey dove on the airship as it climbed. His first two drums of Brock-Pomeroy ammunition had no effect, but the third set the airship aglow and it soon fell at Billericay. Strasser radioed his crews to bomb as planned. A second super airship was lost that night, and this strengthened the German general staff's opposition to airships. The bloodbath on the Somme reinforced the army's argument that the 7,000 men who were now in Strasser's command could be put to better use elsewhere.

On October 1st, 11 raiders set out for England but only one reached London. It was commanded by Heinrich Mathy a national hero and ace airship captain. Wulstan Tempest of Perdue, Sask., spotted the L-31 at 12,700 feet and climbing. He had a slight height advantage and the nearest anti-aircraft bursts were three miles away. Tempest was fighting a defective fuel pump as he sacrificed his height advantage in a dive. "I gave a tremendous pump at my petrol tank and dived straight at her ... tracer bullets flying from her in all directions ... the airship started to burn and shot past me like a roaring furnace."[23]

Mathy's death and the heavy losses took the soul out of the German airship division and raised further opposition in Berlin. The Kaiser told the admiralty to stop the raids. The army instigated the order and this set off a spasm of inter-service rivalry. Senior naval officers who never did believe in the airships as a weapon now rallied against the intrusion by the army into naval affairs, but they did exercise much tighter control over airship operations. Strasser could no longer select targets or plan his own raids. Airship operations became restricted to recon-naissance or the occasional raid on the Midlands.

The fortunes of the Airship Division continued to decline. But the irony of the last days showed that airships might have significantly changed the course of the war had they been used to track Allied shipping. In mid-May 1917, Robert Leckie spotted the L-22 on a scouting mission. His observer, J.O. Galpin, poured incen-diaries into the Zeppelin, and as they turned away with a gun stoppage the airship began to glow and then burn.

Basil Hobbs of Sault-Ste. Marie, Ont., who paid his way to war by learning to fly at the Wright School in Dayton, was up on a routine patrol a month later. He was three hours out of Felixstowe when he spotted an airship off the Dutch coast. Hobbs managed to get the flying boat above the airship and dove. His three gunners opened fire and the airship fell into two flaming halves.

Three nights later, Lt Loudon Watkins of Toronto, took off in an RFC BE12 to intercept the L-48 that had crossed the coast at Orfordness. It was a mission that started badly for the Zeppelin commander Franz Eichler. As was custom, the divisional band played them off as they left from Nordholz. However, this time the base drum split. Then Eichler had to circle for hours as they approached the English coast. The starboard engine quit and his compass froze so he descended and bombed the naval base at Harwich. The airship was under attack by another aircraft when Watkins approached and slid under the giant and tilted his twin Lewis guns upwards. On the L-48, the machinist's mate, Heinrich Ellerkamm, heard the rattle and saw tiny blue flames dance among the gasbags above his head. The collar of his fur coat sizzled and started to burn as explosions rocked the ship and threw crewmen into a pile on the gondola floor with a 600-foot blaze roaring above them. "The benzine and oil tanks had burst ... oil was run-ning about like liquid fire. My coat was burning on my back. I was imprisoned in a cage, the bars of which were a glowing red-hot mass."[24] When the L-48 hit land, Ellerkamm rolled free of the twisted mess and returned to rescue the watch officer. Of the 21-member crew, they were the only survivors.

The German army introduced its Gotha bombers in 1917 and airships were no longer considered a serious threat in England. Yet Strasser still had the influence and the drive to get funds for bigger airships. The first of the super airships came to strength in mid-1918. The L-70 was almost 700 feet long and well armed with a speed of 75 m.p.h. at 22,000 feet. It had a range, which would take it to New York City and back, and this is precisely what Strasser wanted to do. He argued that such a raid would panic the Americans.

Early in August 1918, Strasser attacked the Midlands with the L-70 and four smaller machines. Robert Leckie was the acting executive officer that night at Great Yarmouth RNAS base when the alarm sounded. He dutifully scrambled more than a dozen machines, and when Maj Egbert Cadbury raced for the last DH4 aircraft, Leckie became an instant observer. They took off and spotted the raiders over the Wash where Leckie's Brock-Pomeroy bullets turned the L-70 into a glowing sun that incinerated Strasser and crew.

The other machines jettisoned their bombs and withdrew. It was the last of 306 sorties against England with the final cost of 57 machines and 500 crewmen. Of the 57 airships, 38 were destroyed in accidents and 19 by enemy action. Anti-aircraft fire was responsible for the bulk of the destruction, but Canadians were largely involved in the annihilation of six of the 12 airships brought down by aircraft from England. Crew losses almost equaled civilian losses in England where 550 people were killed. Yet in spite of the grim statistics, Strasser had been able to inspire his crews to the end.

From the Allied point of view, the airship war ended with a sense of irony or poetic justice. Charles Rumney Samson, the man Winston Churchill sent to Belgium in the early weeks of the war to fight airships, was back in the innovation business. After a period in the Mideast, Samson endured a stint at the admiralty. Then he took command of the RNAS base at Great Yarmouth. In 1918 an admiral sought out Samson to develop a means of getting an aircraft off a barge at sea. Samson worked out the grand plan, which called for a Camel with skids instead of wheels to be flown off a barge being towed behind a ship. Samson gunned the Camel and it shot forward but the skids fouled on the trestles that supported the track. The Camel shot into the water and the barge ploughed over it. When Samson recovered, he decided that perhaps it was a job for a younger man and selected Montrealer Stuart Culley.

Five days after Leckie brought down the L-70, Lt Culley flew a Camel with wheels off the barge being towed at 30 m.p.h. by HMS *Redoubt*. His target was a German airship that had been observing the British task force for some time and whose information enabled German aircraft to destroy three motorboats.

Culley made a successful takeoff and 50 minutes later was stalking the airship at 18,000 feet. He pulled up underneath the airship and fired a drum but his second gun jammed as the fighter stalled and spun down to 2,000 feet. As he glanced up, the airship was flying away, but yellow flame had sprouted from three places. It was later known that Culley had flown past the last German airship to fall in combat. He later recalled: "Maybe had I not glimpsed their faces when I flew by the gondola, I would have been less affected by their ghastly fate ... I was horrified and sickened by what I had wrought."[25]

## BOMBERS OVER ENGLAND

Although German airships were servicing the fleet in 1918, the airship war had lost its impetus by 1917 and the German army was training bomber crews near Ostend. On May 25, 23 Gothas left bases around Ghent for the first sweep against England. When the formation reached Gravesend, it encountered towering clouds that guarded London like a fortress. The Gothas jettisoned bombs on Folkestone, killing 95 and wounding 195. Thirteen of the dead and 76 of the wounded were Canadians from Shorncliffe, Man. Although the raid failed to reach its target, more civilians were killed than in any airship raid of the war.

Louden Watkins and W. Humphreys of Parry Sound, Ont., were among the 74 pilots to feel the frustration of being out-climbed and out-flown by the raiders. Watkins sighted a Gotha, but could not get up to its height; and Humphreys chased one 20 miles, but couldn't catch it. However, within three weeks Watkins destroyed an enemy airship. The first attack convinced Bomber Commander Ernst Brandenburg that the Gotha was a deadly match for the weak and uncoordinated British home defences.

Powered by two Mercedes 260 h.p. engines, the original Gothas cruised at 90 m.p.h. usually above 16,000 feet with a daylight bomb load of 660 pounds. With a crew of three, it had machine guns fore and aft and a scatter gun that shot downwards through a trap near the tail. Implications of the first Gotha raid were slow to penetrate official London. Brandenburg sent 22 against Sheernes dockyard on June 5th as a dress rehearsal for a strike at London. Sixty-five assorted British machines took off, but only five got within range of the enemy formation and none brought down a raider although artillery fire damaged one causing a forced landing.

On June 13, Londoners heard the sound of approaching Gotha's 10 minutes before 17 of them flew over the city. Brandenburg reported visibility that gave them a clear view of the Thames Bridge, a railway station and the Bank of England. Anti-aircraft fire was moderate and poorly directed and the aircraft circled and dropped their bombs with no hurry or trouble.

Over 90 British aircraft were aloft but many like the BE12s or BE2bs of #37 Squadron were merely wasting fuel because neither machine could get above

12,500 feet. The London raid got the attention of the War Council, which met that afternoon and determined there should be an increase in the number of aircraft. A panic conference wishfully recommended increasing RFC strength from 108 to 200 squadrons, but the only effective action was to pull two of Trenchard's best fighter squadrons home from the front.

After being decorated with the Blue Max, Germany's highest award, Brandenburg was injured in a plane crash and confined to hospital for many months. He was succeeded by Rudolph Kleine. Kleine's first raid came on July 4th when 18 Gothas hit Harwich and did considerable damage to the Felixstowe naval station. Canadians flying out of Dunkirk with the RNAS were among the pilots who had better luck against the Gothas because the bombers descended as they approached the coast. Alexander Shook of Tiogo, Ont., shot down one bomber as it returned from Harwich and the flight of Camels, which he was leading, added two more. Shook later shared in the destruction of another Gotha.

With riots in the streets, and an uproar in the British House of Commons, pressure increased for more aircraft and reprisal bombings of German cities. A committee was set up to prepare two reports. The first called for strengthened air and anti-aircraft defences; the second called for a unified air service and an independent bombing arm.

Trenchard recommended depriving the bombers of their bases by the capture of German pockets on the Belgian coast. Failing this, he favoured strikes on enemy sheds and equipment but felt that reprisals on German towns would only lead to more counter-raids. Kleine's assessment of the July 7th raid on London was that the anti-aircraft fire was more accurate and enemy airmen were more aggressive. Although home defence machines had little success up to this point, the bomber wing's losses from accidents, anti-aircraft damage and fighters from Dunkirk left Klein wondering how soon the losses would become unacceptable.

The appointment of Brig-Gen E.B. Ashmore to London defence intensified Kleine's concerns about acceptable losses. Ashmore added three squadrons to the defence of London and improved anti-aircraft defences. On August 12th one Gotha dropped out of formation as they crossed the English coast and bombed Margate. Harold Kerby, who flew at Gallipoli, and M.R. Kingsford of Toronto were part of a patrol which went up from the RNAS station at Walmer in Ireland. The patrol pursued the Gotha to Zeebrugge on the Belgian coast but lost it because it crash-landed on a beach. On the way home, Kerby flew towards anti-aircraft bursts at Southend and found a homebound Gotha formation. He engaged the bombers and drove one down into the water where it turned over on impact. He reported: "One of the occupants I saw hanging on the tail of the Gotha, I threw him my lifebelt and did two or three circuits."[26]

Kleine lost six aircraft in the raid and nine days later Kerby was credited with another Gotha. The Germans switched to night bombing on September 3rd and were virtually unopposed. The War Cabinet threw up its hands when both the RFC and RNAS maintained that the new Camel and SE5 fighters were too unstable to fly at night. Top fighter pilots were posted to home defence squadrons ringing London and underwent intensive night flying exercises.

Although a few pilots like Redford Mulock did have night flying experience, the fighter aircraft, in addition to being extremely sensitive didn't have instrument illumination. The training program had hardly begun when the Germans launched the harvest moon strikes during the last week in September. London was hit on five of six raids in which fighters failed to bring down one bomber although anti-aircraft fire accounted for four. Five home defence machines crashed on landing. Of the 151 missions flown by home defence, only five pilots thought they saw bombers. The harvest moon raids featured another German technological triumph as Giant Straaken R.VI bombers joined the Gothas. The Giants carried more than three times the bomb load of the Gotha but in subsequent months the pace of the raids slackened even though no Giants were ever shot down.

To some extent the bomber force was diverted to the continent in preparation for the Ludendorff offensives of April 1918. In the last raid on London seven of 45 bombers were shot down. For a loss of 61 Gothas, the German bombing campaign killed 1,413 and seriously injured over 4,400 others. Absenteeism in British factories hit 70 per cent following the raids and home defence measures occupied more than 15,000 troops. In diverting its bombing force to the Western Front, the Germans were investing in tactical bombing while in England by the fall of 1917 the government thirsted for retaliation through strategic bombing and would continue to tie up personnel even though no more aircraft raids were forthcoming. The irony of the German failure of strategic bombing is that it was a major factor in leading the British into the same type of warfare.

## THE STRANGE SAGA OF STRATEGIC BOMBING

While the RFC fought to a deadly gridlock with a powerful enemy over Flanders, a war of words had been raging in London since the first bombs fell in the spring of 1917. Gen Jan Smuts made a study of the situation and recommended the RNAS and the RFC be amalgamated and an additional independent bombing force be established to strike back at Germany. The revenge motive became a popular issue in England, but on the Western Front Boom Trenchard snorted at the Smuts Report because it meant that precious resources would be diverted to the bomber force instead of supporting the land battle.

Cabinet ordered immediate raids from Nancy, in eastern France, and Trenchard detached two squadrons and borrowed one from the RNAS to set up #41 Wing.

Lt-Col C.L.N. Newall's day-bombing squadron, including five Canadians, flew DH4s out of Banville-sur-Madon while two night-bombing squadrons were based at Ochey, France. Half of one such squadron were Canadians who flew obsolete FEs that had a small bomb load and a ceiling of only 9,000 feet. The naval squadron flew Handley-Pages which had a bomb-load of 1,000 pounds and a remarkable endurance of eight hours.

The strategic bombing campaign opened on October 7, when DH4 day-bombers took off for steel works at Saarbrucken-Burbach. Four days later, #55 Squadron was out again bombing factories and railroads at Bous. After bombing, 11 DH4s were jumped by 10 Albatros fighters and the two-seaters brought down four of the enemy's best. Daniel Owen, a Nova Scotian from Annapolis Royal was a flight leader with #55 Squadron who had an eye shot out but managed to land behind enemy lines. About 150 Canadians would eventually fly with what became the Independent Air Force and a third of these would become casualties.

Handley-Pages from the naval squadron hit the Burbach works and FE2bs from #100 Squadron raided rail yards between Falkenburg and Saarbrucken where four more Canadians went missing. The naval squadron lost almost 50 per cent of its aircraft in the one mission. Out of a force of nine, two went missing, one wrecked and one was damaged beyond immediate repair. Gordon Flavelle of Lindsay, Ont., flew his first operation and his log entries suggest a night of confusion. "Dropped bombs on target ... could not see results for clouds. Lost ourselves on way back. Crashed machine near St. Dizier ... nothing left but tail and fuselage."[27]

Two squadrons were added to the force in February. It became known as VIII Brigade as work got under way on five aerodromes in the Nancy area to accommodate anticipated extra aircraft. Within a month, Trenchard resigned as chief-of-staff of the proposed RAF and a new air minister offered him the job as head of the Independent Air Force. The man who had developed Allied tactical bombing suddenly found himself the proponent of strategic bombing. Trenchard was promised 34 squadrons, but at no time did bombing strength exceed nine. Although now part of the RAF, Trenchard showed a marked lack of enthusiasm for Maj-Gen Sykes, the man who succeeded him as chief. He had less time for Syke's headquarters staff and the targets they selected from London. So he usually ignored both.

Sykes wanted to hit German chemical and industrial production, particularly the steel and ironworks that flourished in centres such as Frankfurt, Metz, Coblenz and Mannheim. But Trenchard usually concentrated on railroads, transportation links and aerodromes, targets more directly involved with the land battle. In fact, about 75 per cent of the Independent Air Force's targets were tactical rather than strategic.

Trenchard became an enigma who had little apparent faith in strategic bombing and saw the Independent Air Force as a political device enabling politicians at home to boast that they were bombing Germany. Yet he soldiered on against obstacles and broken promises at home and growing opposition over Germany. When British ground forces were doing badly during the Ludendorff offensives in the spring of 1918, the air minister asked Trenchard to start a big fire in one of those German towns. The attack on Metz-Sablon could be interpreted as a response to the air minister's request.

Two Canadians flew as observers when 14 FEs went against the railhead in a night raid. Seven bombs fell on the main track, seven munitions wagons exploded and 15 cars burned. About 20 tracks were damaged while a second train exploded burning itself out. As well, an exploding gasometer blew the top off a nearby building. During a period of 23 days, as the Ludendorff offensive was driving the Allies back to Amiens in the north and close to Paris in the south, V111 Brigade flew 200 sorties in support of their troops. When #55 Squadron hit Saarbrucken on May 16 one DH4 was lost and three observers wounded as they were attacked by 30 fighters. The introduction of the DH9 with an extremely unreliable engine added to everybody's troubles.

On another raid on Metz-Sablon towards the end of the month, five of 12 DH9s had engine trouble. But the force, which officially became the Independent Air Force on May 8, intensified its activity and in six months carried out 110 additional raids. On July 31st, 12 DH9s from #99 Squadron flew out to bomb Mainz. The new machines were a replacement for the efficient DH4 day-bomber but an engine prone to failure made the DH9 a classic dog of an aircraft. During one month, the force lost 14 machines to enemy action and 59 to accidents.

The flight to Mainz added fighters to the pilots' problem with chilling results. Three of the 12 DH9s crash-landed before reaching the front. The others were attacked by 40 fighters as soon as they crossed the lines. Heavily engaged, the bombers swung toward Saarbrucken as an alternate target and four were shot down on the way. Five bombed Saarbrucken and turned for home, but three more were lost to fighters in German air space. Ten aircraft were missing when two survivors got back to base where the crews immediately volunteered to "go back and finish the job."

Canadians were a significant component of most squadrons and prominent on #104 Squadron with J.B. Home-Hay of Wadena, Sask., and Torontonian E. H. McKay, each of whom led a flight of DH9s towards Mannheim. One of the 12 machines was shot down by anti-aircraft as soon as they crossed the lines and enemy scouts hovered overhead waiting for a chance to attack. When J. Valentine's engine quit, the fighters attacked, but Valentine managed to land before being destroyed. McKay developed engine trouble over the Vosges Mountains and was forced down. The remainder went on to Mannheim where fighters attacked them during their bombing run. The squadron dove to 6,000 feet where it broke up and the scouts pounced. G. Pickard of Exeter, Ont., was shot down and Home-Hay made a forced landing. W. Bottrill of Hamilton, Ont., assembled the scattered formation by tying a handkerchief to the scarf mounting of his Lewis gun. Four machines of #104 Squadron followed him home but seven did not. #110 Squadron lost seven of its 12 aircraft in a strike on Frankfurt and the squadron was wiped out operationally. D. Atkinson and K. Wilkinson both of Toronto were among the survivors. By October many operations were being made in support of American and French troops, but as the range of the Handley-Page bomber improved, pressure also grew to bomb Berlin.

A group under Redford Mulock had been formed to bomb Berlin but delivery of their Handley-Page V/500 bombers was delayed. The so-called strategic bombing campaign of the Independent Air Force flew 508 raids in which 382 men were killed, wounded or missing, One hundred and forty machines were lost over enemy territory and 320 behind Allied lines. About one-third of the 150 Canadians who flew with the force were casualties. The bombing was politically motivated, ill defined and its execution marred by conflicting views. Most of Trenchard's targets were not strategic but simply distant and the entire operation lacked the precision of his air policy on the Western Front. Analysis of bombing reports tended to be overly optimistic. For instance, the admiralty attached significance to an early report that observed that bombing was causing special prayers to be raised in German churches. This invited the conclusion that the process of strategic bombing was a clumsy and expensive way of leading an enemy to God.

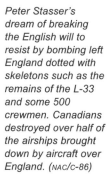

*Peter Stasser's dream of breaking the English will to resist by bombing left England dotted with skeletons such as the remains of the L-33 and some 500 crewmen. Canadians destroyed over half of the airships brought down by aircraft over England. (NAC/C-86)*

**TOP:** *Voisin biplane flown by F/S/L Rudolf D. Delamere (right) of Toronto, one of two Canadians who served with the RNAS in East Africa during the Frist World War. This photo was taken at Mbuyuni, British East Africa, in May 1916. (CAF)*

**ABOVE:** *Innovator Charles Samson turned a channel ferry into a carrier for seaplanes, which were winched aboard. His force in the Mid-East included a number of Canadians. (IWM)*

**OPPOSITE PAGE:** *Late in 1917, a number of Canadians were among the airmen who moved from the Western Front to Italy were they experienced a different kind of war. (IWM)*

# ᔕ WORLD TRAVELLERS AT 21

*ALTHOUGH MOST OF THE* Canadians ended up on the Western Front, a number followed a war that spread like a rash. Some three weeks after the outbreak of war, Winston Churchill, first lord of the admiralty, sent Commander Charles Rumney Samson and 10 pilots to the continent to harass the Hun. Samson's men hit the enemy from the air and from the ground. They bombed Cologne and an airship shed at Dusseldorf, and armed busses hit enemy columns, confusing them with fast moving armoured vehicles. Samson was an inventive pirate at heart who cared little for admiralty conventions, and was just the sort of man Churchill later needed to provide air support for the Gallipoli operation.

During April of 1915, Samson moved another strange assortment of men and machines to a new location. When Naval Three squadron began unloading aircraft on the island of Tenedos all but five were dead on arrival. Pilots lived in the crates that some reckoned to be as airworthy as their aircraft and, although the war was only seven months old, the first Canadian pilots soon joined them. Churchill was one of the prime movers in the Gallipoli campaign to force a passage through the Dardanelles in order to link up with the Russians on the Black Sea. The plan, according to the admiralty, was to send a number of British ships up a narrow channel, weave through minefields and knock out heavy guns on the cliffs on either side. It was a scenario written for *Boy's Own Adventure* and an early version of the Dieppe raid.

Eighteen British warships, four French battleships and a number of auxiliary ships bombarded Turkish forts on February 19th. About the only noticeable result was that the commander of the attacking force broke down and had to be replaced. In a later attempt, four battleships struck mines and the admiralty decided that army support was needed to take the Dardanelles. The British assembled four divisions, including the Australian and New Zealand army corps while the French organized a feint on the east shore of the Dardanelles. Samson's group was at Imbros, south of the peninsula, when Harold Kerby of Calgary joined them in the third week of March 1915. Kerby would later bring down two Gotha bombers, but when he checked in with Samson, he had but 15 hours of flying time. He soon began logging hours because it took 40 minutes to get to the peninsula where the landings went in on April 25th. Samson flew over a landing site at Sedd-el Bahr and saw the sea run red for 50 feet from shore as thousands of brave men died because isolated groups were thrown into the maw of Turkish rifle machine-gun fire.

As the campaign dragged on, Samson's small force ranged guns for the navy and did observation. But long hours in the air, poor living conditions on a bug infested island and the navy's lack of appreciation for airmen created frustration. Naval gunners bombarding targets they could not see depended on aircraft for information on where their shells were landing, yet when the airmen ordered major changes, naval gunnery officers often ignored them.

Samson's men had moved to Imbros where they were repeatedly bombed, and by September the Fokker Eindecker with its synchronized gun began to take its toll. The rains of October brought cold, dysentery and fever. Kerby succumbed to the latter but worked his way back to England and France.

The Royal Newfoundland Regiment occupied a spot on Kangaroo beach for three months before they became part of the general evacuation. The ill-conceived campaign cost the British some 57,000 casualties of which about 10,000 were victims of disease. Churchill resigned as a result of the costly fiasco, and although Charles Rumney Samson lost a friend in a high place, he continued to soldier on in his unique fashion. In May 1916, he went to sea in a converted steamer cum aircraft carrier and sailed the Aegean and Mediterranean. Pilot Melville Dover of Winnipeg, was with the carrier in August when a force of 11 seaplanes hit a rail junction. Samson had found the key to tactical bombing but the navy brass didn't know how to use it. The French were more responsive and during the summer of 1916 the carrier *Ben-My-Chree* did a lot of steaming around looking for work.

Toronto's Alfred Nightingale joined the carrier at Port Said in August. Two months later, he was part of a force of four spotting for guns shelling a Turkish stronghold when he and another pilot were shot down by a Fokker Eindecker. Nightingale crash-landed and was rescued, but two months later he and his observer were taken prisoner when he was shot down again. Frederick Henderson of Toronto, also flew from Samson's carrier for five months, during which time they hit a bridge and delayed delivery of heavy guns to Baghdad. A number of Canadians also flew with the wing that replaced Samson's original squadron on Imbros. Cecil Bronson of Ottawa, won the Distinguished Service Cross for an attack on a heavily defended German cruiser although his bombs failed to sink it. A similar award went to John Devlin, also of Ottawa, for an attack on a rail bridge.

Canadians also served with RFC squadrons, which were drawn into the confused conflict where the real enemies within the hostile country were heat, cold, thirst, disease and savage Bedouin tribesmen who were impartial as to whether they were killing German or British foreigners. The war spread throughout the Middle East like a make-work project and Canadian airmen became part of its complexities. Lt James Owen of Annapolis Royal, N.S., ended up with an RFC squadron in Macedonia flying BE12s. In mid-February 1917, Owen and Britisher Gilbert Murlis-Green headed for a shoot out at Drama in Greece. It was like the OK Coral with wings. They were after Rudolph von Eschwege, a German ace recently condemned to that theatre of war. Von Eschwege met the BE12s and shot Owen down while Murlis-Green had trouble with his gun but escaped. Owen glided to a landing behind the lines where he set fire to his aircraft before being captured by the Bulgars. A mob hauled him into court where he was tried for burning the aircraft, an offence that could have brought him death. But von Eschwege successfully pleaded his case. Owen survived as a POW but the man who saved his life was dead within a month.

While the *Ben-My-Chree* was unloading cargo early in 1917, the ship was ripped by four Turkish shells. She burned for half an hour before Samson issued the order to abandon ship. A number of pilots continued the war in places whose names they couldn't spell. Samson spent a period at the admiralty counting beans. He was depressed to find that the admiralty considered aviators untrustworthy and somewhat inferior. After a period in purgatory, he was put in command of Great Yarmouth station. Here he continued to experiment, pushing the frontiers of aviation ahead.

## THE GENTLEMAN'S WAR

As soggy weather closed over exhausted armies in Flanders late in 1917, the British were called upon to assist the Italians who had made 11 assaults on the Isonzo River but had failed at a cost of over half a million casualties. Then, with German reinforcements, the enemy launched some 35 divisions against the Italians at Caporetto in the mountains of northeastern Italy. It opened with a massive mortar, artillery and gas attack in late October, and among the attackers was a young

Capt Erwin Rommel who led the Wurttemberg Mountain Battalion. During the attack, Rommel's mountain troops penetrated to a ridge behind the Italian line and waited for the retreat. According to Rommel, the retreating Italians were well received. But the retreat soon became a flood of soldiers and refugees as 750,000 people fled and the enemy advanced 75 miles. This was the situation that the British and French were called upon to support in the fall of 1917. Allied troops were soon on their way to re-establish the shattered front and the RFC was brought in.

In early December, Lt Tommy Williams of Woodstock, Ont., was among the airmen of five RFC squadrons being transferred from the Western Front. Williams recalled years later that, "They had a nice gentleman's war going down there but then they were invaded by a bunch of barbarians from the Western Front."[28] Although there were occasional glimpses of chivalry between airmen on the Western Front, by the end of 1917 those glimpses were extremely brief and rare. The first thing the Canadians heard about in Italy was the legend of Major Francesco Barraca, an Italian ace who was caught behind the Austrian lines. When a flight of 14 Austrian planes blocked his path, he attacked and shot one down. The Austrians were so impressed at the Italian's courage, they gathered around him and formed an escort, which crossed the lines and flew with Barraca to his home base.

Many things about the Italian war were different. The engine of Williams' Camel quit at 16,000 fleet over the Alps and he was forced to glide for miles through foreign Alpine gorges and passes. For crews of the RE8s who did artillery spotting and reconnaissance, the mountains meant hiding places for enemy troops and artillery. The mountainous terrain, which spread over three sectors of the front, not only concealed enemy artillery, but the confusing contours of the mountains made it difficult for crews to report where Allied shells were falling.

The three Camel squadrons and two RE8 squadrons originally contained 29 Canadians while an estimated 60 were to serve in Italy over the next year. The first RFC operation occurred in late November. The photographic mission by an RE8 had four Camel pilots as escorts. One of the pilots was "Bill" Barker of Dauphin, Man., who had three victories when he arrived in Italy and would add 43 more on that front. Another Camel pilot was Clifford McEwen of Griswold, Man. McEwen would finish his Italian tour with 22 victories, one shared and one possible. He would also haunt thousands of airmen in another war as Black Mike, commander of the RCAF Six Group. On their first Italian operation, the Camel pilots were attacked by 12 Albatros fighters. Encountering some difficulty at 10,000 feet, Barker brought the battle down to deck level where the spirited Camel had an advantage and scored his first victory in Italy.

Although the first operation for the Camels was escort duty behind enemy lines, the Trenchard doctrine of Distant Offensive Patrols soon permeated the squadrons, and they were flying offensive patrols behind the lines and regular patrols over the Italian front. The offensive patrols soon led to the location of major Austrian airfields, and this in turn led to bombing attacks that were more of an inducement or a challenge to get the enemy in the air than a tactical device.

On Christmas Day, Barker and Lt Harold Hudson from Victoria, found an Austrian field where they dropped a "Merry Christmas" message. As they approached, a party in the Austrian mess was showing signs of bottle fatigue. A few die-hards clustered around the piano as the Camels came back to drop another package. This time small bombs rained down on hangars, machine shops and aircraft. The fighters flew so low their wheels bounced as they turned and laced the hangars with machine gun fire. The raid apparently did little to discourage the party-goers yet somewhere over the next 24 hours Operation REVENGE was hatched with alcoholic enthusiasm.

Early on Boxing Day, over 30 Austrian planes crossed the lines, weaving across the sky at all altitudes. The general path of the intruders seemed to take them towards the RFC base at Istrana, but every now and then an aircraft dropped its bombs and turned back. It was later concluded that this was not a new bombing technique but a consequence of the two nights of celebrating. There was bombing of sorts on the aerodrome and then the invaders continued to roam aimlessly around Istrana. Six planes came down and Williams spent most of the day "picking prisoners out of the fields like potatoes." One pilot reported finding a small Austrian machine crashed with the pilot apparently dead, but when they approached they heard snores.

On New Year's Day, 10 RE8s, with 10 Camels as escorts, hit the German 14th Army H.Q. at Vittorio. Barker drove down one aircraft and sent another crashing into a mountain. Throughout the winter the RFC gained control of the air but not without cost. The balance swung in the allies' favour when, in March, enemy squadrons were sent to the Western front to support a spring offensive. On three fighter squadrons, 10 Canadians achieved ace status with five or more victories and accounted for 150 downed aircraft.

Before dawn on June 15, 1918, an Austrian barrage opened along 80 miles of the front. Under cover of smoke, mist and gas fumes, the enemy crossed the Piave River in several places and made limited advances into the British sector. The RAF responded by bombing and strafing troops trying to cross the river on pontoon bridges. Lt Williams recalled: "We were down low enough to see the expressions on their faces...so low that the blast of bombs just lifted our aeroplanes."[29] During the night the Austrians repaired some of the damage to the bridges but the RAF knocked them down again the following day. This set the pattern for seven days of battle. The Austrians withdrew in darkness on the night of June 22nd-23rd.

A new squadron of Bristol fighters was formed in Italy with Bill Barker commanding. It contained nine Canadians and during the summer lull on the ground, it continued to fly aggressive reconnaissance and army co-operation missions. But there was little air combat. As part of the build up to an Allied attack, Camels from #28 and #66 Squadrons hit an advanced flying school south of Udine. Stan Stanger and McEwen were credited with three Albatros and Williams got one while several other aircraft and hangars were destroyed on the ground. In the ground attack that followed, the RAF devastated the retreating Austrians. "The sights on the Pordenone road moved the victorious British to horror and pity...mile after mile the road was flanked with the wreckage of troops and transport, shattered guns and wagons, the mangled remains of drivers intermingled with those of the horses..."[30]

The gentleman's war gasped itself out on November 4th.

**ABOVE:** *In the final stages of the war on the Western Front, German aircrews concentrated on ground attacks and the RAF responded by assigning fighters to enemy troops that were now on the move. In many respects the summer of 1918 was the birth of the Blitz. (DND/PL-6411873)*

**OPPOSITE PAGE:** *Although no precise figures are available, it is estimated that at least one quarter of RAF/RFC operational crews on the Western Front were Canadian by the summer of 1918. Billy Bishop commanded #85 Squadron at that time. (DND/AH-558)*

*In the last one hundred days, Canadians in the air joined those on the ground in bringing about the enemy's...*

# 🎩 GÖTTERDÄMMERUNG

*AT THE CLOSE OF 1917,* the useless fighting at Passchendaele had exhausted the British 3rd and 5th armies, and the collapse of the Russian Czar meant that thousands of German troops were transferred to the Western Front where Gen Ludendorff was planning a spring offensive. Throughout the winter Ludendorff massed 74 divisions against 31 British divisions on a 70-mile front and air activity quickened in spite of the weather.

The Germans had 170 more aircraft than the 750 serviceable machines of the RFC and RNAS. In February 1918, the British began experimenting with multiple squadrons similar to those that Richthofen had been using for eight months. His *Geschwader*, or wing, consisted of four squadrons of scouts with the mobility to provide heavy firepower at any point along the front. But when the RFC sent three squadrons of fighters into German territory, the results were less than satisfactory. German fighters simply flew eastwards until the RFC machines ran low on fuel and had to turn for home; then the German scouts followed the retreating aeroplanes and picked off the stragglers.

Day-bombers became far more aggressive during 1918. Although Andrew McKeever of Listowel, Ont., led the way by posting 31 victories, in the fall of 1917, Ken Conn of Almonte, Ont., figured in 20 victories in a Bristol Fighter between June and November of 1918. Montreal's Wilfred Beaver accounted for 15 of his 20 victories during the spring and summer of 1918 as well. Alfred Atkey, a former reporter for the *Toronto Evening Telegram*, remains an enigma. The

RFC credits him with being instrumental in 38 victories, but many of these were acquired by his different gunners. On two occasions, Atkey's machine scored five victories in a day.

While air activity intensified during March, intelligence was slow to recognize the gravity of the enemy build up in spite of observation reports. On the other hand, observation reports eight hours before the massive attack reported no unusual activity.


## LUDENDORFF OFFENSIVES

Early on the morning of March 21st, 500 guns blasted the British lines. Every calibre of weapon from trench mortar to super heavy field artillery fired a combination of high explosive and gas shells. They smashed trenches and dugouts, ripped up communications lines and shattered the entire front to a depth of 20 miles. By 9:30 a.m. German troops moved through the mist, rifles slung over their shoulders and stick grenades at the ready. Armed with flame throwers and light machine guns, they had no intention of battling trench lines. Their job was to infiltrate and the by-passed pockets of resistance were the responsibility of follow-up units.

The fog and mist grounded hundreds of rugged, two-seaters whose crews were especially trained in ground attack. Seven squadrons were airborne later and saturated the British lines with grenades and machine gun fire. While the concept of the *Blitzkrieg* may have evolved over months, it was in full flight that afternoon of March 21, 1918 when German troops marched four abreast on open roads. RFC fighters attacked the troops so aggressively that some pilots brushed wheels on the backs of the men below. The sight of an enemy marching in the open was something pilots had never seen before. According to Maj Sholto Douglas: "Pilots for the first time in their experience ... were presented with perfect ground targets ... the only effective defence against these low-flying fighters was a concentration of entrenched machine guns. Time and circumstances usually prevented the Germans from assembling such defences."[31]

Fighter pilots like Don MacLaren of Vancouver resented the ground attacks because it meant missing air combat and the nature of the low-level work meant that traditional skills had much less to do with one's survival. At 50 feet in a battle zone the bullet which got you did not necessarily have your name on it, but was probably addressed to "to whom it may concern."

MacLaren was one of eight Camel pilots sent out to destroy a railroad gun some five miles behind the lines. He went in at 200 feet, putting two bombs into the railway truck and two on the rails. On his way home, he spotted an enemy two-seater which he had sent down near Douai. He then attacked an observation balloon leaving it burning, while taking down another two-seater. In seven months MacLaren would be credited with 54 victories.

For the first time since the beginning of the war, the British Expeditionary Force was in retreat. For the RFC, this was a replay of the retreat from Mons where a squadron would fly several missions a day only to return to a field to find it had been overrun. The RFC suffered heavy aircraft losses as fields were overrun and machines abandoned. Then word came down from RFC Headquarters: "...squadrons will bomb and shoot up everything they can see on the enemy side of this line. Very low flying essential. All risks to be taken. Urgent."

The Germans continued to advance, but as early as March 25th reports indicated that they could no longer provide continuous air protection for their troops. Raymond Collishaw commanded #203 Squadron and mounted six sorties on March 27th while Alan McLeod of Stonewall, Man., took off with observer Arthur Hammond to bomb and strafe troops around Bray-sur-Somme.

They were part of a flight of six Armstrong Whitworths but became separated from the others in heavy fog. McLeod landed and got directions and flew on alone. A Fokker Triplane guarded the artillery battery that was part of the target and McLeod attacked it, enabling Hammond to shoot it down. Seven more fighters jumped out of cloud and a second enemy aircraft went down. Then another Triplane raked the intruder, wounding both men and setting their aircraft on fire. McLeod dove for the ground and the bottom fell out of the rear cockpit. Hammond climbed up to the rim of the cockpit and continued firing although his left arm was useless. He sent down a second Triplane but flames forced McLeod out onto the port wing. Neither man wore a parachute because at that time War Office warriors had decided that if aircrew wore parachutes they would lose too many aircraft.

As a consequence, Hammond stood on the cockpit rim of the burning machine firing at the enemy while McLeod reached into his blazing cockpit to put the aircraft into a slideslip helping to draw the flames away. But the third Triplane followed them down, wounding both men. Hammond had six wounds as McLeod pancaked in no man's land and his plane slid to a blazing stop with flames licking at eight bombs. Both men were thrown clear and McLeod grabbed the unconscious observer and dragged him to safety as the bombs exploded. He was later awarded the Victoria Cross.

By March 28th, the Germans had driven inland 40 miles and taken 80,000 prisoners when the advance suddenly lost impetus. During the German attack, Canadian ground forces were scattered throughout British units and one of the final encounters was the cavalry charge of the Strathconas at Moreuil Wood. Lt Gordon Flowerdew led the charge on the strong enemy positions and lost 70 per cent of his men. He died of wounds the day after the attack, but the German thrust had been stopped in that section.

The advance stopped seven miles from Amiens and the enemy failed to split the British and French lines. An over extended line of advance and heavy casualties from air activity were given as reasons for failure to break through to the coast. Considering, the state of the British army and the lack of support from the French to the south, it is not unreasonable to conclude that air power was a major factor in turning the tide in the land battle. But another curious situation was involved. Shortages in Germany had deprived troops of the most basic of supplies. When they began to overrun British stores, the excellent discipline of the German soldier broke down. The advancing troops concentrated on looting instead of precise military objectives. Over the next two months the Germans would attempt several offensives. The first of these came to the southeast of Amiens as Ludendorff probed the 5th Army strength at Roye and Montdidier where the RFC lost 39 aircraft in one day. At Arras, to the north of France, the RFC lost another 52 aircraft as the enemy then tested the Ypres sector.

On April 1st the Royal Flying Corps and the Royal Naval Air Service were amalgamated to become the Royal Air Force. Hardly anybody noticed in the field but London was in chaos. Maj.-Gen Hugh Trenchard, the man who headed the RFC in France for much of the war, briefly commanded the RAF but quit after a few weeks because he couldn't get along with Air Minister Lord Rothermere. Frederick Sykes was appointed in Trenchard's place and this caused Gen Sir David Henderson, the man who commanded the RFC since the outbreak of war, to resign. Then within a month of Henderson's departure, Rothermere resigned as well.

On April 9th the Germans attacked the rail junction of Hazebrouck. The British 2nd Army occupied the sector, but the centre of a 12-mile line was held by Portuguese troops who were confused and unenthusiastic about being an ally of Britain if it meant fighting. When the Germans moved against them, they dispersed faster than the morning mist and the route to the Channel was open. In the confusion of the breakthrough RAF #208 Squadron, formerly Naval Eight, was grounded at La Gorgue. Believing the Germans were about to overrun the aerodrome, the CO had the squadron Camels stacked in the middle of the field and burned. The incident illustrates why RAF losses were so high as over 22 airfields were overrun in three weeks.

## WHO WAS THE VICTIM?

On the morning of April 21st, pilots of #209 Squadron at Bertangles should have stayed in bed. Fog hung over the Somme valley like a snug shroud and the silent Camels waited patiently while some pilots tried to get back to sleep and others groused about the new uniforms they'd have to wear in something called the Royal Air Force. Roy Brown's ulcers needed attention again and if there had been two words for the condition of the pilot from Carleton Place, Ont., it would have been "combat fatigue." In addition to ulcers, Brown suffered from a back injury sustained in a crash while training. Yet since going on operations with Naval Nine over a year earlier, he scored 12 victories and wore the DSC. In spite of the stress, Brown was a competent flight commander but the presence of a new man on the squadron added complications to his life that he didn't really need.

He had known Lt Wop May in Edmonton, and when May reported to the squadron he was short on training and Brown became a big brother although he had more on his plate than he could handle. May had struck up a conversation with a lorry driver when he left the pilot's pool at St. Omer. The driver was familiar with the delights of Amiens and presumably May got a guided tour, which made him two days late at Bertangles. The commanding officer was about to send May back to whatever fate awaited when Brown interceded and May was assigned to Brown's flight. As they waited for takeoff, Brown kept reminding May to stay on top of the fight, which was almost a sure thing, and under no circumstances was he to descend.

Twenty-five miles to the east at Cappy, Manfred von Richthofen was reciting the same words to his cousin Wolfram. Many of the assembled pilots had a hangover because the night before they celebrated the Baron's 80th victory. At 10:30 a.m., April 21, 1918 Brown and May shuffled along duckboards to their aircraft and Brown led three flights of five Camels each up thorough the mist.

Near Le Hamel, Brown saw two Australian RE8s under attack. Signalling to May to stay on top, he led the rest of his group down and the engagement that followed enabled the Australian photography machines to escape. While this was happening, Richthofen led 20 fighters into the sector where the German lines cut the Somme. Drawn by anti-aircraft fire from British guns, the German fighters dived into the fray while Richthofen circled above looking for a victim.

May remained at height and noticed an enticing Fokker doing the same. He had a slight height advantage on Wolfram von Richthofen and couldn't resist. Guns blazing, he dove on the Fokker and missed. Wolfram spun down through the vortex and May's guns jammed as he dove through the mix of wheeling machines. But as soon as he broke clear, bullets and blue smoke snapped about his head. Glancing over his shoulder, he saw the most feared sight on the Western Front: Manfred von Richthofen's red Triplane was on his tail and the Spandeaus were blinking him to eternity. May's inexperience became an asset because his flying was so erratic the Baron didn't know what the Camel would do next. Unfortunately neither did May. They dropped to tree-top level and May was trapped over the Somme. Brown had just disengaged from two Fokkers when he saw May under attack. He dived onto the Baron's tail as they skimmed the Australian lines and fired a long burst.

The Baron stood in his seat to look back and then collapsed. He went down with a bullet in his chest and the Triplane made a rough landing behind the Australian lines. Brown flew back to base and filed a report, claiming a Fokker Triplane. By noon, Wing was involved and a strange public relations battle erupted with Brown an innocent victim at its centre. Brown claimed a red Triplane and the RAF was pleased to credit him with bringing down Richthofen. The Australian Army Corps disputed the claim and still does. Australian ground gunners and even the crews of the two photography aircraft claimed the Baron. The incident brought the war to a halt in the Australian sector and an orgy of report writing followed, much of which was contradictory.

Australian Sgt. C.B. Popkin, who claimed to have shot Richthofen down, said the Fokker was pursuing the Camel overhead when he started shooting at it. The Fokker then abandoned the pursuit, turned to attack Popkin and was brought down by a second burst of Popkin's machine gun. Popkin then went to the crashed machine, examined the body and saw "at least three machine gun bullets through the body." The official medical report said one bullet entered Richthofen's chest going from right to left in a slightly upwards trajectory.

Lt. George Travers inspected the wreck: "I went over with three officers and had a look at the plane and also the driver who was dead, a machine gun bullet had passed from the left side of his face and near the bottom jaw and came out just behind his right eye."[32] A third report said there were bullet wounds in the knees, abdomen and chest.

In the middle of the critical battle, the Australians made a media event out of Richthofen's funeral thereby enhancing their claim. Brown collapsed shortly afterwards and although his health gradually improved, he lived for decades with abuse and accusations that he was nowhere near the scene when the Baron went down. The irony of the event is that the arrogant killer of 124 Allied airmen went to his grave with the pageantry of a hero while the airman who only reported what he saw became the object of derision.


## THE AIR MACHINES

The first phase of the Ludendorff offensives marked the ascendancy of aircraft into the land battle just as the Battle of Midway in 1942 would establish a dominant role for aircraft in a naval battle. The enemy's use of ground-attack aircraft devastated British troops in the early phases of the action, but failure to provide advance landing strips as the assault line lengthened diminished the effectiveness of the *Schlachtstaffeln* in the later stages. The British use of Camel and SE5 fighters in a ground attack role became a major factor in stopping the advance.

T.O.M. Sopwith chalked the design of a fighter on the wall of his workshop and six weeks later the Sopwith Camel emerged. With a speed of 115 m.p.h., the Camel's weight was concentrated within seven feet of the nose. Magnificently agile, the torque or twist from the 113 h.p. Clerget rotary motor made the Camel no machine for the timid. But as one pilot said: "Once you conquered her she was your friend for life."

Alex Shook scored the first of 1,294 victories for the Camel. When Don MacLaren of Vancouver, reported to #46 Squadron in the fall of 1917, it had just converted to Camels. During the winter, MacLaren was assigned to strafing in the Cambrai sector. Winter weather also restricted flying and MacLaren did not score a victory until March 6th. The Ludendorff offensive saw MacLaren back on low-level ground attacks. Yet by early October, he had destroyed 54 machines.

The original production record of the Royal Aircraft Factory was spotty, but in the summer of 1917 it came up with a winner when it produced the SE5 fighter. It was still an effective machine almost a year later when Bill Claxton of Gladstone, Man., reported to #41 Squadron. He got three words of advice from the veteran pilots: "Dive and zoom." The SE5 pilot's hope was to catch his prey in a dive, destroy him and then zoom for altitude.

Consequently, the pattern of offensive patrols was to approach the lines at up to 19,000 feet and dive on prey. Claxton's first victory was a balloon and in May he brought down a Fokker. A good shot with a deadly instinct for deflection shooting, he brought the machine down with a few short bursts. Fred McCall of Vernon, B.C., joined them and teamed up with Claxton to become one of the deadliest duos in aerial warfare. Claxton brought down 21 aircraft in a month and three days. Towards the end of June, the pair took on 40 hostiles and after an hour-long battle, each Canadian claimed three enemies. On June 13th, Claxton followed an enemy too close to the ground as it crashed behind the lines. His machine was riddled with ground fire and limped towards the lines where he crashed in French territory. Three days later he was jumped by Fokker Triplanes while bringing down an enemy fighter. Although his machine was severely mangled, he made it back to base however he was shot up again the next day while bringing down another fighter.

On the last of June, Claxton destroyed six enemy aircraft while McCall got five. Claxton had 37 victories and McCall had 35 when their luck ran out. They were attacked by 40 aircraft and Claxton went down with a serious head wound. A German doctor performed an intricate operation, which saved Claxton's life. McCall became seriously ill and was hospitalized in England. Although the period from the end of the first Ludendorff thrusts until mid-August was technically times of regrouping by both sides, three Canadians in two fine aircraft ran up 116 victories.

During this same period, Billy Bishop brought his #85 Squadron to France. Although he chafed under the administrative duties of a squadron commander, within three days he destroyed three enemy aircraft. Given somewhat abrupt notice that he was being posted back to England in two weeks to help organize a Canadian air force, Bishop brought down 25 aircraft in 21 flying days. Three of these were downed in the last 30 minutes of his final patrol.


## BREAKOUT FROM AMIENS

During the summer months, Gen Sir Henry Rawlinson, who had taken over command of the 5th Army, submitted a plan to Field Marshal Haig. The enemy had brought in long range guns that threatened their position at Amiens and Rawlinson proposed to push the enemy back a moderate distance. It was never intended as a major counter-offensive, and what happened to it became a classic case of a failure to communicate.

Haig took the plan to Marshal Foch, the Allied commander, who not only endorsed it, but also embellished it. While Rawlinson envisaged an advance of eight miles, Foch called for gains of 30 miles and Haig failed to convey the new objectives clearly to his commanders. This applied to Air Commander L.E.O. Charlton, whose air plan covered only one day. While troops were assembled, German aerodromes became prime targets for Camels, which dropped modest bomb loads and then reverted as fighters. Night intruders haunted German aerodromes for hours, waiting for bombers to return. One squadron accounted for 21 bombers on the intrusions foreshadowing intruder operations of WWII.

In mid-July, Raymond Collishaw and Leonard "Tish" Rochford hit the aerodrome at Dorignies. Collishaw strafed three aircraft being pulled from a shed and shot down a two-seater coming in for a landing. He returned to base where he rearmed and re-fuelled and then flew back to inspect the damage. This time, however, he was jumped by three fighters but ended up shooting down one of them. Rochford went up later and destroyed two Fokkers.

Among the troops being assembled in great secrecy were the Canadian Corps and the Australian Army Corps, who both now enjoyed a dubious reputation on both sides of the line of being formidable storm troops. On the eve of the British attack, the RAF had 800 aircraft while the Germans had 385 machines in the sector, but to the south in Champagne, the enemy had an additional 850 machines.

Shortly after midnight on August 8th, two Ontario pilots were early starters in the drive that ended in final victory. Gordon Flavelle of Lindsay, Ont., and William Peace of Hamilton, Ont., made several attempts to get their Handley-Page twin engine bombers off the ground. They finally got off and flew by compass to the front lines where they started a three hour routine of flying back and forth. Their mission was to drown out the sound of some 400 tanks that the British were assembling. It was a tactic Raymond Collishaw would use in North Africa in WWII.

Some 2,000 guns hit enemy positions and waves of bombers struck enemy aerodromes, but because of heavy mist, results ranged from fair to disappointing. The mist kept corps machines grounded until 9 a.m. and only then were they able to observe artillery fire and do contact patrols. In the early hours of the attack, clumsy tanks became vulnerable to anti-tank guns and almost half of the 67 tanks received direct hits. This reinforced the need for air protection and 24 Camels were assigned to the tank corps, providing one machine for every 2,000 yards of front.

The rapport between pilots and tank crews became a very personal thing. American Lt William Lambert spotted an Allied motor column and a tank moving towards anti-tank guns which glinted from a hedge. Wheels skimming the ground, he flew across the path of the column and fired a warning bust. Then he destroyed the gun.

N. Goudie of Kamloops, B.C., flew his RE8 over about 100 enemy troops on a sunken road while his observer snapped off a steady stream of fire until the infantry took over. Communications between tanks and aircraft was tenuous. Although a direct wireless link was technically possible, there were simply not enough sets to go around. A wireless central information bureau received calls from aircraft in Morse code and then transmitted them to appropriate artillery batteries.

After a slow start because of weather, the RAF enjoyed its finest hour and air support was the most extensive of the war. Contour flying fighters strafed disorganized troops and sought out anti-tank guns with 25-pound bombs. Throughout the morning the RAF owned the air and Allied forces continued to make gains. Then confusion set in over final objectives as corps commanders paused to consider the next move. Canada's Gen Currie had no specific instructions, but decided to go on anyway. Other commanders did the same but some did not and the attack lost its impetus and co-ordination as a result of Haig's failure to clearly define the new objectives.

Shortly after noon, Brig-Gen Charlton got orders to abandon his air plan and concentrate on 11 bridges over the Somme. The RAF commander in France, Maj.-Gen John Salmond, feared the enemy would be using the bridges to escape. He was half right. The enemy was using the bridges by late afternoon, but to bring in reinforcements.

The four-squadron Richthofen wing, under temporary command of Lothar von Richthofen, flew in that afternoon from Champagne. Lieutenant Ernst Udet broke his flight long enough to shoot down a fighter on contact patrol. They landed at a German drome for fuel but the base commander refused to part with any. While they argued, the RAF struck and Udet reflected on the sad sight of the once proud Richthofen group herded together like a gaggle of hens. Udet then got off long enough to shoot down an intruder but ran out of gas and had to make a dead stick landing. Two hours later, he got a third machine.

In spite of British confusion over objectives, significant gains were made on the first day. Canadian troops gained 12 kilometres and took 5,000 prisoners, but the enemy poured reserves over three of the Somme bridges and what was probably the most savage air battle of the war resulted. Over 360 RAF machines went against the bridge at Brie, but it remained standing and on the first day 97 machines were written off. Ground attacks were resumed on the second day but momentum had been lost and enemy resistance stiffened. In four days, 700 sorties and the loss of 154 machines failed to destroy the bridges.

Responsibility for the RAF failure rested not with the gallant crews, but with the vagueness of Haig's order and the consequent change in the battle plan. Losses were particularly heavy during the four-day attack and the total for August came to 240 aircraft. The Richthofen *Jagdeschwadern* lost 39 of 50 experienced pilots defending the bridges and while the British could replace their losses, the Germans were now past the point of no return in both men and material.

In spite of the disaster in the air, the Canadian Corps advanced 22 kilometres and took 9,000 prisoners. Gen Ludendorff later called the day of the attack "the black day for the German army in the history of the war." There was a brief pause in the ground war as the Canadians shifted to another sector, but the air war intensified.

On August 10th, Hank Burden of Toronto led a fighter patrol west of Bray and encountered six enemy scouts. Burden brought two down while four spun earthwards to escape. One of his victims was Eric Loewnhardt, Germany's third ranking ace with 53 victories. Burden's group later attacked 20 hostiles and he destroyed another. Then on an evening patrol Lt Burden, Billy Bishop's brother-in-law, sent two more down.

The Canadian Corps smashed through the Drocourt-Quéant line on August 23rd in a drive that would take them to Mons and to the end of the war. But the German air force, although defeated, was deadly to the end. During the last 100 days the RAF lost some 700 aircraft. Canadians were credited with four of the last 16 enemy machines to fall. George Mackay of Mimico, Ont., shared a victory with A.B. Rosevear and H.H. Gilbert of London, Ont., as they brought down an observation aircraft in the same Dunkirk sector where in 1915 Stracham Ince brought down the first of 1,500 aircraft that would fall to Canadians. In the final hours of combat, Frank Taylor of Toronto, and William Jenkins of Montreal, each brought down a Fokker D-V11 H. Oldham of Yarder, Sask., accounted for another.

Long crowded roads which led through a wasteland of four years of war were the target for #46 Squadron Camels as they bombed a retreating supply train, leaving a smoking mess of men, horses and wagons in its wake. The Camels circled at treetop height for a strafing run and George Dowler, a Calgary school-teacher, collided with another aircraft. He was the last of 1,388 Canadians to die and possibly the last RAF airman to die.

Until the last minute, some bomber crews were briefed for operations. According to Vivian Voss, crews at Bersie were warming up the engines of their Bristol fighters when the tall figure of the commanding officer reeled across the field, waving his arms like a novice skater. All within sight could read his lips, "The war's over! The war's over!"[33] Pilots switched off and crews climbed down to let the adrenaline of war run its course. Beyond the gigantic wasteland where 10 million had died, Canada was awash in a tide of nationalism. Yet some 13,000 Canadians flew operationally and 1,388 died without identity as Canadians. While most would be returning home a few would be caught in the bizarre legacy of a politician who had long since left the scene.

*Standing on the wing of his blazing aircraft, 19-year-old Alan McLeod managed a crash landing while under attack by eight fighters. He and his observer were wounded several times, but brought down three enemy machines. (PAINTING BY DON CONNOLLY)*

**ABOVE:** *Major William Bishop, VC, DSO and Bar, MC, and DFC. (DND/PA-122158)*

**OPPOSITE PAGE:** *Crews of the first Handley-Page V 1500 were assigned to Mulock and awaited orders to bomb Berlin if the peace talks failed in November 1918. (DND/PMR-71-401)*

# SAM'S BIZARRE LEGACY

*THE MAN WHO GAVE* a civilian $5,000 in 1914 to form a one-plane air force but resisted supporting aviation for the rest of his term of office left a bizarre aviation legacy. Although Sam Hughes' term of office was but a bad memory in 1918, his long arm reached across the years to inspire history with a dash of mayhem. Prime Minister Robert Borden has the distinction of being the only leader in history to wait until after a war to form an air service. The Canadian initiative finally came after the war when Canada formed two squadrons in England. But the admiralty had also formed something called the Royal Canadian Naval Service and the comedy of errors which resulted saw Borden allowing both services to lapse like unwanted magazine subscriptions.

Long before his enforced departure in the fall of 1916, Sam Hughes, minister of Militia and Defence, commissioned a study of Canadians in the British flying services to Montreal businessman Grant Morden and Capt. K.E. Kennedy one of the first Canadians to fly in France.

Kennedy had served as an observer and a pilot and was familiar with the problems that confronted Canadians. Morden reported to George Perley, the Canadian high commissioner in London. His paper was critical of the inequities suffered by Canadians in the British air services and raised the question of Canadian squadrons at the front. Morden discussed the paper with Gen Sir David Henderson, head of the RFC. Later Gen Sefton Brancker called a conference with the Australians and Canadians to discuss the paper. Australia set up its own air force early in the war, but Canada had consistently refused the British invitation to do the same.

The Canadian high commissioner snuffed out the last traces of Sam Hughes, and for a brief period the question of a Canadian flying corps lay dormant. Then Borden began getting phone calls from influential Canadians in all parts of the country. In England, he was approached by several airmen who broadened his horizons on the inequities suffered by Canadians in the RFC. He found out that Canadians were discriminated against in promotions, forbidden to wear Canada badges and received no recognition as Canadians citizens. Borden was seized by the fact that Frederic Wanklyn, the Canadian who taught Cuthbert Hoare to fly, was still a major while Hoare, now head of RFC training in Canada, was a colonel en route to a major-general's rank.

Whereas Borden had previously been indifferent to the concept of a Canadian flying corps or Canadian squadrons, something now touched a nerve. He became an ardent and angry proponent of a Canadian air arm and demanded that Perley and Militia Minister Sir A.E. Kemp investigate. Gen Sir Richard Turner operated a clearing house for Canadian military matters in London and came up with an estimate of 35 per cent for the number of Canadians in the RAF. Although a high estimate, most guesses were 25 per cent, it was useful in linking the concept of the Canadian Army Corps to the desirability of having Canadian airmen support Canadian troops.

Gen Sir Arthur Currie, commander of the Canadian Army Corps, agreed that Canadians were best served by Canadians. Billy Bishop and Redford Mulock were strong advocates of Canadian airmen being part of the Canadian Corps, but the experienced commander in Mulock warned of probable difficulties the Canadian Air Force would have in getting suitable aircraft from the air board. Mulock, a former squadron commander and professional engineer, was obviously remembering the frustrations of Boom Trenchard during Bloody April when he was inundated with a stream of near useless aircraft.

Although the RAF went to great lengths to deny it, there was a substantiated belief that Canadians worked under senior officers who did not understand them. As indicated, Bert Wemp and other Canadians were ordered to go on English parade at an RNAS base. Part of the problem was that all British flying services were established on social class. One popular criticism of the RFC was that it had "become a mixed crowd with fewer public school entrants." In 1918, the British secretary of state replied to the challenge in the House with the assurance that every effort would be made to popularize the RAF within public and private schools.

For years Charles Grey, the bombastic editor of *Aeroplane Magazine*, promoted class warfare. "There is an idiotic theory that a man is too old at 30 to fly and that the howling little bounder of 20 is going to make a better officer aviator than the thoroughly sound sportsman of 32. The youngster may fly more reck-lessly till his nerve breaks just as a mongrel dog will go yapping into a fight till he gets a damned good hiding, but he will never make an officer and will never fly after a bad smash in the way the better class man will do."[34]

On most squadrons, Canadians lived well below the salt. Denis Winter records the view of one Britisher as follows: "Old Hambley is a very bad Canadian and if I wasn't out here I should have difficulty seeing any good in him at all. He was uncouth and used to bring terrible Canadians into the mess, and the major wanted me to get rid of him at one time but I said I would not. He drinks too much, wears side whiskers and sometimes a dirty stock. But he is a splendid fellow and I have the utmost confidence in him over the line."[35]

By the spring of 1918, the Canadian government relented to growing pressure and reversed its negative stand on an air service. It signed a broad agreement with the air ministry but this came as the RFC and the RNAS were being amalgamated and while the RAF was not opposed to the Canadian action, the unification of the two British services was the top priority. Movement towards a Canadian air force went on hold as the RAF tried to pull the pieces of the two competing air units into a unified whole.

It was at this point that the admiralty launched its final black joke. It issued warnings of increased submarine danger off the Canadian coast, warnings that were never substantiated but led to a drive to get untrained Americans to fly patrols off Canada's East Coast. Negotiations between the RN commander for North America and the Yanks concluded that air stations should be built at Hali-fax and Sydney from where the Americans would fly airships and seaplanes. When the Canadians were brought into the picture, it was a *fait accompli* as Canada paid for the air stations. By mid-August the station at Baker Point outside of Halifax became operational, but patrols over a six-week period failed to spot one subma-rine. In an apparent attempt to rationalize this double-assault on its sovereignty, the Canadian government formed something called the Royal Canadian Naval Air Service (RCNAS). While the inexperienced Americans began flying patrols out of Nova Scotia the men who wrote the book on Coastal Command such as Redford Mulock, Basil Hobbs or Robert Leckie languished abroad.

The establishment of the RCNAS raised temperatures in the Canadian Military Overseas Headquarters where officers had been negotiating in good faith to form an air service. Billy Bishop had been brought in to help organize the proposed Canadian Air Force (CAF) and saw the formation of a second air arm as absolute futility and completely opposed to RAF policy. Gen Turner agreed and passed the sentiment along to the minister of the militia. The RCNAF died a quiet death shortly after the war, but plans moved ahead for the CAF.

Nine days after the Armistice, one Canadian bomber squadron and a fighter squadron were formed in England. Two weeks later, Andrew McKeever took command of the fighter squadron while Walter Lawson headed up the bomber squadron.

Redford Mulock had been offered command of the two units but refused. However, he did provide a blueprint for the organization, which was later ignored in Ottawa. Bishop returned to Canada and it soon became apparent that the CAF lacked a sense of mission or command. It was simply two squadrons flying exercises in inadequate aircraft, and while this eroded aircrew morale, a more serious problem afflicted the ground crew.

One group of trainees went to the RAF station at Halton Park where they refused to obey orders to drill. This followed a session when a RAF NCO drilled them in mud to the delight of army onlookers. Discontent spread to Upper Heyford in England, where Canadians refused fatigue duties assigned by British officers. Canadian aircrew officers had little time or inclination to enforce discipline and many legitimate grievances of other ranks were overlooked in the confused organizational structure.

For two years, the CAF created the illusion of an air force, but it was simply a way of keeping personnel in two squadrons at RAF expense. When the British asked Canada to pick up the costs of operating the squadrons in 1920 Canada failed to do so and the last link with our aviation heritage was broken. On July 1st, as most Canadians sat on porches drinking lemonade or listening to "The Land of Hope and Glory" at the local bandstand, the last of Canada's aces without an air force began packing to return to a land whose government had denied them recognition.

**LEFT:** *Col. Redford Mulock, DSO and Bar, CBE, and Legion of Honour. (DND/RE-20434)*

**OPPOSITE PAGE:** *The Curtiss flying boat on a lonely northern lake was a perfect symbol of Canadian aviation in the years between the wars. (NATIONAL AVIATION MUSEUM)*

*Veteran pilots and surplus machines*
*open Canada's frontiers in...*

# ぐ THE YEARS BETWEEN

*SIX MONTHS AFTER THE* Armistice, former RNAS pilot Stuart Graham cranked up a surplus Curtiss flying boat in Halifax and flew to Lac La Tortue in Quebec's St. Maurice valley. The four-day trip covered some 650 miles and was the longest cross-country flight up to May 1919. It was also the start of the world's first bush operation as an influx of veteran pilots and a host of surplus aircraft would soon create a new era in Canadian aviation.

The seaplane that Graham flew was a war assets machine left behind by the Yanks, but donated to the Canadian government. American born, forester Ellwood Wilson borrowed two of the idle machines from the government and hired Graham to fly them to Laurentide Co. paper mill's base on the St. Maurice. Throughout the summer the aircraft were busy on forestry patrols, searching for fires and photographing in hours what would take years to cover on foot. The Laurentide Air Service became an independent operation and the world's first bush charter service, but Laurentide's success soon boomeranged. The Ontario government hired Laurentide to map 20,000 square miles of timber, and a job that normally would take six years was done in 160 hours. The Ontario government decided to form its own air service and lured Roy Maxwell and other key personnel to the Ontario Provincial Air Service (OPAS) and three years later Laurentide Air closed down.

The British gave Canada well over a hundred aircraft and two dirigibles and the Americans turned over much of the equipment they had on the East Coast. For some time after the war it sat in crates at Borden and Halifax. Their presence and the surplus of privately owned aircraft prompted the federal government to form an air board in 1919 and the following year a non-permanent Canadian Air Force. During the summer of 1920 a month-long refresher course attracted the first group of summer airmen who were part-time auxiliaries.

The real impetus, however, came from men like Doc Oakes. Geologist, mining engineer and former RFC pilot, Oakes was among the OPAS pilots who flew some 170,000 patrol miles and spotted 600 fires in 1924. When gold was discovered at Red Lake the next year, Oakes and pilot Tommy Thompson quit their jobs and mushed a dog team to Red Lake where they established a claim. They later sold their claim to buy a Curtiss Lark and start Patricia Airways. Soon they were flying freight, passengers, and mail out of Sioux Lookout to Red Lake. With financial backing from James Richardson of Winnipeg, Oakes expanded the operation which became Western Canada Airways.

A permanent RCAF was formed in 1924 and for over a decade most of the flying was civilian in nature as the force became a service unit for government departments. RCAF operations and the saga of bush flying blended as aviation became the great impetus to northern development.

During this period most of the RCAF's allocations were devoted to operations in forestry, mining, fishing and mapping. It suffered during the depression and it was not until war clouds began gathering in Europe in the mid-thirties that the RCAF was able to expand operations such as coastal patrol and army co-op activities. When Germany invaded Poland on September 1, 1939 the RCAF had 270 assorted aircraft, but only 19 Hurricanes were fit to share the air with the machines devastating Warsaw. Only two of these Hurricanes were operational. About 400 RCAF had been assigned to the RAF on loan, but a much larger number of Canadians were in the RAF as volunteers. They were the cattle boat brigade. Like the generation before them, these young men went overseas to join the RAF. Most had acquired some flying experience at clubs across Canada and some were in action a few hours after Prime Minister Chamberlain's announcement that Britain was at war.

*OPPOSITE PAGE:* *Bristol Blenheims were in action from day one and so were Canadians in the Royal Air Force.* (IWM)

*"Run Rabbit Run" topped the charts in England
and appeasement set the tone during...*

# THE WINTER
# OF THE PHONEY WAR

*ENGLAND AND FRANCE RESPONDED* to Adolf Hitler's invasion of Poland by declaring war and while there were many brave speeches both countries stopped short of land contact with the enemy. France soon had five million men in uniform in some 85 divisions on the Western Front alone, facing some 36 German divisions. Except for one brief foray, this massive army languished behind the Maginot Line while the British sent four divisions to France. Allied inaction as Poland fell and the manner in which Hitler intimidated the Allies during the winter of the phoney war led to a popular ditty which said it all about Allied strategy. It advised the rabbit to run, run, run and deprive the farmer with the gun of his fun, fun, fun!

However, the RAF responded from day one and Canadians were involved.

John Sproule of Brandon, Man., and Robert Stephenson of Victoria, boarded crew buses and made their way out to fly Whitley bombers on two different squadrons. A force of 10 bombers flew to Hamburg, Breman and nine other Ruhr cities, but instead of bombs, the Whitley's carried 5.4 tons of leaflets. As if any Germans in the target cities cared, the leaflets outlined Neville Chamberlain's reasons for going to war. Within a month, the people in Berlin who were celebrating the collapse of Poland were also subjected to tons of paper as the RAF launched its leaflet war.

On shipping strikes crews were ordered to take the greatest care not to injure civilians. If a German warship was tied up to a wharf where civilians might be present, it was not to be bombed. On the second day of the war, F/Lt Phil Goulder of Calgary was part of a force of 15 Blenheims and 14 Wellingtons, which flew through gusty rain at wave-top level towards Wilhelmshaven and Brunsbuttel. Five of the Blenheims failed to find the target and five others were shot down as they attacked the *Admiral Scheer* and the *Emden,* which lay at anchor at Wilhelmshaven. One of the Blenheims crashed onto the *Emden* inflicting minor damage. Sgt. Albert Prince of Vancouver became the first Canadian to die when his aircraft crashed on the home journey after being shot up on the bombing run. Prince was listed among the RAF's first 17 casualties.

In the attack on Brunsbuttel, two Wellingtons were lost with no damage to enemy shipping. In the two sweeps, 22 aircraft reached the target and seven were shot down. Five nights later, Alfred Thompson of Penetanguishine, Ont., was shot down to become the first Canadian POW. He had flown two operations before his country was at war. As indicated, most of the Canadians were part of the cattle-boat brigade, the several hundred Canadians who were in the RAF when war was declared. Although the RCAF had some 400 officers attached to the RAF, there was no record of the hundreds of cattle-boaters on operations: the RCAF didn't know they were there nor did they care where they came from.

Before the end of September, five of 11 machines failed to return from an operation. Canadian Max Coste's Hampden was shot down into the sea, but fortunately the Calgarian was picked up by an enemy destroyer. John Griffiths of Niagara Falls, who joined the RAF in 1926, was a wing commander with #99 Squadron when it was assigned to raid Heligoland and the Terschelling Islands in mid-December. Part of a larger force, the Wellingtons found a convoy north of Wilhelmshaven but because of low cloud were unable to bomb. Fred Lambert and John Dyer both of Wilkie, Sask., were part of the squadron which, circled for half an hour amid heavy flak and fighter attacks. Five of 12 Wellingtons fell to fighters and a sixth crashed near its base. Griffiths was awarded the first Distinguished Flying Cross given to a Canadian following this operation.

Archibald Guthrie of Reston, Man., led a squadron of Wellingtons on a raid that shattered the illusion that all bombers get through. When Sqd/Ldr Guthrie called crews of #9 Squadron to a briefing on December 18th. John Challes of St Catharines, Ont., and William MacRae of Regina, were among the assembled crew captains. The briefing covered a three-squadron strike on shipping at Schillig Roads and Wilhelmshaven on the north coast of Germany.

Twenty-two Wellingtons rendezvoused off Kings Lynn about 10 a.m. and headed through overcast. As they swung down the Heligoland Bight, there wasn't a cloud to hide behind. Some 70 miles from the coast, the bombers were picked up on the enemy's new Freya radar in one of the first enemy interceptions of the war. They were jumped by fighters and then ran into heavy flak near Bremerhaven.

The Wellingtons fought their way to the target area that was empty of ships. They then peeled off to approach Wilhelmshaven from the southeast where they spotted several enemy ships at quayside, which were so close to shore that Guthrie, mindful of orders, was unable to attack. The commander of the force, Richard Kellett, then ordered the three squadrons to abort the operation.

Once out of flak range, the Wellingtons were jumped again by fighters. A Wellington in the lead section fell in flames and another broke apart in mid-air while a third spiralled into the sea trailing smoke. In the long fight that followed, the bombers claimed a number of enemy fighters, but 10 Wellingtons were lost during the attacks and two went down in the sea later. As well three crash-landed on the English coast. Fifteen of 22 aircraft were lost in the futile operation, and most of the remaining seven aircraft had dead or wounded onboard. The Guthrie and Challes crews were killed and MacRae made a crash landing on the British coast. He was awarded the DFC but was killed two months later.

In the activities of December 14th and 18th, half of the 34 Wellingtons sent out were destroyed. What the disaster at Wilhelmshaven ultimately proved was that the RAF had neither the machines nor the training for successful daylight bombing. Bomber Command crews soon became minions of the moon although shipping attacks continued. There were many phoney aspects to the war that winter. RAF crews were shot at if they strayed over Belgium or Holland, and the winter was characterized by French timidity and lack of co-operation, a desire not to antagonize the Nazis and a pervasive illusion that somehow peace was about to break out.

During the winter of the phoney war, most RAF activity was against enemy shipping. On April 4th, Wilson Donaldson, of Lethbridge, Alta., talked Don Middleton of Dauphin, Man., who was also a pilot, into flying as his navigator on a shipping strike. Their Hampden sank an enemy destroyer, but they were shot down and both ended up in a POW camp. After one escape, Donaldson was sent to Colditz where he endured a mock execution.

On April 7th, 12 Blenheims spotted a large German fleet, including the *Scharnhorst* and *Gneisenau* at sea. Bombing was ineffective and Canadian pilots Roy Gayford, of Bassano, Alta., and Art Whitencamp, of Stenen, Sask., were lost in the attack, the first of many to die seeking the *Scharnhorst*. The previous day, Whitencamp had been awarded the first Canadian member of the Order of the British Empire (MBE) for pulling members of his crew from a burning aircraft.

The Finns had resisted gallantly all winter when the Russians sent five armies against them late in November. Britain and France promised aid, but their somewhat devious strategy was to secure Swedish iron ore by moving through Norway and Sweden in order to confront the Russians in Finland. Norway had become important to the Allies because of its ports that not only provided the enemy with iron ore from Sweden, but also threatened Britain's Atlantic lifeline.


## NORWAY INVADED

There is no doubt that Norway was invaded on April 9th, but the fact that it was invaded by the Germans and not the British might well have been a matter of poor timing by the British. As Charles Lamb, a Fleet Air Arm pilot put it: "Our mine laying was in nightly demand, generally at the request of sinister little men in bowler hats, carrying dispatch cases."[36] When the British and French informed the Norwegians that three mine fields had been laid off their coast, within minutes Oslo also got word that a Polish submarine had sunk a German transport and among the survivors was the first wave of troops bound for Norway.

The Germans occupied Denmark virtually without firing a shot. For some reason, this prompted Prime Minister Chamberlain to proclaim that Hitler had missed the bus. Although Norway was slow to respond, resistance stiffened. But two Norwegian ships were blown out of the water in the northern port of Narvik and minutes later German troops occupied the town which surrendered. British naval superiority then turned the occupation into a siege as 10 German destroyers were sunk and much of Maj. Gen Eduard Dietl's invading force was lost.

The Germans took aerodromes at Stavanger, Trondheim and Oslo and soon a stream of Ju-52 transports brought in thousands of paratroops. British and French troops then made landings at Namsos and Narvik to the North and #263 Squadron provided critically needed air support.. Led by Sqd/Ldr Baldy Donaldson, the ancient Gladiators lifted from the deck of HMS *Glorious* in a snowstorm some 180 miles out to sea and reached a frozen lake south of Trondheim.

First patrol next morning was delayed as carburettors froze and frozen tires locked wheels into the ice. Then relays of Ju-88s and He-111s struck repeatedly. Ground crews fought to release the aircraft, but ultimately only two made it off. Throughout the morning, they rearmed and labouriously refuelled the machines from four-gallon drums. Within a few hours, 10 of 18 Gladiators were destroyed. The others engaged in continuous combat and shot down several enemy machines, but by evening only five RAF aircraft remained.

The shattered #263 Squadron withdrew to another landing ground and flew a sortie next morning. Five went out and only three returned. By noon of the second day, only one Gladiator remained and, with fuel exhausted, the pilots managed to catch a ship to Scotland. The squadron returned about a month later launched from HMS *Furious*. Three Glads ploughed into a mountain and the squadron turned back to face its first carrier landing in an Arctic storm. The Gladiators got ashore next day and flew 50 sorties in the Narvik area. They were reinforced by Hurricanes a week later and were immediately thrown into an attack on Narvik. The two squadrons fought off heavy German air attacks, flying 80 sorties in a day, as work progressed on disabling the port. But the crisis in France forced a withdrawal of troops and the squadrons provided air cover for the soldiers and then prepared to leave. The Gladiators landed on the HMS *Glorious* on June 8th and the Hurricanes all managed a landing as well. Lacking arrester hooks, pilots strapped bags of sand to the tails of their aircraft to hold them down when they hit the deck. The next day the *Glorious* and two other ships were attacked by the *Scharnhorst,* the *Gneisenau* and the *Hipper.* The *Glorious* was sunk and the pilots of #263 Squadron disappeared without a trace. Among the missing were F/Lt Alvin Williams of Toronto and F/O Phil Purdy of St. Stephen, N.B.

Prime Minister Chamberlain resigned and Winston Churchill took his place on May 10th, the day a much larger disaster started to roll through the Ardennes and further north into Holland and Belgium.


## THE SHORT HEROIC LIFE OF THE BRAVE BATTLES

"You can't send a kid up in a crate like that!" The sentiment became a cliché after WWI and a grim reality in September 1939 as the RAF sent its first squadrons to France. The young men who flew to war in Fairey Battles and Lysanders inherited a heritage of neglect and lack of vision on the part of the RAF and paid with their lives during the short heroic life of the Advanced Air Striking Force (AASF).

The AASF consisted of 10 squadrons of Fairey Battles and two squadrons of Blenheim bombers. The Battle was 50 m.p.h. slower than the enemy's Me-109 and also more awkward and much more poorly armed. The Blenheims were also easy prey for the Me-109s. In one of the first engagements, five Battles were jumped by a flight of Me-109s and four were shot down. Two squadrons of Hurricanes were brought in to provide fighter cover for the AASF whose role was essentially to provide tactical bombing. The RAF also provided an air component to work with the army. It consisted of five squadrons of Lysanders, four Blenheim squadrons and two Gladiators squadrons.

Winter encounters had shown the Hurricane to be a stable and reliable gun platform, but the Me-109 left the Hurri behind in a dive and on the climb. RAF pilots would try to compensate with aggressive turning. Mark "Hilly" Brown of Portage la Prairie, Man., was the first Canadian to fly with #1 Hurricane Squadron and scored his first victory over a Dornier-17 in November 1939. During an attack on an enemy bomber in early March, his wooden propeller was shot away, but he glided 30 miles to a landing at Nancy. In April, Brown shot down two Me-109s, and the call his squadron got at about 3:30 a.m. on May 10th became the final wake-up call for the British.

Brown flew a patrol to Metz where his section took turns disabling a Do-17.

Then they returned to base where there was a long delay. After nine months, the enemy was on the move but the RAF was on the ground. The inactivity was not of its making. The French were so intimidated by the thought of German reprisals that it was 11 a.m. before they grudgingly agreed to the bombing of German troops. But they insisted that such bombings had to be on Allied territory. This soon proved to be no problem for the RAF because bombing opportunities soon exceeded the force's potential to deliver as German armies struck Holland and Belgium. The enemy flew some 500 Ju-52 transports with airborne troops to key airfields in the Hague and Rotterdam while parachutists secured key positions in the Amsterdam-the Hague-Utrecht triangle known as Fortress Holland.

In Belgium, nine gliders swept onto the roof of the strongest fortress in Europe. Fort Eben Emael was situated at the junction of the Meuse River and the Albert Canal and was supposedly manned by 1,500 troops. Some 80 Germans went to work with grenades, other explosives and flame-throwers. Parachutists reinforced them and soon the fortress was in German hands. Parachutists also took two bridges a few miles to the north at Maastricht, which provided a highway for German forces pouring into Belgium and an access into Northern France.

German bombers, meanwhile, hit some 70 Allied aerodromes but fortunately the RAF was then airborne. By afternoon, over 30 Fairey Battles took off with delayed action bombs for a low-level attack on German columns. Thirteen fell to flak and all were damaged. Earlier that morning, F/O Allan Angus of Winnipeg, Man., had closed on a Ju-88 while on patrol with #85 Hurricane Squadron. His fire was accurate but so was that of the German gunner. No sooner had Angus sent the Ju-88 crashing into the woods that the engine of his Hurricane began spitting glycol. He rode the machine down to a crash landing and got back to base in time for another patrol the next day. During the next seven days, Angus would bring down five enemy aircraft, making him the first Canadian WWII soldier to rank as an ace. Unfortunately the day after he was awarded the DFC, he was shot down and killed.

Among the Canadians who were involved in operations were Fl/Lts Eric Parker of Vancouver, Arthur Roberts of Vernon, B.C. and Al Matthews of Moncton, Ont. Parker was killed and Roberts and Matthews became POWs. Canadian-born Sqd/Ldr Harold Mitchell, flew with #87 Hurricane Squadron and shot down two Dornier 17s the first day and was credited with two enemy aircraft the next. The bridges over the Albert Canal became key objectives. On the second day, crews of #114 Squadron were boarding Blenheims for an early takeoff when nine Dornier -17s skimmed the treetops at Conde-Vraux and destroyed six of the parked bombers while badly damaging the others. The Belgian air force attempted to bomb the bridges, but lost six of nine aircraft on the way in and none of the survivors hit the targets. Twelve Blenheims flew from England later that day, however four were shot down and none hit a Maastricht bridge.

Air Marshal Sir Arthur Barratt, commander of RAF forces in France, was now under intense pressure to blow up the bridges because senior brass was convinced that the full thrust of the German advance would fall on Maastricht. Although destruction of the bridges was seen as critical, Barratt was ordered to send nine Blenheims out to strafe troops on the road from Maastricht to Tongres. They ran into fighters and seven were lost.

The loss of the Blenheims virtually wrote off Barratt's medium bomber force and the bridges still stood. He then called for volunteers and six crews sat through the final briefing. It was short and to the point. The bridge at Veldwezelt and the one at Vroenhoven were to be destroyed at all costs. Norman Thomas and Donald Garland were each to lead a section of three against the bridges. Garland was for a low-level on the Veldwezelt Bridge while Thomas opted for dive-bombing the one at Vronhoven.

One of Thomas's aircraft failed to get off because of hydraulic trouble. The second machine had Canadian aircraftsman Gordon Patterson of Woodrow, Sask., flying as wireless air gunner. As Thomas started his dive on the bridge, enemy fighters attacked Patterson's aircraft. In Les Allison's *Canadians in the RAF*, Patterson later recalled: "Before we could dive we were hit by three Me-109's which I eventually shot down, but we were so badly damaged my pilot, F/O Davey, ordered us to bail out. I had been hit ... in the right forearm and left leg. When I bailed out, I hit the tail and very badly smashed my right forearm." Patterson was awarded the first DFC to a Canadian, but was taken prisoner that night in Liège.

Thomas picked up flak as he dived and pulled out some 20 feet above the trees. His bombs did no apparent damage, but the engine coughed and he was forced to land. The crew became prisoners within minutes. Meanwhile at the Veldwezelt Bridge, Garland led his section through a screen of flak at 50 feet. P/O David McIntosh's Fairey Battle was hit and burst into flames, but he held course for the bridge and the navigator got the bombs away. The Battle crashed and the crew dragged the injured McIntosh from the burning wreckage. Then another Battle executed a suicide run onto the bridge. Flak blew pieces off the aircraft as it ran in but the bombs fell short just before the Battle hit the bridge. Overhead, the last Battle stood on its tail, climbed briefly and then stalled and plunged to the ground. Although there is no proof, it was assumed that Garland and Gray made the run on the bridge. They both were awarded a Victoria Cross but the third man in the crew was not mentioned. The bridge was damaged but German engineers had it back in operation within hours.

F/Lt Hilly Brown and F/O Roland Dibnah, both of Winnipeg, along with F/O Dick Lewis of Vancouver were three of the fighter pilots who engaged Me-

109s at Maastricht that day. Brown and Lewis each destroyed two enemy fighters. The German officer who captured McIntosh is said to have commented on the insanity of the British as follows, "You British are mad. We took the bridges early Friday morning. You gave us the whole of Friday and Saturday to build up our Flak entrenchments all around the bridge, and then on Sunday ... you came here with three planes and tried to blow the thing up."[2]

The perceptive analysis was a fair comment, not on the RAF, but on the lack of communications between Allied commanders. The French army continued its movement towards the north in spite of reports from its air force that hundreds of tanks were massing for a drive south near Dinant. On the 14th, French squadrons went against the enemy in the Sedan, but were soon put out of action. By then the AASF had lost half its serviceable bombers.

On the fifth day, the crisis shifted to the Sedan area. Late on May 13th, Gen Erwin Rommel's Panzers crossed the Meuse at Dinant and by the next morning Panzers had broken through the Ardennes and were pouring across the Meuse on pontoon bridges. Throughout the day, the RAF sent all its bombers against Sedan bridges, but they flew into intense flak and were sitting ducks for swarms of Me-109s as 40 of 71 aircraft were lost.

F/Lt Gordon Clancy of Semens, Sask., led a flight of five Battles and only one returned, with Clancy staying behind as a POW. Two permanent bridges were hit and two pontoon bridges destroyed, but a modicum of success at high cost in the air was offset by failure of land forces to exploit the advantage. In six days, the Advanced Air Striking Force lost 103 of its 159 aircraft and the remnants retreated westward to Troyes and the Le Mans area. With help from squadrons based in England, they remained operational until June 13th when 38 Battles bombed and strafed enemy troops on the banks of the Seine. They lost six machines in their last operation bringing the total losses to 115 aircraft. During this period Hilly Brown scored 12 victories. While leading his flight against nine Me-109s on June 14th, he destroyed one but his aircraft was damaged and he landed near Caen. By the time he got back to base, his squadron had withdrawn to England.

In the first weeks of the war, Prime Minister Mackenzie King saw immense political gains at low cost by having Canadians serving in the RAF recruited into a Canadian squadron. About two months after the declaration of war, #242 Squadron was formed, but it never became part of the RCAF. When the Blitzkrieg started, it was flying Hurricanes out of Biggin Hill. Although not an official part of the AASF, it joined the force on the continent by mid-May and shared in its ordeal.

F/Lt John Sullivan of Guelph, Ont., was the first to be killed on May 17th. The next day F/Lt Lorne Chambers was shot down. The Vernon, B.C. native survived but was badly burned and suffered a broken back. Within a week John Graafstra, of Souris, Man., and Andy Madore of Saskatoon, were killed and Joe Smiley of Wolseley, Sask., was shot down. By the time of the evacuation at Dunkirk, the squadron had scored a number of victories at a terrible cost. Over half the original 22 pilots were killed, missing or wounded.

Winston Churchill, who had taken over as British prime minister on May 10th, got a call from French Premier Paul Reynaud on May 15th in which he begged for 10 more fighter squadrons. Churchill met with the combined chiefs of staff within two hours and all were at the point of agreeing with Reynaud's request. The head of Fighter Command, Air Chief Marshal Sir Hugh "Stuffy" Dowding, startled Churchill and the War Cabinet with a telegram and letter stating that while 51 squadrons was once considered inadequate for home defence, he was now down to 36 squadrons and Churchill wanted to send 10 to France.

On the day the enemy destroyed 40 AASF aircraft, Holland was negotiating its surrender. A hundred Heinkels flew over Rotterdam and 54 of them dropped 97 tons of bombs on the heart of the city, killing some 1,000 inhabitants. There is some evidence that a breakdown in communication between the Luftwaffe and negotiators may have been responsible, but in addition to the dead, 78,000 people were left homeless two hours before Holland officially surrendered.

When Douglas Bader took over #242 Squadron, he met a sullen group of survivors who somehow felt they had been betrayed. When Bader suggested the pilots tidy up for mess, Stan Turner, who had shot down seven aircraft, icily observed that they had been in a war and didn't have shirts, shoes or ties. In the final days in France, it appeared they had been deserted, separated from ground staff, shunted about aimlessly with each pilot somehow responsible for his aircraft while waiting for a phone call that never came. Most pilots flew to England, but many airmen literally had to hike or steal boats to get home. Those who made it to Dunkirk suffered a final ignominy as the evacuation added another tragic note to a dark moment in history. The total campaign cost the RAF 959 aircraft of which 447 were fighters, but in addition to the loss of life, the tragic consequence was a breakdown of trust between the army and the air force. Although the RAF had been fully engaged and suffered appalling losses, the army suffered from intense enemy air action. At the time of evacuation, some airmen were literally thrown off ships by irate soldiers. In England, Fighter Command's Dowding waited for the storm to break and derived some consolation from the fact that they were now alone. King George VI agreed with Dowding. He wrote to his mother on June 27th, five days after France's surrender. "Personally, I feel happier now that we have no allies to be polite to and to pamper."[3]

**TOP:** *Gladiator crews of #263 Squadron took on impossible odds in Norway, but after a valiant struggle all were lost at sea. (IWM)*

**ABOVE:** *Fairey Battles of the Air Advanced Strike Force bore the brunt of the Blitz as Hitler's forces overran Europe in three weeks. The total campaign cost the RAF 959 aircraft. (IWM)*

**OPPOSITE PAGE:** *With the British army disorganized and equipment abandoned in France, Hitler looked for a quick victory over Britain. The first phase was a massive air assault. (PA-803925)*

# ☙ WHEN BRITAIN STOOD ALONE

*"Born of the sun, they travelled a short*
*while towards the sun, and left the vivid*
*air signed with their honour."*
*~ Stephen Spender*

*ON JULY 10, 1940,* two weeks after the fall of France, RAF Fighter Command scrambled five squadrons to intercept 64 enemy aircraft over Dover. They destroyed 12 and lost three in what is considered to be the first encounter in the Battle of Britain. Duncan "Alex" Hewitt of Saint John was killed attacking a Dornier 17 the next day over Portland, and became the first of some 20 Canadians to die in the air battle that decided the course of history.

The Luftwaffe aircraft made 34 attacks on shipping in as many days and most of the 261 aircraft lost fell to Air Vice Marshal Keith Park's fighters from 11 Group. Because of its location, Park's group would later bear the brunt of airfield attacks and the defence of London. Although Britain now stood alone, Hugh Dowding, the salty chief of Fighter Command, sighed with relief. Entanglements in France had left him with an estimated 750 Spitfires and Hurricanes to counter some 2,800 machines, but now he could pursue his own battle plan.

After his July losses, Hitler tried to give the battle a new spin by declaring

August 13th Eagle Day, and predicted that the new attacks on airfields would cripple the RAF and pave the way for an invasion within two months. At the time there were probably some 80 Canadian fighter pilots in Britain. Twenty-one were with the newly arrived RCAF #1 Squadron and 16 flew with the badly mangled #242 Squadron. The other pilots were volunteers who had gone to England before the war and were scattered throughout the RAF. It should also be noted that hundreds of Canadian aircrew were flying in other commands or theatres of operation.

Eagle Day opened with 1,485 German sorties against ports and assaults on Detling and Eastchurch airfields, and for the next two days, airfields and radar stations were hit. Joe Larichelière of Montreal, became an instant ace when he destroyed six machines in two days, but on the third day he was killed. The day after Larichelière's death, Harold Mitchell of Mount Hope, Ont., downed three to bring his total up to seven. Kenley airfield became a major target on August 18, as 36 bombers approached while nine Dorniers, unseen on radar, skimmed the Channel bound for the same field. A second group of 60 bombers and 150 fighters followed and Kenley was knocked out of action for two days while 60 bombers hit Biggin Hill which remained operational.

Over 100 Stuka dive-bombers hit radar stations on the south coast from Gosport to Ford. The field at Ford was put out of action in the engagement that cost the Luftwaffe 24 aircraft. In four days, the Germans lost 180 planes. However, British losses also grew in August. In a 10-day period prior to September 6th, Fighter Command lost 248 machines with 231 pilots killed or wounded. Pilots were even more difficult to replace than aircraft. Although 250 pilots passed through Operational Training Units in August, they lacked gradual battle experience and many became easy victims.

Most of the pilots of #1 Squadron were from the Montreal area and had arrived from Canada after the evacuation from Dunkirk. The Squadron's first action was an unfortunate disaster in which a flight of 12 Hurricanes mistakenly attacked three Coastal Command Blenheims. Two were shot down before Sqd/Ldr Ernie McNab of Rosthern, Sask., was able to get the confused attackers to withdraw. Two days later, McNab led the squadron into its first action against the enemy as 12 Canadians attacked 30 Dorniers and McNab saw one victim burst into flame just as he was forced to land as his own aircraft was hit. R. Edwards shot the tail off another Dornier before he was killed, becoming the first RCAF fatal casualty, although other Canadians had died before him. In its first contact with the enemy, the squadron destroyed three and damaged four bombers.

Ernie McNab led by example. By October, he was the RCAF's first ace and was awarded the RCAF's first Distinguished Flying Cross. Gordon McGregor, 38, was the oldest Canadian pilot in the Battle of Britain, but one of the first to score a victory. He shot down a Dornier over Biggin Hill late in August and later accounted for five enemy aircraft. Among the Canadians in the RAF was Johnnie Kent, a veteran of the campaign in France, who became a flight leader with Polish #303 Squadron. By mid-October, "Kentowski" had four victories, and when posted to non-operational duties within a year, his score stood at 13. Mark "Hilly" Brown, who flew with RAF #1 Squadron, had 14 personal victories and several shared by the time he took command in November.

While fighting over France, #242 Squadron had lost 13 pilots, but Canadian veterans provided a high level of leadership for replacements. Willie McKnight, Edmonton, went into the Battle of Britain with eight victories and Stan Turner, Toronto, had six and two probables. Robert "Slim" Grassick of London, Ont., Noel Stansfeld of Edmonton, and Victoria's John Latta were other veterans whose drive to have at the enemy matched that of their new leader Douglas Bader. The impatient squadron was scrambled on August 30th and ran into about 100 bombers over North Weald. Willie McKnight accounted for two of the 12 aircraft destroyed.

The outcome of the entire war may have hinged on an accident when stray German bombs fell on London on August 24. In retaliation, the RAF bombed Berlin and Hitler's act of retaliation was to turn the wrath of the Luftwaffe against London. In so doing, he probably snatched defeat from the jaws of victory. According to Winston Churchill, "Extensive damage had been done to five of 11 Group's forward airfields. If the enemy had persisted ... the whole intricate organization of Fighter Command might have broken down."[39]

Against the advice of his senior commanders, Luftwaffe Reichsmarschall Herman Göring switched tactics. London became a target and more fighters were brought into play hoping to now destroy the RAF in the air. Some 950 aircraft hit London on September 7 and returned that evening, leaving the city in flames. But before the flames died, day bombers were back to set the pattern for the next week. Fighter Command was caught off guard by the change of tactics and for at least three days, heavy cloud also prevented ground observers from tracking enemy formations. Fighter Command's brief failure to respond with its customary aggressiveness led Göring to misread the situation and mount a 1,700-plane raid on September 15.

Designed to break the back of Fighter Command, the operation started shortly after midnight. Five major raids pounded London during the day, and as lazy contrails chalked the blue that Sunday, Britons looked up and tried to decipher their fate in the tracings. The next day, the *Daily Express* announced that 175 enemy aircraft had been shot down, a number that later checked out at about 56. But it was a decisive moment as Hitler postponed invasion plans, which he eventually cancelled. The entire war took on a different character, but the air battle continued and on September 27, the RCAF #1 downed eight invaders. Days shortened and nights gave way to bombing, sending some seven million Londoners to shelters or subways. A million children were taken from their homes and sent around the world. The Battle of Britain segued to the Blitz as 300 enemy bombers fell over England in October. Liverpool, Southampton, Portsmouth became designated targets and in mid-November 500 bombers hit Coventry, killing over 550 people.

The young men in the Spitfires and Hurricanes showed incredible determination in winning the Battle of Britain, but Bomber Command also contributed by flying several missions against invasion barges in Channel ports. Members of the Women's Auxiliary Air Force were also key figures under fire at isolated radar posts as well as busy airfields. But it was the fortitude of the average citizen that won the Blitz that followed. By the spring of 1941, 43,000 civilians had been killed and 51,000 seriously injured. Their spirit of resistance paraphrased Churchill's promise to fight on the beaches and never surrender.

## TOTAL BATTLE OF BRITAIN LOSSES

| Total Losses | RAF    905 | Luftwaffe    1733 |
|---|---|---|

## THE GRUMPY OLD MAN WHO SAVED BRITAIN BUT WAS FIRED

Before he took on Göring's Luftwaffe in 1940, A/C/M Sir Hugh "Stuffy" Dowding had many battles with the Air Ministry as he tried to enforce his views on how to defend Britain. When he undertook the greatest battle since Trafalgar, the grumpy, old man of Fighter Command considered his status as an "unsatisfactory domestic servant under notice." He wasn't far wrong. Dowding's conflict with authority dated back to the Battle of the Somme in 1916 when he commanded the Headquarters Wing of the RFC. Col Dowding then asked Brig-Gen Hugh Trenchard, RFC commander in France, to withdraw one of his squadrons, which had taken heavy casualties.

Trenchard withdrew the squadron and sent "Dismal Jimmy" Dowding packing. The stigma haunted Dowding for two decades, but he kept it alive with frequent brisk exchanges with Air Ministry officials as he tried to drag the RAF out of the lotus days of air pageants and parades. Most of the senior command subscribed to the Trenchard illusion that the bomber would always get through. Few stopped to consider how bombers would get through if navigators couldn't navigate or drop a bomb in the right place. As for the fighter arm, pilots were taught to fly pretty formations, but they weren't taught to fight and their machines were from some forgotten era.

Dowding sent out a wake-up call in 1936 when, as head of research and development, he got designs for Spitfires and Hurricanes approved. He was appointed head of Fighter Command that year and his determination to use the latest technology, including radar, to build up a force that could defend Britain became his only concern. His enthusiasm for that task rattled cages at the Air Ministry and soon there were open suggestions that he retire.

During his first months as chief of Fighter Command, Dowding's hypothetical scenarios saw France as the enemy but later, in spite of Prime Minister Chamberlain's brave pronouncements at Munich, it became obvious to the 56-year-old Dowding that Herman Göring and the Luftwaffe would be the enemy. Dowding's original plan for the defence of Britain visualized 52 fighter squadrons, but once war was declared, his numbers fell increasingly short because of foreign engagements such as two squadrons in Norway and six in France. On May 10, 1940, German Panzers started rolling westward and four additional Hurricane squadrons were sent to France, leaving 36 squadrons in Britain.

After a chaotic five days, Churchill got a phone call from the French premier who lamented: "We are defeated!" Two hours later, Churchill met with his chiefs of staff to discuss his plan to send 10 more squadrons of Hurricanes to France. As indicated, Dowding bluntly put it on paper, saying if his fighters continued to defend France there would be none left to defend Britain. Churchill relented although it was against his nature. According to some sources, Dowding was convinced that a grudge was born at that instant which determined his future.

When the first German attacks against England hit the south coast, a radar network of 21 stations became of critical importance. Radar picked up enemy bombers and fighters over the Pas de Calais. Only 25 minutes would elapse before they were over RAF stations and of this time it took the best RAF squadrons up to three minutes to scramble and 15 minutes to climb to 20,000 feet. This left a very narrow time window to seek out and destroy the bombers.

Reports of the enemy's approach were fed to a filter room at Fighter Command headquarters near London and developments were relayed to various sectors. Hence, the entire defensive operation was under very strict central control with radar at its heart. German Luftwaffe General der Flieger Adolf Galland later wrote: "The British had an extraordinary advantage which we could never overcome throughout the entire war: radar and fighter control. For us ... this was a surprise and a very bitter one."[40]

While #11 Group drew most of the enemy attacks, a dispute over tactics broke out between the commander of the hard-pressed #11 Group, A/V/M Keith

Park and Trafford Leigh-Mallory, the somewhat political air vice marshal of #12 Group to the north. Dowding insisted that there was insufficient time to scramble squadrons from #12 Group and have them intercept the enemy, but Leigh-Mallory was given to Air Ministry intrigue and also objected to having his group play second fiddle to Park's. After one acrimonious exchange, Leigh-Mallory boasted that he would get Dowding's job.

Park asked Leigh-Mallory for help when enemy forces hit his airfields at Debden, Hornchurch, and North Weald, while his own aircraft were engaged to the south. When #12 Group Spitfires got to Debden, the field had suffered extensive damage. Park was very critical of the slowness of Leigh-Mallory's response and four days later, Leigh-Mallory's force failed to locate enemy bombers over Biggin Hill, which underwent two severe bombings. Meanwhile, Sqd/Ldr Douglas Bader repeatedly ignored orders to patrol the less active northern sector and Leigh-Mallory encouraged his poaching forays to the south by giving him command of five squadrons.

On the last day of August, the Luftwaffe flew 1,300 sorties against Park's fields. They hit Hornchurch and Biggin Hill where the sector operations room was hit and telephone lines cut for the second time in two days. In less than two weeks, Dowding lost 466 fighters while 231 pilots were killed, wounded or missing. Among the survivors, exhaustion was setting in as some flew four operations a day and all were constantly on call.

The air staff bureaucracy as well as the Luftwaffe was closing in on Dowding. Leigh-Mallory was mustering support for the "Big Wing" theory when Hitler shifted his air attack to London. Some 900 German aircraft hit London's East End, overwhelming Fighter Command that was geared to attacks on airfields. Bombing continued into the night and next day, but by then Park's fighters pounced and the effectiveness of the German bombing fell off.

The raids killed 2,000 Londoners and wounded 10,000, and by September 15th, Göring made his final bid. He launched everything that flew in two assaults, and Park threw 10 squadrons at the first wave while Douglas Bader left his assigned area in the north to lead the Duxford Wing to London where they ripped into the second wave. German fighters ran low on fuel and abandoned the fight and at least 30 bombers fell from the sky.

Two days later, Hitler postponed invasion plans and Stuffy Dowding won the Trafalgar of the air. But he was about to lose a critical battle to enemies at home. On October 17, a meeting of RAF brass – at which Sqd/Ldr Bader and Leigh-Mallory were present – approved the "Big Wing" concept of grouping five squadrons. The minutes indicated "it would be arranged for #12 Group Wings to participate freely in suitable operations over the #11 Group area." This translated as a personal defeat for Dowding and Park, the men who had saved Britain. About a month later, both were relieved of their command. Park went to southeast Asia and Dowding, of all people, was sent on a diplomatic mission to Washington.

## THE BRIDGE GROWS WINGS

During the Blitz, Canadian Lord Beaverbrook became responsible for aircraft production and his priority obviously was Spitfires and Hurricanes to replace the heavy losses. Bomber Command was in dire need of replacements because it had lost the equivalent of half its front line strength during the Battle of France. Although some 240 Hudsons had been delivered from Canada by ship, with increased enemy submarine activity, the chances of safe arrival fell to 50 per cent. Beaverbrook then turned his considerable energies to delivering bombers across the Atlantic by air.

It was an idea that grew by avoiding officialdom and calling on the best of the old boy's club. George Woods-Humphries, former manager of Imperial Airways, was persuaded to recruit the first few pilots such as British Overseas Airways Corporation's Capt Don Bennett. Sir Edward Beatty, a friend of Beaverbrook and president of the CPR volunteered the services of the CPR, and offices were set up in Montreal's Windsor Station. Former bush pilot Punch Dickins became director of recruitment and launched a net that would attract pilots from at least six countries.

By November 1940, Bennett had trained six crews and was ready to challenge the Atlantic. Pilots were either British or American, but six radio operators were Canadian. Seven Hudsons took off from Hattie's Camp, Nfld., on a blustery evening while a band played "Nearer My God to Thee." All 22 men were glad to be clear of the dismal swamp people were starting to call Gander. They touched down at Aldergrove, near Belfast, next morning and Ferry Command became a reality.

The seven Hudsons were the first of 10,000 aircraft delivered across the Atlantic and Pacific. Aircraft flown across to North Africa would become a major factor in the success of the counter push from El Alamein. As the war progressed, Ferry Command underwent various transformations and became a blend of service and civilian personnel. But for a non-combatant unit, it suffered appalling casualties. An estimated 560 of its 1,100 aircrew were killed.

## CANADA TAKES WINGS

As Britain faced the reality of a shooting war in the spring of 1940, Canada was gearing up for a mammoth undertaking. Much of the planning and survey work on the British Commonwealth Air Training Plan had been done during the winter and bulldozers moved in by spring. The RCAF's strength at the declaration of war was 4,061 personnel and the training plan called for a tenfold increase in size merely to provide trained personnel to keep things moving at 74 depots and flying schools.

C.G. "Chubby" Power, Canada's minister of National Defence for Air, was responsible for recruitment and training. Transport Minister C.D. Howe energetically directed aerodrome construction and 17 civilian flying clubs agreed to provide elementary flight training. The aircraft program was directed by Ralph Bell, an executive who reported to Howe. Bell experienced his first setback when Britain was unable to deliver 1,500 Avro Ansons promised as advanced trainers. A shipload of Ansons was ordered back to England while in the mid-Atlantic. Insiders reckoned that if Britain depended on the Anson for defence then the situation was indeed even worse than the new Prime Minister Churchill's promise of blood, sweat and tears.

Howe attacked the problem by buying up all the engines an American firm could produce and established Federal Aircraft to produce the Ansons for training potential bomber pilots. He solved the problem of training fighter pilots by having Noorduyn Aviation produce over 100 Harvards a month. And if there was one sound which came to say it all about Canada's war effort, it was the sound of a distant Harvard changing pitch in the frosty air anywhere from Summerside to Medicine Hat.

A/C Leckie came over from England to become another key player as he was named the RCAF's director of training. Seven training camps, or "Manning Depots" as they were called, began to receive recruits during the winter and by April 1940, the first draft of British Commonwealth Air Training Plan (BCATP) students arrived at the Eglinton Hunt Club in Toronto which had been turned into an Initial Training School (ITS). From the perspective of the new recruit, the Manning Depot was the first stop on his way to war. Here he got a haircut and a winter cap that slid down over his ears when he bashed the parade square. He learned to make his bed with tidy hospital corners and if he happened to be at #1 Manning Depot in Toronto, he quickly adjusted to the permeating stench of cattle manure. The bull pen at the Canadian National Exhibition grounds was a major centre of activities, and generations of cattle had left happy mementoes of better times in various patterns on the floor.

Recruits parading outside were constantly exposed to aircraft doing circuits and bumps from nearby Toronto Island. The endless stream of aircraft were flown by tall, blond, Norwegians who would quickly be swaggering around Sunnyside wearing a white aircrew flash in their caps that soon became a beacon for babes. The time an individual spent at a Manning Depot depended on how well the entire training treadmill was moving and also the demand for certain trades. Most were assured that the Air Force would find some backwater shack that needed guarding and this meant a period on guard duty and a chance to search for the evasive Southern Cross and find only the Big Dipper in the Northern sky.

Although a recruit may have originally been selected as pilot or observer when he signed up, some seemingly unwritten law gave the RCAF authority to con certain groups into other trades. This exercise went according to demand. One group had successfully completed training at the Initial Training School, but instead of going through as pilots or observers, all were packed off to become wireless air gunners.

In the spring of 1941, there was a sudden demand for radar mechanics. The exercise went something like this: a recruit was examined and tested for aircrew. Then some genial administration person congratulated him and said: "By the way there's another course coming up ... most interesting ... good possibilities for commissions ... dealing with radar." The word *radar* was usually uttered with a knowing yet secretive wink. The deal was if the applicant didn't like the course, he could always re-muster to aircrew.

Hundreds, later thousands, took the difficult course and went on to vital ground crew work. But a number followed Slim Grassick's lead. Slim soon became disenchanted and wrote the final exam at the University of New Brunswick in less than 90 seconds. A stunned physics professor read Slim's paper to the class that hadn't quite completed reading the first question on a superheterodyne. The perplexed academic read: "There'll always be an England and I intend to buy lots of war bonds. Somewhere there's a Spitfire waiting for me and I damn well want to find it!"

By fall, Slim had hundreds of followers who returned to Manning Depots. Some, like Slim, got to re-muster, but as candidates were reviewed alphabetically, many of those in the bottom half of the alphabet became a cropper on December 7, when Japan hit Pearl Harbour. The priority became defence of the West Coast and the RCAF responded by sending bodies with no training and less aptitude to defend Canada. Numbers alone solved immediate public relations challenges.

One such group had inadvertently given high-speed rescue launches as the second choice on their interviews. Soon they found that their first experience with boats ended up taking them up the Inland Passage to absolute isolation at Alliford Bay in the Queen Charlotte Islands. Instead of streaking across the English Channel, this group's first encounter with war was scraping endless barnacles and leaving no buoy in the northwest theatre unpainted.

However, in spite of many detours, the flow to Initial Training Schools grew steadily. For potential pilots, the schools were a psychological obstacle course. The idea was to emerge with a recommendation for pilot training. It wasn't enough to flex one's muscles like Buster Crabbe or memorize where each valve was during the intake stroke. There was the constant danger of obscure interviews. Bland-faced, wingless administrative officers asked hypothetical questions, the answer to which assuredly determined if one became a pilot or observer. Tall candidates tended to scrunch during such interviews because every now and then rumour had it that the RCAF was only taking short pilots. The conveyor of such information usually confirmed it with, "Billy Bishop isn't very tall is he?" Those who survived ITS and the demon Link Trainer took either of two routes: they went to one of 26 Elementary Flying Training Schools (EFTS) or became observer trainees at one of 10 schools. At EFTS, the trainees did battle with the mighty Tiger Moth (or Tigerschmidt as it was affectionately referred to) or Fleet Finch and counted off the hours to solo.

Those who survived EFTS moved to service flying in either Harvards or Yales if streamed as potential fighter pilots. Bomber candidates trained on Ansons or Cranes. After cross-country flights on the prairies, British students often returned in confusion and abject fear of being washed out because of poor map-reading. Ogilvie Oats had grain elevators sprinkled all over the prairies with the name "Ogilvie" standing distinctly tall. British student pilots and navigators checking landmarks invariably saw Ogilvie, but failed to find it on a map. Confusion grew by the second because there were few other landmarks as distinctive as the elevators, and if they flew on they came to another Ogilvie. Canadian trainees would nod sympathetically as the distraught Britishers later told their story, but there is no record of anybody ever actually telling a Brit that Ogilvie was a guy who made oats.

The first draft of BCATP trained pilots went overseas in March 1941. While the BCATP was to be phased out in March 1943, by 1942 it became obvious that the end of the war was nowhere in sight and the scheme was expanded. At its peak, the plan operated 97 schools with 184 support units. It turned out 131,533 aircrew graduates in eight categories from the Commonwealth and France, Belgium, Holland, Norway, Czechoslovakia and Poland. Of these 72,835 were Canadian. The reaction of Canadian communities to the BCATP soon became a home-grown symbol that the phoney war was over.

**ABOVE:** *By November 1940, Don Bennett trained 22 civilians for the first flight of bombers across the Atlantic. It was the start of Ferry Command, which would later deliver 10,000 aircraft overseas. (PMR-85475)*

**RIGHT:** *Air Vice Marshal Sir Hugh "Stuffy" Dowding. (IWM)*

**ABOVE:** *During the Battle of Britain reinforcements for Malta were not available. In 1941 two carriers launched 48 Hurricanes at maximum distance from Malta and 36 pilots were lost. A later Spitfire launch was more successful, but within 72 hours of reaching Malta every machine was destroyed or unserviceable. (PL-14940)*

**OPPOSITE PAGE:** *When Italy launched its bombers on Malta, three ancient Gladiators rose to meet raids of 200 aircraft for three weeks. They were joined by four Hurricanes three weeks later and the fighters met odds of 10 to one. (PL-14940)*

# ✍ THE WAR WIDENS

*Faith, Hope and Charity take on the*
*Italians in Malta's ordeal*

*A FEW WEEKS BEFORE* Hitler's Panzers rolled across Europe in 1940, the HMS *Glorious* steamed out of Malta and left four packing cases on the wharf. Curious Maltese longshoremen eventually investigated the cases and found they contained four ancient Gloster Gladiator aircraft. The RAF managed to breathe life into three of the Fleet Air Arm machines that became Malta's air defence as France fell and Italy then declared war on France and Britain.

When Italian bombers struck Malta on June 11th, three old Gladiators were all that rose to meet them. F/Lt William Joseph "Timber" Woods and two companions drove the first wave back out to sea, but the second formation closed on the port of Valetta. Woods got in a burst at a bomber, which sped away leaving the biplane a sitting duck for enemy fighters. He then sent a sleek Macchi fighter diving for home with a long trail of smoke tracing its course back to Sicily. This was the overture to the 29-month siege of Malta, a few rocky islands strategically located in the middle of 2,000 miles of the Mediterranean. About the size of London, it had a population of 300,000 that was heavily dependent on outside sources for food.

The British chiefs of staff had declared it indefensible, but Churchill saw it as the key to the Middle East because it provided a potential base from which to protect British shipping and harass enemy supply ships to North Africa. But in the spring of 1940, as Italian raids continued from nearby Sicily, all that stopped the enemy were three Gladiators that became known as *Faith, Hope* and *Charity*. For three weeks, the fragile trio rose to meet raids of 200 fighters and bombers.

They were first joined by four Hurricanes that were en route to the Mideast, and for two months the seven fighters were meeting odds of 10 to one. The Gladiators intercepted 72 hostile formations and shot down 37 enemy aircraft. Later that summer, 12 Hurricanes were flown in from the carrier *Argus* but disaster hit a second batch of reinforcements that fall. The *Argus* slipped through Gibraltar, but stood off at maximum distance from Malta because of possible enemy action. A Fleet Air Arm machine escorted the fighters and pilots had been briefed on a weather report that was sadly out of date. What should have been a tailwind was a headwind and long before they reached Malta, the fighters had exhausted their fuel and were falling into the sea. Nine of 14 pilots and their machines were lost.

The assault on Malta came just prior to the Battle of Britain and demands on the RAF's limited fighter strength also came from North Africa. Official reinforcements were slow in reaching their target, but an assortment of aircraft bound for other parts were seconded, diverted or otherwise assigned to Malta. Gradually a bomber and reconnaissance force was built up and strikes against enemy shipping grew. Photos taken by a Maltese aircraft induced the Fleet Air Arm to mount a raid on Italian shipping at Taranto. Swordfish struck from 170 miles out and sank three battleships, two auxiliaries and left two cruisers listing. The Italian navy never recovered from the losses and spent most of the war trying to evade the British fleet. A Japanese official was sent to Taranto to study the damage and the techniques used by the raiders. His report became a primer for Pearl Harbour some 13 months later.

Disaster continued to dog British efforts to launch fighters from aircraft carriers. In June 1941, the *Ark Royal* and *Victorious* sent 48 Hurricanes off their decks. They took off at maximum distance and the RAF pilots used statute miles to compute distance to Malta, while Fleet Air Arm escorts used nautical miles. The formations flew south of Malta and this time 36 pilots and fighters were lost. Yet RAF and Fleet Air Arm aircraft took a heavy toll on enemy shipping during the summer of '41, sinking over 160,000 tons or about 50 per cent of shipping encountered. By fall, Beauforts and Sunderland flying boats were observing and photographing enemy ports.

Early in 1942, the Luftwaffe was flying 10 to 15 attacks a day on Malta in a major blitz and by February the island had suffered from 2,000 enemy sorties.

Stan Turner was brought in as CO of #249 Squadron in February, but by the following month, Malta was down to three fighters. Two months later, the USS Wasp loaded 48 Spitfires in England and sailed through the Straits of Gibraltar to within 600 miles of Malta. The carrier turned into the wind and Martlet fighters provided cover as the Spits prepared to takeoff.

The first machine to attempt it was flown by an officer known as "The Confectioner" because he considered anything a piece of cake. On this particular takeoff his role was to show the others how it was done. His Spit trembled as he applied full boost. Then when he released the brakes, a sudden torque hit the machine sending it sliding sideways 90 degrees and popping over the edge. Somewhere in the 60 feet to the water, "The Confectioner" managed to gain air speed, but the other machines took the long way down the runway.

Although 46 Spitfires reached Malta, they landed amid dust from an air raid and within three days every machine was either destroyed or unserviceable. The battle for Malta now reached critical proportions as a major Allied convoy failed to get through and fuel was brought in by submarine. The survival of Malta was dependant on three factors: the growth of an air defensive and offensive force; the resolution of the natives to resist; and the ability of the merchant navy to provide essentials for survival, including food.

A number of pilots arrived in Malta by the summer of 1942, of which nearly one-quarter were Canadian. W/Com Hilly Brown commanded fighter operations until he was shot down by anti-aircraft fire in a raid on a German field in Sicily. At the time of his death, he had scored 20 victories. Wally McLeod, of Regina, got 13 victories in 18 weeks and Robert Wendell "Buck" McNair fulfilled the promise shown in the Battle of Britain. Although George "Buzz" Beurling of Verdun, Que., showed few of the leadership qualities of the above, his deadly ability at deflection shooting enabled him to score 28 of his 32 victories from Malta in four months before being shot down and wounded.

The bombing of Allied convoys created critical shortages of food and supplies. In one attack in June, 15 vessels were lost and in August another convoy fought its way through attacks by submarines, E-boats and dive-bombers. All 14 ships were seriously damaged and nine were sunk. The experience of the tanker Ohio puts things into perspective: Early on the morning of August 12th, a torpedo blasted a 24 by 27-foot hole in her side and seconds later the engine room was ablaze, but tons of rushing sea water helped control the fire. Part of the extensive damage was to the instruments and steering, but the engines were still growling and the captain eventually managed to close on the distant ships of the convoy.

The Ohio was sailing in line with a merchant ship when it was hit by a bomb and blown apart. It spread a tower of flame across the water, which a second ship ploughed through. Thirty-four members of its confused crew jumped into the sea of flame, thinking their ship had been hit. The *Ohio* was so close that one of its kerosene tanks was set ablaze, and within an hour, a second wave of Ju-87s struck and this time the *Ohio* took a 500-pounder in the bow. Two sticks of bombs straddled the wounded tanker, lifting it out of the water.

It rocked, rattled and rolled, but continued towards Malta. Then a second Ju-88 hit the sea and bounced aboard the poop deck. This time two boilers blew out and the engines ground to a halt. The *Ohio* underwent further bombing for two hours and attempts to take her in tow failed because of her damaged steering gear and severe structural damage. She drifted for three hours; down to the bows in water and listing sharply with the engine room flooding six inches an hour while kerosene mixing with water added additional danger to the flooding.

Some 70 miles from Malta, the tanker and its precious cargo was near death when three ships took her in tow. Spitfires from Malta met further air attacks, but a 1,000-pound bomb pitched the *Ohio* out of the water where her screws were torn out of alignment and the plates began to buckle. One final attempt to tow the wreck was successful and the cargo finally arrived in Malta on August 16th.

By November 1942, the major siege of Malta was lifted. Some 5,715 bombers had killed an estimated 1,500 civilians. At times the lack of oil made it impossible to operate water pumps as buildings burned. However, the people persevered and the navy endured brutal convoy action as the RAF built up its defensive and offensive strength. Malta then emerged as a key base that dominated the central Mediterranean and became an important element in eventual victory in the North African campaign.


## NORTH AFRICAN THEATRE

Malta was the gateway to the Mediterranean, Egypt and the Suez Canal. Far beyond Malta, A/C Raymond Collishaw commanded a force of nine squadrons in the front line of the defence of Egypt and the Suez Canal. As the Italians flew the first raid against Malta, Collishaw's Blenheims struck at the Italian airfield at El Adem, near Tobruk. A ceremonial parade to celebrate Italy's entry into the war was unceremoniously dispersed, and Collishaw's planes returned later to destroy 19 enemy aircraft.

Canada's second ranking ace in WWI with 61 victories, Collishaw had remained in the RAF and saw distinguished service in Russia, the Middle East and on Royal Navy aircraft carriers. When Italy entered the war, he was in command of four squadrons of Blenheims and one each of Gladiators and Lysanders, a fragile network designed to protect Alexandria, Cairo and the Suez Canal.

Collishaw was determined to establish an aggressive philosophy from the outset. On the third day, Vernon Crompton "Woody" Woodward of Victoria shot down his first bomber followed by a fighter. By the end of the month, he added two more fighters to a total of 20 destroyed and five probables. Woodward was another of the Canadian cattle-boaters who were scattered around North Africa.

Italy's action came as France collapsed and Britain braced for invasion. A/C/M Sir Arthur Longmore was responsible for some 4.5 million square miles of territory. With extremely limited resources and little chance of getting reinforcements from England, Longmore was cautious. Although Collishaw's losses had been relatively minor, Longmore saw little chance of replacing aircraft or even getting parts for damaged machines. He therefore asked Collishaw to fight a less aggressive war. Although the relationship between Collishaw and the commanding air officer was good, the Canadian's pilots took a dim view of being muzzled.

Collishaw then resorted to light-hearted deception and psychological warfare to outfox the enemy and maintain morale. The Italians had failed to take advantage of a six to one majority and Collishaw turned to one-upmanship when somebody found a store of ancient fragmentation bombs. They were put into boxes and loaded onto lumbering Bombay transports for nightly excursions over enemy encampments. Each aircraft had 200 unstable bombs that had to be fused individually in flight. Then they were tossed out the door, the total process took at least a minute a bomb, which meant that each aircraft spent more than three hours over the target and had to refuel during flight. The empty fuel drums were then tossed overboard and the consensus grew that the drums did more damage than the bombs. But the operation did keep the enemy awake and the offensive spirit alive.

The only modern aircraft Collishaw had access to was a Hawker Hurricane called "Colly's battleship." In order to create an illusion about Allied resources, he had it dragged from base to base leaving it exposed to the lens of Italian reconnaissance cameras. To further this ruse, Collishaw started an industry among Jewish settlers in Palestine who built a host of dummy aircraft, which he had scattered around his advanced airfields. As the Allies stalled for time and hoped for reinforcements, Italian Marshal Graziani moved 215,000 troops and 280 aircraft into nearby Tripoli in preparation for a strike at Gen Sir Richard O'Connor's 40,000 men.

In addition to facing invasion at home, Prime Minister Churchill ran into a problem with the admiralty while trying to get reinforcements to O'Connor's superior, Gen Sir Archibald Wavell. The admiralty declined to send reinforcements through Gibraltar because slow moving tank transport ships would expose the fleet to bombing. Instead, they moved an armoured brigade around the Cape of Good Hope and up to Alexandria. It arrived two weeks after Graziani's advance on September 13th when his armies moved 50 miles to the east where they occupied Sidi Barrani and built up supply lines. Graziani also built a line of fortifications extending some 40 miles inland from the coast road and even added a pipeline.

The British withdrawal meant that the RAF lost forward landing strips that were critical to the land war. The bombers then had to fly beyond the range of fighter cover while a lack of refueling bases substantially cut down bomber range. Although these were essentially RAF problems, the manner in which they impacted on the ground war resulted in a relearning of old lessons long forgotten by the most senior command.

Collishaw and O'Connor established headquarters in adjacent buildings and an extremely close rapport developed between the air and land arms. Both remembered the lessons of the previous war when the Ludendorff offensives almost separated the British and French armies. Intense German air support during the Ludendorff drive gobbled up RAF fields and aircraft making British troops vulnerable to attack. But as the line of advance lengthened, the enemy failed to move his aircraft forward and the impact of the air attack diminished. In the British counterattack, air support became a key element in the drive.

While this philosophy may seem obvious in retrospect, it was discarded during the years between the wars as tactics became a matter of personal agendas. In spite of the valiant work of the Advanced Air Strike Force, a unified air-ground policy was missing during the fall of France. Collishaw and O'Connor re-established a rapport that made the doctrine of air-support a critical part of the land battle.

When Gen Wavell and A/C/M Longmore concluded plans for Operation COMPASS in the fall of 1940, it was determined the advances of Collishaw's airfields would determine the timing of O'Connor's offensive. At a time when air and land commanders seldom talked to each other, the concept was revolutionary.

Although the Fleet Air Arm strike against the Italian fleet at Taranto on November 11, 1940, decisively shifted the balance of power in the Mediterranean, a month later the Germans moved Fliegerkorps X down to Sicily and shifted the balance right back. With 330 first-line aircraft and highly-trained crews who had learned their dive-bombing skills in Norway, the Luftwaffe challenged the British fleet soon after its arrival. A major attack on British ships crippled HMS *Illustrious* as six 1,000-pound bombs pierced the deck, destroyed nine aircraft and set the carrier afire. Although eight attackers were shot down, the carrier was circling out of control when another strike by Italians fell short. Two and a half hours later, the Junkers returned, but their earlier losses made them less aggressive. A third attack on a battleship was unsuccessful and the *Illustrious* limped into port by late evening. The engagement proved conclusively that the dive bomber had arrived as an offensive weapon.

The Italians invaded Greece in late October, but within three days, the Greek army was holding the invaders in check. Churchill, who was obsessed with foreign intrigue since the disaster at Gallipoli in 1915, longed to establish a presence in Greece, and his political ambition soon reflected on the action in North Africa.

In early December, Gen O'Connor was ready to strike back at the Graziani forces that had been consolidating for three months. Collishaw borrowed a page from the night in 1918 when British, Canadians and Australians prepared to breakout from Amiens. At that time, two Canadian pilots pushed their heavy Handly-Page bombers aloft in driving rain and flew at low level over the British lines for three hours to drown out the sound of tanks being assembled for the attack.

Collishaw had Bristol Bombays pounding a beat where Gen O'Connor's Matilda tanks had assembled. The tanks swept through Graziani's encampments and drove the Italians back 250 miles to Benghazi and beyond. Collishaw's bombers struck Italian airfields and fighters screened the battle area and swept the desert ahead of the advancing British troops.

George Keefer of Charlottetown shot down his first enemy aircraft on December 7th and would ultimately add 17 more during his three tours accounting for 400 operational hours. In two months, O'Connor destroyed 10 Italian divisions, took 130,000 prisoners, 400 tanks and 800 guns. The British sank or disabled 35 ships and 1,100 aircraft were abandoned or shot down. On the second last day of the offensive, fighting centered around Sollum where Charles "Deadstick" Dyson of #33 Squadron was reported to have shot down seven enemy aircraft in one engagement. While O'Connor's troops prepared to expel the last Italians from Libya, Collishaw's meagre forces had literally crippled the Italian air force with a loss of only 26 aircraft.

But political considerations took the edge off the victory and sprinkled it with confusion. Churchill told Wavell: "Nothing must hamper the capture of Tobruk, but hereafter all operations in Libya are subordinated to aiding Greece."[6] O'Connor ended up over 200 miles beyond Tobruk, but didn't get the support he needed to deliver the knockout punch because it conflicted with Churchill's plan. Greek Prime Minister Ioannis Metaxas had persistently refused British troops on his soil because he feared German retaliation, but he did agree to air support. Collishaw was forced to send five squadrons to Greece in December as O'Connor's drive was getting under way.

A month later, Metaxas died of a heart attack and within nine days, Churchill convinced his successor, Alexandros Korizis, to accept British troops. The day O'Connor was forced to break-off his round up in Cyrenaica, General Erwin Rommel arrived in Tripoli with the first of his Afrika Korps, and the Germans were at a loss to understand why the British had not exploited the Italian defeat by securing Tripoli. Churchill's political motives took precedence over military realities and the British made the fatal mistake of diluting meagre forces until Wavell was left with only one infantry division and half an armoured division. Ultimately, Collishaw had to send eight squadrons to Greece.

On April 6th, the Germans struck through Yugoslavia. In one attack on RAF fields in Greece, the Luftwaffe destroyed 30 Hurricanes and Blenheims and wiped out #113 Squadron. Fl/Lt John MacKie of Vernon, B.C., who had scored seven victories, was killed while trying to take off in a Hurricane at Eleusis. Robert "Bob" Davidson of Vancouver shot down a Cant bomber while flying Blenheims with #30 Squadron and Lloyd Schwab, Niagara Falls, Ont., took over #112 Gladiator Squadron which was reduced to three aircraft. Arthur "Jimmy" Cochrane, of Vernon, B.C., also flew with #112 Gladiator Squadron at a time when they repeatedly faced odds of 20 to one. He later commanded the restructured squadron.

Woody Woodward destroyed an Italian Fiat while escorting Blenheims on April 5th and the next day was temporarily grounded as his flight took off. When he did get airborne, he attacked four enemy bombers and destroyed three. Many of Woodward's flights were in the company of his commanding officer, Sqd/Ldr Pat Pattle. Pattle and Woodward became legends during April. Estimates of Pattle's victories range from 40 upwards and Woodward was finally credited with 20 confirmed, five probables and two destroyed on the ground. Their last battle together occurred on April 20th when 100 enemy aircraft attacked RAF bases and the last 15 Hurricanes rose to meet them. In the extended air battle, 22 enemy aircraft fell while the RAF lost five including Pattle.

Seven survivors eventually flew to Crete where the British experienced another Dunkirk. Sunderland flying boats had evacuated hundreds of Greek and British troops to Crete, which was soon hit by 1,300 aircraft in support of 3,000 parachutists. Wavell lost 30,000 of his best men in the Greek misadventure and the German Afrika Korps also pushed across North Africa to the gates of Tobruk. In a shuffle in the British Command, A/V/M Arthur Coningham replaced Raymond Collishaw. Of the eight RAF squadrons sent to Greece, only six aircraft got back to Egypt. In the final days of the Greek disaster, the RAF's failure to provide cover for the evacuation revived bitter memories of Dunkirk and heightened tensions between the airmen and the other services.

The only positive aspect of the dark summer of '41 was a British victory in Ethiopia that re-opened an old Imperial Airways route across central Africa. This meant that Hurricanes arrived in West Africa in relative safety and were flown in stages some 3,500 miles across the continent. Soon Ferry Command was flying in bombers as well as fighters from America, which were to become key elements in turning the tide.

The desert war became like a football game where two strong teams pushed each other the length of the field, but didn't have the energy to score. By the fall of 1942, word went around that the chiefs of the army, navy and air force were actually speaking to each other. When Montgomery opened his offensive at El Alamein, tactical air power was a key element in the battle plan. Boston, Baltimore and Mitchell bombers saturated enemy airfields, armour and supply dumps. They got close cover from Kittyhawks, Tomahawks and Hurricane fighter-bombers while Spitfires flew top cover. It was the birth of what later became the Second Tactical Air Force that provided taxi-rank service to ground troops in Normandy.

*As the war spread to North Africa a number of Canadian "cattle-boaters" became involved. Woody Woodward fought in the desert and in Greece where he had 20 confirmed victories and five probables. (PL-19348)*

**TOP:** *The Catalina Flying Boat had the range to make it an effective search weapon. But somewhat cumbersome, it tended to be vulnerable to heavy submarine anti-aircraft fire. (PL-10008)*

**ABOVE:** *A Liberator, flown by Canadian crew from Gander, Nfld., closed the gap on the Atlantic run which had long been a hunting ground for enemy subs. (IWM)*

# ❧ BATTLE ABOVE THE ATLANTIC

*In the Battle of the Atlantic, Canadians sank 61 U-boats, considerably more than the 33 they were officially credited with. But little is known about the role of the Canadian airmen.*

**IN 1939, THE RCAF** started its marine war well back in the queue. It lacked aircraft, armament, technology and experience. The British could provide little help because RAF Coastal Command had only 34 aircraft, which could range 500 miles from shore. With the fall of France, Germany occupied every port from Norway to Spain. This meant that *Grandadmiral* Karl Dönitz could launch his subs a greater distance into the Atlantic. Although German U-boats of the period had to surface frequently to recharge, the RAF then had no means of locating them in the dark.

Canadian progress on the East Coast was slow. In June 1941 Sqd/Ldr C. Annis of #10 Squadron made the first attack on an enemy U-boat. He made a low level pass on U-573, and although the depth charges fell close, they failed to explode because a crew member had neglected to set the fuses. The submarine war then became a team-effort where every member of the crew played a vital role. A great deal of training lay ahead, and Annis became a major figure in developing such crews. Among other Coastal Command pilots who flew interminable patrols searching for elusive subs, was Sqd/Ldr. Norville Small who was convinced that the current system of patrols was wasting thousands of air hours.

During the Battle of Britain, Radio Direction Finding (RDF) enabled pilots to remain on ready until alerted by the RDF and guided to a target. Small was instrumental in having the system adopted by Eastern Air Command (EAC), and on July 31, 1942, he scored the first of the EAC's six victories when he sank a sub off Sable Island. Coastal Command crews were extremely vulnerable to weather or engine malfunction because there was little hope of making an emergency landing. Six months after sinking the first sub, Sqd/Ldr Small and his crew went missing on a flight out of Gander.

Although Eastern Air Command is officially credited with sinking six enemy subs, the total sunk by Canadian airmen is probably closer to 30. In addition to the squadrons operating out of Canada, seven were assigned to RAF Coastal Command and #162 Squadron, which accounted for six U-boats, also served overseas.

Most of the RAF's Coastal Command activity was part of Britain's counterattack on German shipping. Unable to strike in mid-ocean, it hit in Norwegian waters, the North Sea and the Bay of Biscay. In addition to convoy escort, activities included mining the waters as well as direct attacks on ships and U-boats.

On October 31, 1941, #413 Squadron was assigned to a photo-reconnaissance of the Norwegian coast. The target area was well beyond Allied fighter range and heavily patrolled by enemy fighters. W/Com R.G. Briece, who had just brought the squadron up to operational level, insisted on joining the crew of the Catalina selected for the operation. All went missing.

Within a few weeks, four Catalina's were destroyed in a storm. On the North Sea raids, #407 Squadron lost 12 Hudsons but would go on to sink five U-boats. Canadian squadrons overseas would sink 15 enemy subs.

As indicated, two Canadian squadrons were assigned to the Pacific. With the United States in the war, German subs were diverted to the Atlantic seaboard where they sank 500 ships in six months. The summer of '42 also became one of the saddest in our history as U-boats invaded the St. Lawrence and sank 22 ships, forcing its closure to ocean traffic. U-boats also roamed Newfoundland waters and sank two iron ore ships some 20 kilometres from St. John's. The *Caribou*, a ferry from Dartmouth to Port Aux Basques, was sunk with a loss of 136 civilians. It was not the RCAF's greatest hour, but on the other hand, in the last half of '42, the U-boats were back in mid-Atlantic. They were now armed with flak guns making aerial attack extremely dangerous. They also adopted the technique of assembling in packs when a convoy was spotted. In October, F/Lt R. F. Raynes of #10 Squadron sank the U-520 and Eastern Air Command would go on to four more difficult victories over an elusive and powerful enemy.

RAF Coastal Command concentrated on German exits from home ports, and Canadian squadrons sank nine U-boats in that campaign plus six attributed to #162 Squadron. Individual Canadians with RAF Squadrons have virtually been lost to history, but some of the loners were very active. P/O Michael Layton was a Canadian navigator flying with a RAF squadron in June 1942. Some 600 miles from Land's End, his first encounter with a sub brought oil to the surface but no sinking. On October 12th, flying out of Iceland, his three well placed depth charges sank the U-342. Four days later, his crew sank the U-661. A third victory came on November 5th as Layton's depth charges blew the U-132's stern erect as it sank. On December 8th, three Liberators attacked 12 submarines and Layton's aircraft destroyed a fourth victim. Layton went on to become a wing commander and his performance in 1942 was officially described as "unmatched in the annals of Coastal Command." Although victories over U-boats are usually attributed to the attacking pilot, navigator Layton was a key party to four sinking.

The introduction of Leigh Lights on Wellingtons in 1943 was a turning point in F/O Don McRae's career. The Leigh Light was part of a radar detection unit. It meant that on a night patrol, an aircraft honed in on radar until close to the target U-boat. Then a massive 120-million candlepower light zeroed in on the target. Attached to an RAF Squadron, McRae sank his first sub, the U-134, during a night in August 1943. In early September, over the Bay of Biscay, he severely damaged a U-boat that remained afloat although the crew became POWs. In November, while flying a night convoy patrol, he attacked and sank the U-211 from a height of 50 feet.

W/O W. Morton had a somewhat unique experience on his first operation with #423 Squadron. Although he was captain of the Sunderland when they flew out in March 1944, Fl/Lt S. Butler was actually flying when they spotted the U-625, which they engaged, dropping all depth charges. They circled for almost an hour, watching the stricken sub. Then a message was flashed from the coming tower: "Fine Bombish!" The crew then took to dinghies just before the U-boat sank.

In the mid-Atlantic, March 1943 was a bad month with 82 Allied ships lost. Dönitz now had an operational force of some 200 submarines and German construction was almost pacing losses of 15 subs that month. In May, U-boat losses jumped to 41 subs and Dönitz temporarily withdrew from the mid-Atlantic. One of the primary reasons for the withdrawal was the growing efficiency of Coastal Command air cover. Air Marshal Sir John Slessor, head of RAF Coastal Command, made a statement in July of 1943. "History has been made by Liberator Y, the first RCAF aircraft to takeoff from the continent of America on an operational sortie and land in the U.K." F/O Howes and navigator F/O A. Bookman took off from Gander to provide close escort for a convoy some 900 miles at sea. With darkness setting in, Bookman set course for Iceland but as weather deteriorated, they were diverted to Ireland where they landed after 15 hours and 25 minutes. It marked a significant closing of the Atlantic gap.

In August of 1943, F/O Roderick Gray was navigating a RAF Wellington on a night patrol when they spotted a sub on the surface. He switched on the Leigh lights and cannon shells from the U-boat immediately ripped at the Wellington, which was soon burning. They continued the bomb run and Gray's depth charges hit just before the aircraft crashed. Two crew members were killed and Gray suffered a broken leg. The pilot was wounded, an air gunner had a broken arm and Gray's dinghy was the only one available. He insisted that the others use his one-man dinghy and tied himself alongside. By dawn Gray was dead.

During the same period, F/O Arthur Bishop of #423 Squadron also had his aircraft burning from enemy fire as he continued his bombing run. The depth charges scored a hit, but the Sunderland immediately crashed. The six survivors of his 11-man crew took to dinghies and by this time they were sharing the ocean with 53 other survivors from the U-489 which sank. They were all were rescued by HMS *Castleton*.

Dönitz's new subs, equipped with snorkels, were back in mid-Atlantic by September. Snorkel tubes permitted U-boats to operate on diesel rather than batteries of limited endurance, and thus gave the subs much longer range. The subs were also now equipped with an acoustic torpedo that homed in on the sound of a ship's propellers. This device was initially successful, but the British soon countered it with a noise generator that they towed behind ships. The second phase of the Battle of the mid-Atlantic was short and by frall Dönitz withdrew to concentrate on the Allied build-up for the invasion.

In a sense, #162 Squadron became the epitome of RCAF development during the sea war and June 1944 was its finest hour, or month. After moving to Wick, Scotland, it destroyed four subs and shared one sinking during the month of June. On the 3rd, F/Lt E. McBride's Catalina blasted U-477 out of the water. Eight days later, F/O L. Sherman sank the U-980 and 35 crewmen emerged through an oil slick as it went down. On June 13th, W/Com Cecil G. Chapman flew a strike against U-715 as heavy flak disabled his aircraft, Chapman's depth charges sank the U-boat. He ditched, but before they were rescued, three crew members died from exposure.

Nine days later, F/Lt David E. Hornell was completing a 10 hour patrol when he spotted a sub some 1,000 miles out. Flak ripped his Canso as he began the attack and soon the aircraft was burning as Hornell fought to keep it on course.

His depth charges sank the sub, but his starboard engine fell off and he ditched. As the crew evacuated the wrecked flying boat, one dinghy exploded. Seven men had to share the remaining four-man dinghy and Hornell elected to remain in the cold water. Waves 50 feet high later pounded the dinghy and one crew member died of exposure. As hours lengthened, a second man died and Hornell went blind but continued to inspire the crew. Although rescued some 20 hours later, Hornell soon died of exposure but was awarded the Victoria Cross.

On the last day of June, McBride attacked U-487, but his depth charges failed to release. He circled the U-boat and summoned a Liberator, which delivered the coup de grâce. McBride was credited with a shared sinking. In its anti-shipping role, Coastal Command formed three strike wings, which got off to a slow start in 1942, but by 1944 were extremely busy and efficient. Two Canadian squadrons flew with this force and in one strike rocket-firing Beaufighters, including RAF machines, left 15 enemy ships blazing. The strike force was responsible for sinking some 366 vessels.

F/Lt Ken Moore set a speed record for sinking subs two days after the invasion of Europe. During a night attack, he bracketed a U-boat with depth charges lifting it out of the water and shattering it. Minutes later, Moore's crew made a second radar contact. This time Moore attacked from 50 feet. The stricken sub pointed its stern skywards and sank. Elapsed time for the two sinkings was 22 minutes. F/O Arthur Bruneau sank the U-629 three days before VE-Day. Coastal Command was probably engaged in the last action of the longest battle: the U-320 was depth-charged the day before VE-Day and sank the day after. In sinking 185 German U-boats, Coastal Command lost 9,500 men. Canadians probably accounted for at least 28 subs at a cost of over 752 men.

*Splashes from both machinegun fire and depth charges entering the water mark the start of the sucessful attack on U-625 by a Sunderland of 422 Squadron on March 10, 1944. (C-4287)*

**TOP:** *The raids on Hamburg were a turning point for Bomber Command. Canadian Six Group provided 72 aircraft for the raid some German leaders saw as the beginning of the end.* (DND)

**ABOVE:** *The trauma of operational flying is etched on the faces of Six Group at debriefing.* (DND)

**OPPOSITE PAGE:** *Early bomber crews lacked training to do a realistic job, but had the courage to create an aura of bringing the war to the enemy. When the illusion faded, Bomber Command itself was in jeopardy.* (IWM)

# 🐌 BOMBER COMMAND

*On the eve of war only 13 pilots above the rank of flying officer could fly at night.*

*AIR CHIEF MARSHAL SIR* Edgar Ludlow-Hewitt took over Bomber Command in 1937 and inherited a mess. Although he instituted many changes, by the time he was relieved of his command three years later, Bomber Command was still very much in disarray. Ludlow-Hewitt immediately foresaw the collapse of daylight bombing. His statements that Bomber Command was entirely unprepared for war, unable to operate except in fair weather, and extremely vulnerable both in the air and on the ground rankled dormant brass at the Air Ministry, but was completely accurate. Ludlow-Hewitt found only 13 pilots above the rank of flying officer who were qualified to fly at night. Navigation was poor, bombing was virtually unknown and many of the ancient bombs failed to explode while air gunnery was atrocious. Ground crew tradesmen had been assigned to flying duties on a temporary basis, and as such they instantly became observers, gunners, photographers or bomb-aimers.

The official history of Bomber Command concludes, "[W]hen war came in 1939, Bomber Command was not trained either to penetrate into enemy territory by day or find its target areas, let alone its targets by night." When Churchill became prime minister, Hugh Trenchard, the former marshal of the RAF, had been on the retirement list for over a decade, but still cast a long shadow. As the Battle of Britain raged, in a triumph of selective memory, Trenchard urged Churchill to strike back with strategic bombing. Trenchard, it will be recalled, was the man who violently opposed strategic bombing in WW I. The prime minister responded with enthusiastic support, but without the means to follow through.

As mentioned earlier, the day war was declared Bomber Command struck back with 5.4 million leaflets. Within three months, 200 tons of paper fluttered over the streets of Germany, but not a bomb had been dropped. By 1945, close to 600 million leaflets and pamphlets were dropped in nightly raids on Germany and later the occupied countries. This worked out to about 30 leaflets for every person in Western Europe.

The first major strike against Germany came the night after the Luftwaffe bombed Rotterdam as 99 RAF heavies went against rail communications and oil refineries in the Ruhr.

The Ministry of Economic Warfare (MEW) soon published an optimistic forecast. It maintained that after two or three months of heavy bombing, oil production in Germany would be reduced by half a million tons. However, in reality it took three and a half years of bombing to reduce oil production a mere 150,000 tons. Planners at MEW failed to recognize why the RAF was not eager to reveal its bombing results.

The city of Gelsenkircken underwent 28 bombings, but reconnaissance photos showed no serious damage to two oil plants. Bombers went to Munster 14 times in four months, but on only one night did more than 10 bombs fall on the city. However, 10 bombs hit Munster on a night when the target was elsewhere and nobody reported bombing that city. Hamburg was raided 19 times, but suffered only 36 casualties, while Wilhelmshaven suffered only minor damage after 21 attacks.

Central London was bombed on August 24, 1940, and it set off a chain of retaliatory raids. The next night the RAF flew the first raid against Berlin, while on September 7, Hitler sent 900 bombers against London in the first of a series of raids. November 8, was the anniversary of the Nazi bid for power and the date the RAF selected to break up a celebration in Munich. Infuriated at the insult to the Nazi movement, Hitler and Göring sent 500 bombers against Coventry where 554 people were killed and some 6,000 buildings were destroyed.

The RAF responded with a plan to "cause the maximum possible destruction in a selected German town," and the town ultimately selected was Mannheim. The first of what became Pathfinders guided some 120 bombers onto the city and all reported successful bombing on their markers, but reconnaissance photos later revealed scattered bombing and the operation was considered a failure. Night raids followed the German daylight raids against London and within a week, 2,000 Londoners were dead. Up to this point the Germans had weakened the RAF Fighter Command by attacks on aerodromes that inflicted heavy losses in men and machines. But, in the months that followed, Bomber Command sustained British morale as the BBC intoned unsubstantiated details of bombings each night.

When scientists such as R.V. Jones proposed electronic aids to navigation, they were originally ignored. German pilots were guided by beams in raids against England, but Arthur Harris as deputy CAS huffed that Bomber Command used no beams, but bombed as successfully as the enemy deep into the heart of Germany. Churchill became suspicious of RAF claims after Gelsenkirchen came up as a target 28 times in six months, and called for an independent evaluation of bombing results.

From a study of photos D.M. Butt concluded that in the Ruhr valley only one in 10 bombers got within five miles of its target. The commander of 4 Group admitted he had no idea where his aircraft went once they were over Germany. At this point, Bomber Command reluctantly agreed to consider navigational aids.

When Arthur Harris took over Bomber Command in February 1942, he reinforced the belief they would win the war by bombing. As he fought to build up his force, Harris pursued the policy of area bombing as a way of bringing Germany to her knees. Aiming points were not to be specific target areas, but built-up areas. He objected to sharing tasks with other services and somehow had the influence to pull it off. The lack of heavies in North Africa and at Dieppe strained relations with the army and the bomber campaign against German warships in Brest raised hackles in the Royal Navy.

Harris chose the port of Lubeck for devastation because the ancient medieval buildings were made of wood and would burn well. Its only military significance was a training school for submariners and a supply depot. About 150 tons of incendiaries started fires burning 200 acres of the old city and rendering over 15,000 people homeless. Three weeks later, Bomber Command hit another ancient city. Rostock had submarine yards, but it was essentially the wooden homes that attracted Bomber Command. Although the Luftwaffe retaliated with raids on Exeter, Bath, Canterbury and York, the RAF hit Rostock four times and 100,000 people had to be evacuated.

Harris scoured conversion units, Operational Training Units, and his regular squadrons to come up with the magic 1,047 aircraft for a raid on Cologne the night of May 30. Original estimates claimed 350 factories destroyed, but later evidence put the number at 36 wrecked and 300 damaged. The morning after the attack, the sky still glowed from 12,000 fires. Although he lost 40 aircraft this was Harris' finest moment and a sense of euphoria ran through Bomber Command, which was now launched on a campaign to win the war by breaking the German will to resist.

Sixty-eight bombers from Canadian squadrons took part, and the first of four squadrons began to convert to the four-engine Halifax. In June, the French-Canadian Alouette Squadron began what would become 60 years of service to Canada. Although the number of Canadian squadrons increased, the flow of Canadian aircrew to RAF squadrons continued to be an unresolved issue. Bomber Harris was somewhat cool to the idea of sending all Canadians to RCAF squadrons, but had many other issues on his plate at the time.

When Harris sent his attack against Cologne, it countered resistance from Coastal Command and army demands that more bombers be sent to North Africa. Harris sent 956 bombers to Essen, where the bombing was extremely scattered, and in late June a 1,000-bomber force hit Bremen, but results were not as good as at Cologne and losses climbed to five per cent.

Doubts about bombing accuracy haunted Bomber Command and the introduction of Pathfinders provided no immediate solution. Although 78 crews claimed to have bombed the target, no bombs actually fell on the city of Flensburg, but a number fell 25 miles to the north.


## THE CHANNEL DASH

On February 12, 1942, three major ships the *Gneisenau*, *Scharnhorst* and *Prinz Eugen* left Brest harbour to challenge the British navy and the RAF in a Channel dash to Wilhelmshaven. Not since 1690 had such a strong force ploughed through the Straits of Dover and not since the charge of the Light Brigade had the British screwed up an operation so badly.

During the 299 RAF bombings at Brest the *Gneisenau* was hit twice and heavy damage was inflicted on the *Scharnhorst*. Yet the Germans were able to make repairs under the noses of the RAF, and on at least eight different days, engaged in trial runs to test equipment. On the night of February 11, 20 Wellingtons hit Brest where seven destroyers screened the entrance to the harbour as the three major ships prepared to leave. Two hours after the bombing, all ships were at sea, unobserved.

The RAF suspected a German break out and Air Chief Marshal Sir Philip Joubert de la Ferté, head of Coastal Command, predicted it almost to the day. Yet little was done to effectively respond. Neither Joubert de la Ferté nor Vice Admiral Sir Bertram Ramsay, the flag officer at Dover, got the support they needed. First Lord of the Admiralty Sir Dudley Pound preferred to keep the home fleet at Scapa Flow and out of action. A convoy would die on the route into Murmansk, Russia when a similar decision was made five months later.

The German force grew as it moved north in the English Channel on its 120-mile journey. Twenty-four torpedo boats joined the ships off Cherbourg at daybreak and 15 E-boats were added to the protective screen off Boulogne. The air umbrella of night-fighters was replaced by day-fighters and 30 machines were on stand-by at bases along the coast. Incredibly, it was 11 a.m. before the British were fully aware that the battle cruisers were out of harbour. Then like an old Peter Sellers comedy, misadventure followed misadventure.

A Spitfire pilot warned of a large force heading for the Straits of Dover and the Luftwaffe intercepted the message at 10 a.m., but it took the RAF at least two and a half hours to sort things out as a morning of intense confusion followed. A duty controller notified 11 Group Fighter Command that he thought the situation was Operation FULLER, code name for the Channel dash. A precise plan had been laid down for FULLER, but when it came time to put it into operation, there was a slight problem. At fighter base Biggin Hill plans for FULLER were locked away and the intelligence officer responsible was on leave with the key in his pocket. A further delay came because RAF commanders wanted confirmation of the sighting before launching FULLER.

Then they refused to interrupt A/V/M Leigh-Mallory, commander of 11 Group, who was on parade inspecting Belgians at Northolt. Leigh-Mallory now had Parks' job and his headquarters refused a navy request for confirmation that a powerful German force was less than 25 miles away. By noon, 58 enemy vessels steamed at 30 knots through the Straits of Dover. British coastal artillery responded with shots that did no damage and fog obscured the flotilla.

Then Lt-Cmdr Neil Pumphrey led five motor-torpedo boats and two motor-gunboats in against the protective screen, which they failed to penetrate. Admiral Ramsay was reluctant to order Lt-Cmdr Eugene Esmonde to lead five ancient Swordfish on a suicidal mission against the ships. The day before, Esmonde had been awarded the Distinguished Service Order for his attack on the *Bismark* and although not officially ordered by Ramsay, by 12:25 p.m. Esmonde was still sitting in the cockpit waiting for confirmation that there would be fighter cover.

At that point, he took off still not knowing if there would be air cover. The Swordfish orbited briefly off the coast near Ramsgate, but Esmonde, fearing that the flotilla would soon be beyond reach, flew out to sea. The Fleet Air Arm and the RAF were on different radio frequencies and almost accidentally Spitfires of #72 Squadron spotted Esmonde's Stringbags flying through low fog. Other squadrons such as Canadian #401 flew endless orbits at their appointed rendezvous waiting for the departed Swordfish.

Sgt Al Harley of Port McNichol, Ont., flew with a flight of Spitfires that chased their tails over Canterbury, while squadron-mate P/O Omer Levesque, of Mont-Joli, Que., said he heard confusing radio chatter and suspected that the enemy might have been monitoring the broadcasts. Harley later recalled the frustration of delays and then orders to proceed. They left Canterbury, but according to Harley, "We still did not know what we were after, but on reaching the French coast [we] ran into several squadrons of Me-109s."

Meanwhile, Esmonde led his flight through flak in a deck-level approach on the port side of the flotilla. Swarms of enemy fighters jumped 10 Spitfires from #72 Squadron 10 miles from the flotilla and the Swordfish pressed on without fighter cover. The Swordfish torpedo bomber of 1942 had a speed of about 15 miles in excess of the aircraft flown by Baron von Richthofen in 1918. The pilot sat in a forward hump and the observer and the air gunner stood in a barrel-like rear cockpit that had no seats. As Esmonde penetrated the first ring of defence around the ships, flak moderated but enemy fighters swept in. The fuselage was riddled and fire broke out.

A Spitfire pilot got an incredible glimpse of Esmonde's gunner straddling the fuselage and beating at the flames with his hands. Then he returned to his guns as battle cruisers opened fire. Fighters attacked the second Swordfish and the gunner was killed in the first pass. The observer stood in his barrel watching the approaching aircraft. When their cannons blinked, he yelled for the pilot to take evasive action. A shell ripped through the rear of the pilot's cockpit, severely wounding Brian Rose.

It was either shells or the violent splashes of water they sent up that blew the lower port of Esmonde's Swordfish away. The aircraft started to plunge, but righted itself and closed on the *Scharnhorst* while Rose picked the *Gneisenau*, which lay less than a mile away. A burst of tracer fire ripped Esmonde's cockpit. Regardless, with his own life ebbing away, he flew on with two dead men in the back cockpit. He pulled the Swordfish into the wind and released the torpedo as a dozen fighters riddled the biplane. His torpedo sped towards its target and missed. In the second aircraft, the observer screamed to keep the pilot conscious as he released a torpedo at the *Prinz Eugen* that turned sharply. The guns of the cruiser hovered over the battered Swordfish and Egdar Lee yelled at his wounded pilot who flew on to a belly landing. Their torpedo also missed. The third Swordfish dropped a torpedo that missed and then it sagged into the water. The second group flew in a vic formation of three through intense fighter fire. The 109s were now attacking with flaps down to pace the Swordfish. The ships sent up a water-spout barrage that nine men flew into and were never seen again. All of the Swordfish were shot down and only five of 18 crewmen survived.

Harley's Spitfire section chased a Me-109 up through clouds. "I gave the 109 a long burst and Don Morrison, my number two man, gave him a burst as well," he said. The enemy dove into the Channel and the Spitfires broke cloud between the German convoy and the French coast without drawing fire. Levesque's section was not so lucky. The ceiling was low and black with flak as they swept in behind the flotilla on its right flank. The battle became a series of confusing personal engagements. Levesque, the first pilot to bring down an enemy aircraft, scored a fourth victory over a Me-109. Then he was hit at low level, the engine stopped, and his Spitfire plunged in. He pulled back the canopy and stuck his arm out to keep the canopy from jamming as the Spit sank 40 feet. Levesque's head smashed against the gunsight and he passed out. He later recalled that he saw a strange green world where one thought pounded through his brain: "Dying wasn't so bad after all. A crack on the head and it's all over." Then as instruments came into focus in the narrow cockpit, he fought his way to the surface where he floated semi-conscious for 40 minutes. He was hauled aboard a German ship that was not part of the flotilla and when he recovered the first thing he heard was a radio playing four notes by Beethoven which later came to symbolize "V" for victory. However, for Omer Levesque victory was delayed. He was on his way to a prison camp by seven o'clock that evening.

The flight chased a few more 109s until they ran low on fuel, but returned in the afternoon to escort bombers that flew some 242 unproductive sorties against the flotilla. Canadian Coastal Command crews were also involved in the tragic farce when its 16 Group Headquarters tried to communicate with them in Morse code and their aircraft were equipped with radio telephones. Some circled for two hours over Manston, England awaiting fighter escorts that were long at sea. Most of the aircraft failed to find the ships because of poor weather and those that did failed to score hits.

The *Scharnhorst* hit a mine off the Scheldt that slowed her to 27 knots and that evening the *Gneisenau* also hit a mine off Terschelling, but continued. About two hours later, the *Scharnhorst* hit a second mine, but went on at 12 knots to Wilhelmshaven.

When Admiral Dudley Pound phoned Churchill to inform him that the enemy ships had escaped, the prime minister screamed one word into the phone and then slammed down the receiver. "Why?"


## ATTRITION OVER DIEPPE

The same question haunts us today when applied to another operation of 1942. While apologists insist that the lessons learned at Dieppe were a tough necessity, two ghosts from WWI haunt the operation and raise the questions: "How many men have to die before planners learn a lesson?" and "Must such lessons be relearned with each generation?"

At Gallipoli in 1915 the operation failed because of inadequate covering fire, hostile cliffs, and failure to use sufficient capital ships in the narrow Dardanelles strait. The same elements of failure were present in the Dieppe planning which also borrowed heavily from a ghost from the Western Front. In April 1942, the three chiefs-of-staff approved a plan to provide maximum intensity bombing by a force of 300 bombers to support the landings at Dieppe. Bomber Harris rejected it, and maintained that his bombers could not provide the precision necessary to bomb the waterfront and not create chaos in Dieppe.

When Lord Louis Mountbatten took over Combined Operations in March he envisioned commando-style raids on either side of Dieppe. Army representative Gen Bernard Montgomery was in favour of a frontal attack and volunteered the Canadians. He then departed for North Africa, disenchanted with a scenario that was becoming more confused with each passing week. The original concept became a smorgasbord where commanders picked up choice bits but rejected anything that interfered with their personal agendas. The army still opted for a tank landing on a beach where the stones were like baseballs, whereas Bomber Command would not be participating and the navy would provide no major fire power because the admiralty refused to send major ships into the relatively narrow coastal waters.

Air Vice Marshal Leigh-Mallory was senior air officer for Operation JUBILEE. The period since 1940 had been relatively quiet for Fighter Command and as it regained strength the only way to challenge the enemy was in fighter sweeps over the continent. Leigh-Mallory was determined to lure the Luftwaffe into a shoot-out at Dieppe. The first of 730 fighters struck as Lord Lovat's 4th Commando came ashore to silence the guns at Varengeville and cut communications at Quiberville to the west of the port. Lovat's men operated with precise professionalism and quickly became the only unit to achieve its objectives. There was no air opposition and the Spitfires concentrated on shooting up a lighthouse at Ailly. From a tactical point of view, one is left to wonder what the fighters accomplished other than drawing enemy flak. Three squadrons of Bostons bombed gun emplacements on the central front, or Blue Beach, and this was followed by smoke-producing Blenheims. The bombing failed to silence the guns in the cliffs and the smoke became more detrimental to the Canadians than the enemy. It obscured the view of the beach and observers were unable to follow the course of the landings.

Hurricane fighter-bombers with 20-mm canons bombed gun emplacements just east of nearby Puits. A group from Maj Douglas Catto's Royal Regiment had crawled to a position known as Bismark Heights that housed six 88-mm guns from within a cave. The guns were bombed at least four times, but were back in action seconds later. Most of the landings took place without enemy air opposition and this became a matter of grave concern for Leigh-Mallory who wanted to provoke the enemy into battle. Of nine RCAF squadrons involved, the first provided cover for ships standing off shore in the initial phases of the attack. Four squadrons provided escort for American B-17s, which hit a Luftwaffe base at nearby Abbeville, France. The raid put enemy fighters out of action for two hours and was a prime example of how the Luftwaffe might have been grounded for the duration of the raid.

On the way home from Abbeville, Sqd/Ldr Keith Hodson of London, Ont., led 401 Squadron over Dieppe where Dornier- 217s were now making a run on Canadian ground forces. P/O Don Morrison of Toronto closed on a FW 190 and gave it a burst. He was so close debris from the enemy fighter smashed into his Spit, which he nursed down to 2,000 feet before he baled out. His chute snagged on the tail and the doomed aircraft carried him to within 200 feet of the Channel before he was able to snap loose and pull the ripcord. He hit the water like a rock, but fortunately the crew of a RAF crash-boat pulled him aboard. Morrison spent the day under fire while fishing downed airmen out of the drink as the air battle over Dieppe moved into high gear. Three months later Morrison, who shot down six and had five probables, was shot down while doing escort duty for B-17s. He finally managed to get out of the doomed Spitfire, but literally lost his left leg, which remained in the aircraft.

Four of six Hurricanes were lost near Dieppe in an attack on what was believed to be the headquarters of the German 110th Infantry Division. The loss was a sad reflection on Combined Operations' poor intelligence. The 110th Infantry Division had moved to the Eastern Front some weeks prior to the Dieppe raid.

Although battered ground forces withdrew by 12:30 p.m., the air war continued as fighters crossed from England throughout the afternoon and fought until fuel and ammunition was exhausted. Then they returned to base to refuel and rearm. Sqd/Ldr Lloyd Chadburn of Montreal, led #416 Squadron on four such missions that day. He shot down one Ju-88 and damaged another. Although the nine Canadian fighter squadrons involved claimed 10 enemy aircraft, they lost 14 machines and nine pilots. With 3,367 ground casualties, the British stressed their aerial victory, claiming 96 enemy aircraft destroyed and 179 in questionable categories of damaged or "probably damaged." Post-war records show the RAF lost 108 aircraft while destroying 46 enemy machines.

**ABOVE:** *The air war was a race against technology. As Bomber Command moved from early course-setting bombsights (shown above) to complex electronic navigation and bombing aides, so did the enemy. Ted Paulton's crew narrowed the critical gap.* (DND)

**OPPOSITE PAGE:** *Ted Paulton's crew baited a German night fighter to determine the radar code that was directing fighters onto RAF bombers. They were shot down, but uncovered the code.* (B. BARRY)

# MARCH OF TECHNOLOGY

*Closing the radar gap.*

**EARLY IN THE WAR** Herman Göring boasted in a public speech: "If an enemy bomber reaches the Ruhr, my name is not Herman Göring; you can call me Meier!" The 1,000-plane raid on Cologne called for a liberal diet of crow, but it did stimulate defensive measures in the formidable Kammhuber Line that shielded the Ruhr and most of Germany. With the introduction of the first Lancaster bomber in March 1942, and the first use of a navigational device called "Gee," bombers got closer to their targets, but bombing did not improve.

The introduction of a Pathfinder force under Donald Bennett, the man who led the first Ferry Command trans-Atlantic flight in July 1942, led to Mosquitos with target-seeking Oboe and improved bombing.

But when Kammhuber came up with a device that vectored his night-fighters onto straggling bombers, the British were at the short end of the gap.

Of the 7,000 sorties flown by Bomber Command, few crews went out in high hopes of engaging a German night-fighter, but Sgt Ted Paulton of Windsor, Ont., and his crew flew out bombless over a dozen times hoping enemy night-fighters would attack their wayward Wellington. They were part of a new radar investigation flight that nobody had ever heard of and their arrival from an Operational Training Unit didn't shed much light.

According to navigator Bill Barry of Delta, B.C. enthusiasm ran high when they finished OTU with the prospect of going on operations in a four-engine Halifax, a Stirling or even a new Lancaster. "Our hopes were shattered when we arrived at 1474 Flight Gransden Lodge, to find only five creaky old Wellingtons. The unit had six, but one was lost a week earlier. Another disconcerting bit of data gleaned from sly observation was that there was no bomb dump."

Their interview with the commanding officer was full of "pip-pip" and "cheerios," but no hard information. They flew navigation and gunnery exercises, but didn't have a clue as to the nature of their operations. When they asked other crews what it was all about, all they got was a shrug: "You'll know soon enough."

Two weeks after arrival, Paulton's crew were told they were going to Karlsruhe as part of a regular bombing operation. But instead of bombs, they carried a specially trained radar and radio technician who sat behind a lot of strange-looking telecommunications equipment that was installed on their Wellington. They were routed to Karlsruhe with the main bomber stream. "It then became clear that our task was the investigation of enemy radar and radio emissions over the target area," Barry said.

They did 10 more ops with 1474 Flight, which was then the only airborne unit doing radar and radio intelligence. It was later expanded to #192 Squadron, but the heavy secrecy that hung over Gransden Lodge still kept them pretty much in the dark. When Ted Paulton's brother, a pilot with Coastal Command, visited Gransden he wanted to inspect one of the five Wimpys, but Ted waved him off. "If you're caught around that kite they'll probably shoot you," he said.

The war became an electronic chess game. According to Churchill, towards the end of 1942, the British knew how the German defence system worked and developed ways to cope with it, but a major gap existed in British knowledge of the Lichtenstein air interception radar system used on night-fighters. Within the RAF the euphoria launched by the 1,000-aircraft raid on Cologne in May 1942, turned to bitterness and lowered morale as the enemy expanded his defence network and launched a new tactic.

German *Freya* long-range radar stations picked up the bomber stream and then two *Würburg* short-range stations came into play: One system would track a bomber, usually a straggler, while the other beamed a night-fighter onto it. As the night-fighter closed on the target its own Lichenstein radar would click in to track the bomber's progress. The RAF didn't know the frequency of the radar and its bombers became particularly vulnerable to attacks coming from below in cloud. By November 1942, the casualty rate mounted to almost five per cent.

Paulton's crew included navigator Bill Barry, wireless operator Bill Bigoray of Edmonton, rear-gunner Everett Vachon of Quebec City and nose-gunner Fred Grant of Brockville, Ont. After 10 operations, Britisher P/O Harold Jordan was

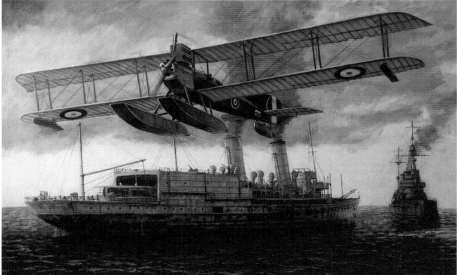

**TOP:** *The Burgess-Dunne made it overseas with the First Contingent but languished in a crate for the rest of the war as the Canadian Aviation Corps was dissolved.* (ROBERT W. BRADFORD, NATIONAL AVIATION MUSEUM)

**ABOVE:** *Within months, the first Canadian airmen were on the Western Front and in the Dardanelles. The aircraft carrier Ben-My-Cree took the war to the mid-East.* (DON CONNOLLY)

**ABOVE:** *While April 1917 saw Canadian troops take Vimy Ridge, the Royal Flying Corps suffered through a bloody month during which it was almost annihilated. The Royal Flying Corps lost 316 men killed or missing; an appalling number of them were lost to accidents. ("VIMY IN THE AIR" BY DON CONNOLLY)*

**RIGHT:** *Better RFC aircraft such as the Bristol F2b enabled the pendulum to swing by the fall of 1917. Raymond Collishaw's "Black Flight" accounted for many of Richthofen's best. In this painting by Clayton Knight, "A Straggler Returns," a British Bristol F2b reconnaissance fighter returns to its airfield. In the rear cockpit, the tail gunner/observer slumps over his Lewis.*

**TOP RIGHT:** *By the Battle for Courcelette, where tanks were introduced, aircraft had adopted a key role of artillery spotting and observation. ("THE BATTLE FOR COURCELETTE, 1918" BY LOUIS WEIRTER, CWM 8931)*

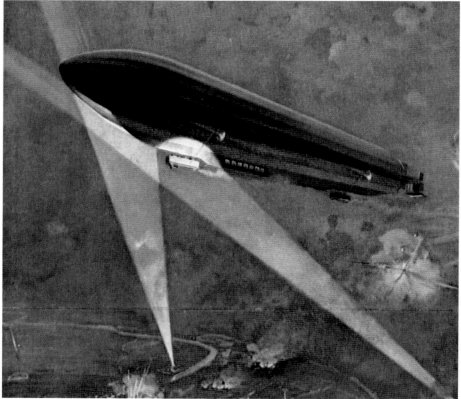

**TOP:** *About half the enemy airships brought down by aircraft over England fell to Canadians. Louden Watkins accounts for the L-48 in the above painting by Don Connolly.*

**ABOVE:** *The Germans lost 57 machines and 500 crewmen in the airship war. Crew losses almost equalled civilian losses in England which stood at approximately 500.* (IMPERIAL WAR MUSEUM)

**ABOVE:** Standing on the wing of his blazing aircraft, 19-year-old Alan McLeod managed a crash landing while under attack by eight fighters. He and his observer were wounded several times but brought down three enemy machines. (PAINTING BY DON CONNOLLY)

**RIGHT:** One of the few bright spots during the summer of 1917 was the performance of Canadians serving with the Royal Naval Air Service. Redford Mulock's squadron helped the RFC survive in April and Raymond Collishaw's "Black Flight" later fought Manfred von Richthofen to a deadlock. (PAINTING BY ROBERT BRADFORD, NATIONAL AVIATION MUSEUM)

**ABOVE:** *On March 30, 1918, the Canadian Cavalry Brigade was ordered to take Moreuil Wood. As C Squadron of Lord Strathcona's Horse, led by Major Gordon Flowerdew, approached the woods, they suddenly faced hundreds of German infantry in a clearing. With sabres drawn, Flowerdew and his men wheeled about and repeatedly charged the machine gun-wielding Germans who eventually broke and fled. One of the last cavalry charges, the squadron suffered 70 per cent casualties, wounded and killed, including Flowerdew, who was awarded a posthumous Victoria Cross for his determined assault. At this time, the Royal Flying Corps had pulled back and was reorganizing. ("THE CHARGE OF FLOWERDEW'S SQUADRON" BY SIR ALFRED MUNNINGS, CWM 8571)*

**LEFT:** *"War in the Air" depicts Billy Bishop in a dogfight against three German biplanes. Flying a Nieuport 17 armed with a Lewis machine gun, Bishop is Canada's greatest ace with 72 victories. (PAINTING BY C.R.W. NEVINSON, CWM 8651)*

*Between the wars, the Royal Canadian Air Force, founded in 1924, was primarily a service unit for government departments related to northern development.* **TOP:** *The Armstrong Whitworth Siskin, along with the Wapiti and Atlas, was used for army co-operation. The Siskin was Canada's only fighter until the Hurricane was introduced in 1938. ("ARMSTRONG WHITWORTH SISKIN — 1930" BY ROBERT BRADFORD, NATIONAL AVIATION MUSEUM)* **ABOVE:** *The Fairchild FC-2 was a bush plane that was a major factor in northern development. ("FAIRCHILD FC-2 — 1927" BY ROBERT BRADFORD, NATIONAL AVIATION MUSEUM)*

**ABOVE:** *While Britain endured the bombing of the Battle of Britain, Canada initiated the British Commonwealth Air Training Plan which ultimately trained 131,553 aircrew. This very successful program ran from 1939 to 1945 and trained aircrews in Canada for the RAF, RCAF, RNZAF, and the RAAF. Unfortunately, there were 856 training fatalities. Pictured is an Avro Anson, a Canadian-built training aircraft at No. 3 Flying Training School in Calgary.*
("CONTROL TOWER" BY PETER WHYTE, NATIONAL GALLERY OF CANADA)

**LEFT:** *"Bombs Over England" by Georg Lebrecht depicts German Stukas striking during the Battle of Britain.* (BAYERISCHE STAATSBIBLIOTHEK)

**ABOVE:** Women played critical roles in the defence of Britain as fighter pilots on key RAF bases met the Luftwaffe's onslaught. Above, a predominantly female crew prepares to launch a barrage balloon. In the First World War these balloons were used for artillery spotting. At the start of WWII, they were used for the defence of British cities. ("COVENTRY, 1940" BY DAME LAURA KNIGHT, IWM)

**RIGHT:** The Spitfire was a key fighter during the Battle of Britain, along with the Hurricane. ("BASE, SOUTHEAST ENGLAND, 1940" BY ERIC RAVILIOUS, IWM)

**LEFT:** *The battle for control of the Mediterranean island of Malta heated up in the summer of 1942 as both the Germans and British saw strategic value in its possession. Here, a Spitfire fighter tries to get an Me-109 in its sights while approaching from above. ("BATTLE OVER MALTA," BY DENIS A. BARNHAM, IWM)*

**OPPOSITE TOP:** *The key island of Malta was subject to fierce enemy attacks from the spring of 1940 until November 1942. In a historic act of defiance, it became key to the defence of North Africa. ("TURNAROUND UNDER FIRE, MALTA" BY LESLIE LOLE, IWM)*

**BOTTOM:** *For much of the war, the German battleship* Tirpitz *posed a threat to shipping in the North Sea. She was sunk in Tromso Fjord in Norway on November 12, 1944 by RAF Lancasters carrying 12,000-pound "Tallboy" bombs. ("ATTACK ON THE TIRPITZ, 1944" BY NORMAN WILKENSON, NATIONAL MARITIME MUSEUM)*

**ABOVE:** *Bomber Command got off to a shaky start but built up strength to where it was able to virtually destroy Hamburg in July 1943. It became a turning point as some German leaders saw the raid as the beginning of the end. Here, four Lancaster bombers can be seen over the starboard wing of another.* (IWM)

 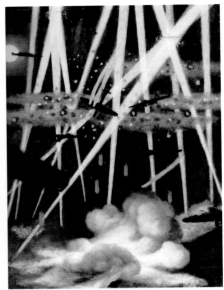

**TOP LEFT:** *Lancaster crew concentrates on its target in the industrial valley of the Rhur. The area bombing campaign then moved against Berlin. (PAINTING BY DAME LAURA KNIGHT, IWM)* **TOP RIGHT:** *German anti-aircraft defences created a well co-ordinated network of flak and fighters over much of Europe. ("NIGHT TARGET, GERMANY" BY MILLER BRITTAIN, CWM 10889)* **ABOVE:** *Canadian Spitfires with the 2nd Tactical Air Force were ashore hours after the D-Day landings. ("NORMANDY DISPERSAL" BY ROBERT HYNDMAN, DND REC 91434)* **OPPOSITE TOP:** *Allied fighters controlled the air on D-Day and airborne troops landed hours before the invasions. ("INVASION PATTERN NORMANDY" BY ERIC ALDWINCKLE, CWM 10679)* **OPPOSITE BOTTOM:** *Following the airborne disaster at Arnhem and Nijmegen, Canadian pilots with the 2nd TAF enjoyed their most productive period of the war. ("GLIDERS IN ITALY, 1943" BY W.A. OGILVIE, CANADIAN WAR MUSEUM)*

**ABOVE:** *The Supermarine Spitfire was arguably one of the most effective fighters of WWII. Receiving constant updates and design improvements, the Spitfire remained in service throughout the war. With a 500-pound bomb attached to the centre of its fuselage, this late model Spitfire is dive bombing a German V-1 "Buzz bomb" site in France. By June 1944, almost 40 per cent of Allied ground and air war efforts were directed at neutralizing the V-1 flying bomb threat. The artist, Robert Hyndman, was also an experienced RCAF Spitfire pilot.* ("DIVE BOMBING V-1 SITES, FRANCE, 1945" BY ROBERT HYNDMAN, CANADIAN WAR MUSEUM)

**OPPOSITE TOP:** *On August 9, 1945, just three hours before the United States would drop the second atomic bomb on Nagasaki, Robert "Hammy" Gray received a change of orders. Flying from the British carrier HMS* Formidable *in his Chance-Vought Corsair, the RCN Volunteer Reserve officer would be awarded Canada's last Victoria Cross when he was shot down after sinking the Japanese destroyer escort vessel* Amakusa *in Onagawa Bay.* ("FINALE - 1945" BY DON CONNOLLY, CWM)

**OPPOSITE BOTTOM:** *Nine Japanese Oscars attacked Harry Smith's Liberator over a drop area in Siam. It was so badly shot up, Smith had to make a tree-top landing in jungle below.* (PAINTING BY DON CONNOLLY)

Some 22 pilots from the RCAF served in Korea while attached to the USAF. Canadian transport aircraft also flew personnel and supplies to Japan. **LEFT:** F-86 Sabre fighters were rugged, versatile, and immediately established superiority over enemy MiGs. (USAF PHOTO) **BELOW:** The Dakota, an adaptation of the famous DC-3 civilian airliner, was the workhorse of the RCAF from 1942 to 1988. (DND PHOTO) **BOTTOM:** Although the North Star transport had a much greater lift capacity than the Dakota, it was unfortunately one of the noisiest aircraft ever built. (DND PHOTO)

assigned as special operator and on December 2, 1942, they were briefed for a raid on Frankfurt. As if the ancient Wellingtons were not slow enough, Paulton's route was deliberately designed to make them fall behind the bomber stream.

"This was to increase the likelihood of being attacked as soon as we left the main stream," Bill Barry explained. It worked! Shortly after they left the bomber stream, Jordan monitored an enemy aircraft following them. The intercepted signals from the night-fighter told him it was transmitting on 492 megacycles, information the wireless operator then sent off to base.

According to Barry, "The Ju-88 closed in and opened his attack; Paulton threw the Wellington into violent evasive action. We lost the attacker momentarily but he was soon back with his cannon fire." As the aircraft plunged, Jordan yelled on the intercom for Bigoray to get off a second message. The special operator was hit in the left arm, but continued to monitor the fighter whose second attack ripped the rear turret.

Shrapnel hit Ev Vachon and the hydraulics that powered the turret were shot away. The Ju-88 shredded the Wimpy with another burst and this time Jordan was hit in the jaw. Bigoray continued to try to raise base until a third attack smashed the front turret. Grant was hit in the leg and trapped in a turret that also would not rotate. Bigoray started forward to help Grant while on his screen, Jordan saw another attack from below and yelled for Paulton to dive. Part of the next burst hit Bigoray in the legs and in the next attack, Jordan was hit in the eye. Bill Barry pulled Grant from the useless turret while Vachon moved from the unserviceable rear turret to the astrodome where he was soon hit a second time.

Paulton finally managed to elude the Ju-88, but when Barry later gave him a course for home, he was flying a very fragile bird. Throttles were jammed and flaps, brakes and undercarriage were useless. Jordan had lost his right eye, Bigoray lost the use of both legs when a cannon shell exploded under his table, Vachon lost considerable blood from extensive shrapnel wounds and Grant had part of a cannon shell lodged in his leg. By the time they reached the English Channel, they had decided to ditch. But Bigoray couldn't walk and would be unable to abandon the bomber before it sank. He was pushed out over the water and his chute delivered him to Ramsgate.

About eight in the morning three fishermen reached the sinking bomber and rescued the crew. The crew survived the mission although Jordan lost an eye and Bigoray was later killed. Jordan was awarded a DSO and Paulton and Barry were commissioned and given DFCs while Vachon and Bigoray were awarded the DFM and Fred Grant received a Mention in Despatches.

The information they brought back was so important that the prime minister mentioned it in his memoir *The Hinge of Fate*. Churchill later said: "On the night of December 2, 1942, an aircraft of 192 Squadron was presented as a decoy. It was attacked many times by an enemy night-fighter radiating the Lichtenstein transmissions. Nearly all the crew were hit. The special operator listening to the radiations was severely wounded in the head, but continued to observe with accuracy. The wireless operator though badly injured was parachuted out of the aircraft over Ramsgate and survived with the precious observations. The rest of the crew flew the plane out to sea and alighted on the water because the machine was too badly damaged to land on an airfield. They were rescued by a boat from Deal. The gap in our knowledge of the German night defences was closed."

**ABOVE:** *The Mohne and Eder dams were breached by the most precise operation of the war. Although damage was extensive, the enemy quickly recovered.* (IWM)

**OPPOSITE PAGE:** *After three years of trying to get officialdom to listen to his plan, Barnes Wallis had to build a bouncing bomb in three months. Some were still hot when delivered to what became the dambusters squadron.* (IWM)

*Canada's Six Group battles for identity
as Bomber Command assaults...*

# ❧ THE UNHAPPY VALLEY

**AIR MARSHAL SIR ARTHUR HARRIS** was in the habit of visiting Chequers, Churchill's home some 12 miles from his residence, and sometimes the discussions would go on until three in the morning. The 1,000-bomber raid on Cologne was an outgrowth of such nocturnal meandering. The magic number was scraped from training units, but the raid gave Bomber Command a positive image. It became a useful propaganda tool for Churchill and also promised more resources for Harris who was soon involved in a program of replacing many of his obsolete bombers with Lancasters. Harris also dangled the notion that he could bring Germany to her knees through area bombing, providing he had enough aircraft. By the end of 1942, he was drawing up plans for an area bombing assault on Germany's industrial Ruhr valley when a political agreement induced him to take delicate evasive action.

Winston Churchill had convinced Roosevelt the Americans should join the RAF at night bombing. But when the two leaders met at Casablanca, Gen Ira Eaker spoke so effectively about the advantages of around-the-clock bombing that Churchill changed his mind. After the conference, a Casablanca directive was issued. It was a masterpiece of gobbledegook and double-talk couched in high-sounding phrases such as "progressive destruction" of the German military, industrial and economic systems and the undermining of enemy morale. A committee was set up to establish priority targets such as oil or aircraft. Harris cleverly managed to pursue his own plans by insisting that somewhere in the night his bombs could be falling on oil refineries, aircraft factories or whatever the commit-tee considered a priority target.

Harris had other problems that summer of 1942, and they centred on Air Marshal Harold Edwards, the tough-talking commander of the RCAF in Eng-land. Edwards had been pushing negotiations for the formation of a Canadian bomber group. While Harris had a high respect for Canadian aircrews, he failed to see any senior commander with the experience necessary to lead an operational group. He had a full plate and was perhaps somewhat shocked the foggy Friday when Six Group became official.

The establishment of Six Group was a boardroom victory for Prime Minister Mackenzie King who demanded that Canadian airmen be accorded some recog-nition. By New Year's Day, Edwards confiscated a 75-room home from a protest-ing Col. Blimp at Allerton Park in North Yorkshire and the new headquarters soon became known as "Castle Dismal." A/V/M G. E. Brookes commanded the group whose first squadrons moved into Middleton, St. George, and Croft. Soon 10 squadrons were scattered about York and Durham counties.

The addition of the Canadian Six Group to Bomber Command now gave Harris some 600 operational aircraft and he decided to launch the Battle of the Ruhr in March of 1943. Essen was the first target in the campaign which included 43 major raids in four months. Mosquito Pathfinders, guided by Oboe, dropped the first target indicators on the centre of Essen. Then backup flares guided three waves of bombers onto the target. Destruction extended over some 160 acres and damaged 50 buildings in the Krupp works. Six Group flew 2,649 sorties with a loss of more than 1,000 aircrew during the campaign. Accidents and early re-turns were alarmingly high, however this was accepted by aircrew and ground crew alike as the cost of learning war.

The Battle of the Ruhr was climaxed with the Battle of Hamburg in which Six Group provided 72 of the 791 bombers that followed Mosquitos in from the sea. For the first time, RAF crews dropped tons of tinfoil or Window, which thwarted German radar, causing searchlights and flak to home in on tinsel. A large number of incendiary bombs lit fires that were burning the next day when the American Flying Fortresses hit Hamburg. Hamburg was one of the few occasions where the American 8th Air Force and Bomber Command showed co-ordination.

The RAF also struck at Essen, but returned for three more attacks on Ham-burg where 40,000 died in a firestorm that destroyed the city. The fire was seen for days from 120 miles away and the fear of terror bombing spread throughout the Reich. The head of the Luftwaffe's Fighter Division, General der Flieger Adolf Galland, later reported that many saw the destruction of Hamburg as the begin-ning of the end. He wrote, "After Hamburg in a wide circle of the political and military command could be heard the words: The war is lost."[43]

# THE NIGHT OF THE BOUNCING BOMBS

Sir Barnes Wallis was a tweedy English aircraft designer with high credentials at Vickers-Armstrong. In the early 1930s, he designed the Wellington bomber with its geodetic construction, which later enabled the Wimpy to absorb intense punishment. But such achievements were merely part of Dr. Wallis' day job. Long before war broke out, he became obsessed with the idea of a bouncing bomb that would destroy massive dams such as those in Germany's highly industrialized Ruhr valley.

By 1939 his specific area of interest was a bomb that would use water pressure as a destructive force on the massive base of dams over 120-feet thick. His basic idea was a drum-shaped bomb with enough backspin to skip over anti-torpedo nets and eventually penetrate to a low depth as it rolled into a dam and exploded. Wallis worked on a way to bring the latent power of water under pressure into play. He peddled versions of his theory around London for three and a half years, but the wall of official indifference was as difficult to breach as the Mohne dam in the Ruhr. At one point, he tried to borrow a Wellington bomber for an experiment, but was rejected. The fact that he had designed the aircraft made little impression on the RAF.

Eventually, he got to test a prototype of the bomb containing a hydrostatic fuse to cause it to explode at the correct depth. In February 1943, a committee finally approved Wallis' concept of a radical bomb dropped from a low level. Immediately this project became a matter of extreme urgency because water levels in the German dams would be receding within about 90 days. At this point all that existed was paper. Dr. Wallis is said to have frequently turned to St. Joseph, the carpenter saint of Nazareth, for guidance in the construction of the bomb. Aircraft had to be modified because the bombs, which resembled an oil drum, were to be carried laterally. As well, crews had to be assembled and trained for the most exacting operation to date. A/V/M Ralph Cochrane was handed the prickly problem of pulling together the details of the mysterious raid with or without guidance from the old carpenter.

At the same time as the project was dumped on Cochrane's desk, Wing Commander Guy Gibson flew his 173rd operation. The 25-year-old veteran had completed his third tour and was due for screening. Next morning, instead of being on leave, Gibson was in the air vice marshal's office at 5 Group trying to make sense of Cochrane's proposal for doing one more trip. About 10 days later, Gibson and Cochrane had personally selected 147 men in 21 crews whom they considered to be Bomber Command's elite, 29 of whom were Canadian. Two of these were in Gibson's crew. Terry Taerum of Calgary was Gibson's navigator and Tony Deering of Toronto was a replacement front-gunner.

According to Wallis' design, the bouncing bomb had to be dropped 245 yards from the dam at 60 feet. A special engine was installed to rotate the bomb and give it sufficient backspin and encourage it to sink to maximum depth. Technicians came up with a simple idea of putting two spotlights under the fuselage and adjusting them so they converged at 60 feet. Each of the target dams had towers 600 feet apart. Elementary geometry was used to create a wooden isosceles triangle with a peephole at the apex and a nail at each corner of the base. When the towers lined up with the nails, the aircraft was 245 yards from the target. Crews worked against the clock, bombing dummy towers at 60 feet.

The briefing on the afternoon of May 16th ended weeks of speculation for #617 Squadron. The assault on the Ruhr dams would be made in three waves. Gibson would lead the first wave of nine Lancasters to the Mohne and if anybody had bombs after the dam was breached, they would fly to the Eder dam to the southeast. The second group of five was to take a northern route and fly down the Zuider Zee to confuse German defences. It would then move on to bomb the Sorpe dam. The third wave could be called in to any of the three dams.

The Mohne dam ran 850 yards at a height of 150 feet and a depth of 140 feet at its base. It was almost half a mile long and retained 134 million tons of water. The Eder dam to the east was even larger and both were of solid concrete while the Sorpe dam was smaller, but controlled a vital water supply to the highly industrialized Ruhr.

The wave going against the Sorpe dam approached from the north and slanted across the Zuider Zee, a land-locked bay that extended 50 miles into Holland from the North Sea. Geoff Rice slammed into it at full throttle. The impact ripped the belly apart and the bomb was torn from its mount, but the Lanc kept flying. Rice turned back. Up ahead Les Munro caught a burst of flak knocking out his wireless. Without radio, Munro could not direct the attack nor follow bombing instructions so he aborted. Australian F/Lt Barlow's aircraft fell to flak and Canadian Harvey Glinz died in the crash. Then Vernon Byers' aircraft was destroyed and fellow Canadian James McDowell died with him. American Joe McCarthy – delayed on takeoff – was the only member of the Sorpe group still flying.

Gibson circled and then attacked. As the Lanc screamed out of the hills, the backspin on the bomb set up a vibration. When Taerum snapped on the belly lights, flak immediately rolled up from the shore. The lights converged and airspeed nudged 240 m.p.h. The Lanc shuddered as the bomb built up speed and Gibson held the machine between the towers while the bomb-aimer sighted through the plywood triangle and waited for the nails to line up on the towers.

The vibration ended with a sudden lurch as the bomb rolled across the water like a bowling ball. The plane leapt the dam and when Gibson looked back, he saw the lake leap back as a wall of water 1,000-feet high towered above him. But the dam had not been breached. John Hopgood, the next pilot, attacked but flak set fire to his aircraft before he reached the wall. The bomb overshot but destroyed a powerhouse downstream. Hopgood went for altitude so the crew could jump, but the flaming wing fell off and the Lancaster fell apart some three miles from the dam. Canadian John Fraser miraculously managed to jump. One other man survived, but Canadian navigator Ken Earnshaw was among those who died. Gibson circled the area with lights on in order to draw fire away from Mickey Martin who was then attacking through heavy flak. He scored a hit but the dam held. "Dinghy" Young – who had twice come down in the Channel – rolled his bomb into the dam, as did Dave Maltby who followed. This time the concrete split and 134 million tons of water swept through a 100-foot gap, creating a wall 25 feet high.

Gibson ordered four aircraft to follow him in a deadly approach to the Eder dam, which lay deep in a ravine. Henry Maudslay hit the parapet, but blew himself up in the process. Alden Cottam and Robert Urquhart became two more Canadians added to the night's casualties. Dave Shannon hit the dam and Australian Les Knight finally scored with the last bomb. This time 200 million tons of water crashed through the breach.

Meanwhile, Joe McCarthy, the only survivor of the northern formation, found and bombed the Sorpe dam. As aircraft from the reserve flight were diverted, Lewis Burpee and Canadian crewmen James Arthur and Joseph Brady were lost. Kenneth Brown reached the Sorpe and, after several attempts, his bomb-aimer Stephen Oancia found the target, but the damaged dam held. Of the 29 Canadians who took part in the operation, 13 were killed and one became a prisoner of war. The aircraft flew back at 50 feet to dodge flak, but it didn't work for "Dinghy" Young who was hit over Holland and had to ditch for the third time. The crew, including Canadian Vincent MacCausland, was lost. Overall, only 10 of the 19 aircraft that left Scrampton returned. Of the 59 missing men, only three survived. Later, 33 men were decorated including a Victoria Cross for Gibson whose conduct in directing aircraft over the dams introduced the master of ceremonies technique used four months later at Peenemünde.

The raid was the epitome of technology, planning, flying skill and courage. But it suffered a 42 per cent casualty rate. About 1,300 people were drowned in the flooding, but over half were Russian prisoners. While considerable damage was inflicted in the Ruhr, it did not have any major or long-term effect on production. Although damage to the Eder dam cut coal production in the Dortmund plants by nine per cent, the dam was back in operation by fall. However, repairing the dams meant some 20,000 workers were diverted from the coastal defences. The precision of the raid had a psychological impact on the enemy and they substantially increased flak defences on the dams. As a consequence of this and the high casualty rate, the RAF did not pursue any further dam raids.

Guy Gibson was grounded for a time, but later went back to action and was killed on an operation where he was flying a Mosquito. Canadian W/Com Johnny Fauquier would eventually take over the #617 Dambuster Squadron, but before doing so he would see outstanding service at a place called Peenemünde.

## CANADIAN DAMBUSTERS

*Survivors:* F/Sgt Ken Brown, P/O Tony Deering, P/O John Fraser (POW), Sgt Chester Gowrie, F/Sgt Don MacLean, F/Sgt Grant MacDonald, Sgt Stephen Oancia, Sgt Harry O'Brien, W/Com Percy Pigeon, Sgt Bill Ratcliffe, F/O Dave Roger, Sgt Fred Sutherland, F/O Terry Taerum, F/Sgt John Thrasher, F/O Danny Walker, F/Sgt Harvey Weeks, Fl/Lt Joe McCarthy (USA).

*Dead:* WO2 James Arthur, WO2 Joseph Brady, P/O Lewis Burpee, P/O Vernon Byers, WO2 Alden Cottam, F/O Kenneth Earnshaw, F/Sgt Frank Garbas, F/O Harvey Glinz, WO2 Abram Gershowitz, F/O David MacCausland, F/Sgt James McDowell, F/O Robert Urquhart, P/O Floyd Wile.

## PEENEMÜNDE

When Werner von Braun got a rocket to fly 119 miles in 1942, it represented the future of aerial warfare. The British were aware of the event, but chose not to see its significance. On the other hand, rocketry was not suddenly thrust upon the world that day at Peenemünde on the Baltic coast. Tales of rocketry had been doing the rounds for decades. During the First World War, Robert Goddard was into rocket experiments, but his native United States was not.

Walter Dorberger was the first to try to bring organization to the work at an army test base. With a limited budget he hired top men such as von Braun and by 1937, a team of 300 moved into Peenemünde. Soon they had a large operational rocket undergoing test flights and the Luftwaffe was farming out related work to one-third of the scientists in Germany. On the brink of war, the German War Ministry called for a rocket that had a range of 150 miles and could drop a ton of explosives on London.

All of the above took place before the war and raises the question of British intelligence and counter-action. Intelligence appeared to have been reasonably good, but counter-action when war was declared was non-existent. The Polish underground provided the British with details of German research and even managed to have slave labourers transferred to Peenemünde so the British were not without information on rocket developments.

The first V1 flew in December 1942, but Bomber Command allowed another eight months to elapse before it struck at Peenemünde. Then oddly enough this was done in the first hours of the day the USAF was planning a massive raid on a ball-bearing plant at Schweinfurt. The original plan was for the RAF to follow-up the American day attack with a night attack. When American Brig-Gen Fred Anderson consulted Harris on the matter he thought he had a done deal. Harris had little time for panacea targets such as aircraft production plants or ball-bearings and he also doubted that his bombers could effectively locate the distant target. After 34 months, Peenemünde became a priority target hours before the American bombers took off for the disastrous Schweinfurt raid.

On the other hand, a clear moonlit night was necessary to locate a number of small buildings, which were located within three areas. On August 17, 1943, a force of 600 took off for a precision raid on a small target. Mosquitos left first and swung south on a course towards Berlin to divert enemy night fighters. At Peenemünde, Group Captain J.H. Searby of 8 Group Pathfinders had drop flares in three target locations, but the enemy immediately covered the areas with smoke. Searby then took over as master of ceremonies and directed incoming waves to their targets.

W/Comm Johnny Fauquier of Canadian #405 Squadron was his deputy and spent 45 minutes circling the target giving a running commentary to the 36 Six Group machines in the final wave. Fauquier was one of the most distinguished bomber pilots in the RAF. Upon completing his second tour as commander of #405 Squadron, he was posted to Six Group Headquarters as an air commodore, but later relinquished the rank to take command of #617 Dambuster Squadron. His performance over Peenemünde enabled Canadian crews to correct original Pathfinder marking errors.

The diversion of Mosquitos against Berlin worked at first but the enemy soon recovered and sent fighters northward. The Me-110s with upward firing cannon hit the final waves and took a toll of 40 aircraft and 32 damaged. The Canadian Six Group lost 12 aircraft – one third of its attacking strength. Although the cost was high, the well-executed raid was considered a success as considerable damage was inflicted on the site and rocket development was retarded four to six weeks. Unfortunately, many of the 735 people killed on the ground were Polish prisoners.

Although the raid delayed the development of both the V1 and V2 programs Bomber Command failed to deliver the knockout punch. A week after the Peenemünde raid, Harris became obsessed with destroying Berlin and ending the war in three months. Two months after the raid, aircraft brought back photos of a V1 on a ramp at Peenemünde, yet no immediate action was taken. The enemy had moved equipment and personnel out of Peenemünde to Poland. In his memoirs Harris states: "There never was, of course, any question of putting a complete stop to V-weapons by bombing Peenemünde. We knew very well by then that if the enemy chose to give first priority to the production of anything, a single attack on any plant could only cause a delay of a month or two at the most."[44]

However, one piece of perplexing history remains: Why did Bomber Command wait three years for the one raid on Peenemünde and stage that raid on the night the Americans asked for help with their attack on Schweinfurt?

**ABOVE:** *Weather did not cooperate when Bomber Harris decided he would try to break the German will to resist by intensive bombing of Berlin. (DND)*

**OPPOSITE PAGE:** *During the Battle of Berlin alone some 587 aircraft did not make it back to base. This represented some 3,750 aircrew of which 3,000 were killed. (DND)*

*Bomber Harris sought victory*
*by breaking the German will to resist in...*

# 🐾 THE BATTLE OF BERLIN

*"UNSUSTAINABLE LOSSES" WAS AN* euphemism for impending defeat, and this is precisely what the 8th Air Force faced when Gen Ira Eaker was unceremoniously shuttled off to the Mediterranean. Fortunately, his successor Gen James Doolittle had a weapon Eaker lacked during the dark summer of '43. The North American Mustang with its long range and fine performance turned the tables on the Luftwaffe. Within four months in 1944, the 8th destroyed 1,000 enemy fighters. No longer were American fighters merely escorts, pilots were now instructed to search and destroy enemy fighters. Gen Adolf Galland, head of German fighters, predicted a total collapse of his day-fighter force.

Although the combined chiefs of staff of the American and British forces were deep into planning the invasion, Harris opened his offensive on Berlin in November 1943. This was by no means the first RAF attack on Berlin and as recently as August, Harris mounted three raids on the German capital as a prelude to the main offensive. He lost 125 aircraft and learned that the night-fighter was effective. He estimated that it might cost 500 aircraft, but by April 1, 1944, devastation in the capital city would be so tremendous that the Germans would surrender. Harris had a free hand in mounting raids on Berlin and 16 on other key cities. While the German day-fighter force was at a low ebb, the night-fighters remained formidable with their radar and upward firing cannon.

The use of Window by the RAF resulted in a German tactic permitting night-fighters to roam at will in search of targets. In addition, the Berlin operation was mounted during the worst possible weather adding to the strain. During the first week of the campaign, Berlin was hit three times along with three other targets. Flying Stirlings, squadrons of Three Group could not get sufficient height and became night-fighter bait and were withdrawn.

The Mark II and Mark V versions of the Halifax soon suffered close to a 10 per cent casualty rate for the same reason. Canadian #434 Squadron was hit with an incredible 24 per cent loss rate in January. Three other Canadian squadrons posted losses of 14 per cent. Harris then had to cut some 250 aircraft or about one-third of his strike force. They were used on other duties such as mine-laying or staging "nickels" or diversionary sweeps. With the approach of D-Day, Bomber Command was to become an instrument of the Supreme Headquarters Allied Expeditionary Force (SHAEF).

Berlin had been severely pounded, but there was no sign of surrender on the eve of April 5th although Harris's prediction of 500 lost crews was to be remarkably accurate. Weary crews dared to relax as they contemplated rest on the second last day of the Battle of Berlin.


## NIGHT OF THE BIG CHOP

March 30th, 1944 was a day of growing apprehension on each of Bomber Command's 77 squadrons. The news was out of an upcoming operation, but little information had surfaced. Experienced hands read bad news as ground crews began topping up gasoline and cutting back the bombload on machines that were readied for a cancelled operation from the previous night. Bomber Command Headquarters at High Wycombe was wrapped in silence as Air Marshal Harris pondered the target. The campaign had gone sour. During the past month, there had been poor bombing results in strikes on Stuttgart, Berlin and Frankfurt. Eleven nights before, he lost 78 bombers and 546 men over Leipzig. This was followed by a raid on Berlin where unpredicted winds scattered the bomber stream and bombs fell on 126 centres other than the German capital, with a lose of 511 airmen. Harris shoved the figures to the back of his mind and selected Nuremberg as the target for the evening. Although the Berlin campaign had not produced the desired results, Harris felt he could achieve a psychological victory in destroying historic Nuremberg.

The route chosen called for bomber streams to converge near Bruges and turn onto one straight 265-mile course and then fly south for some 80 miles to Nuremberg. Seasoned Pathfinder commanders immediately protested the straight course and the fact that it was directed over areas of intense night-fighter activities. There was argument throughout the afternoon among group commanders who saw the straight course as a route to disaster. A Mosquito flew in with a weather report saying the bombers would be flying some 900 miles through enemy sky in moonlight possibly without cloud cover.

In brief, the target had no major strategic importance. The bomber stream would invade areas of key fighter opposition close to two beacons that assembled German fighters. A late-meteorological report called for moonlight on the long approach, but clouds were over the target. Deputy Commander Air Marshal Sir Robert Saundby said: "I can say that in view of the met report and other conditions, everyone including myself expected the C-in-C to cancel the raid."[45] But there was no cancellation.

On eight bomber groups, pilots, navigators and bomb-aimers met in the chill afternoon to work out primary details of the flight plan enabling over 700 aircraft to takeoff from dozens of bases and assemble in a stream that would then challenge the night defences. Another factor that needed to be considered was the matter of timing over the target because a mistake here could get you blown out of the sky by your best friend's bombs. Crews waited in a twilight zone and literally counted off the hours of their life. Bets at poker and seven-toed Pete became extravagantly reckless. Men also made a careful check that good luck charms were in place and ultra-personal documents were out of place. For Canadians, those few hours were probably the worst of Six Group's experience. A week earlier, more than 500 men died in flights over Berlin and now Nuremburg promised to be even worse.

Thirteen Canadian squadrons located in the north of England faced the longest journey of Bomber Command. The 1,600 miles would take some eight hours. Lord Boom Trenchard, who commanded the RFC in France during WWI, had been in the habit of visiting squadrons before a major battle to jolly up the airmen. Typical comment in 1917 was that it was more important for pilots to shoot down a given balloon than to come back. Although officially long gone, on the afternoon of March 30, 1944, Trenchard was up to his old tricks. He visited #103 Squadron at Elsham Wolds and stunned crews when he told them their life expectancy was to be greatly reduced because of the maximum effort. Crews attended a briefing to hear what everybody had feared for hours - the target was Nuremberg.

Six Group put up 118 machines as part of the 782 aircraft that groped towards a rendezvous over the North Sea. Two other Mosquito operations were timed to draw enemy fighters northward, but the fighters refused to be lured by trailing window. Moose Squadron dropped 112 mines off Heligoland with no major opposition. When the Nuremberg force crossed the Belgian coast, it did so in moonlight and the cold air at 20,000 feet left behind clouds of contrails that chalked the path of the bombers.

By 1944, the air war was well into the realm of electronics, and for the Germans it had come full circle. The British had first successfully dropped window – strips of tinfoil – in the raid on Hamburg in July 1943. The impulses, picked up by radar, befuddled the enemy for some time until Maj. Hajo Herrmann convinced superiors that part of the answer was to forget electronics and use eyesight and height to spot the bomber stream. A system developed where FW 190s and Me-109s would fly above the bomber stream and anti-aircraft fire. These "Wild Boar" pilots were effectively able to pick up RAF bombers visually against the glare of searchlights and flares. A second system, known as "Tame Boars," depended on electronics. Their Me-110s were directed to the vicinity of the bomber stream by ground control and then pilots took over by airborne radar and infiltrated the bomber stream.

On the night of the Nuremberg raid, the first German move was to launch 246 night-fighters. Tame Boars from the 3rd Fighter Division were directed to radar beacon Ida that lay directly in the path of oncoming bombers. Most of the Me-110s were equipped with twin cannons mounted to fire upwards. The bombers were swept by an 80 m.p.h. tailwind as the Luftwaffe fighters closed for the greatest night battle of the war.

Helmut Schulte crept under four bombers and destroyed all of them with only 56 rounds. Martin Becker didn't have the upward mounted cannon or Schrage Musik and had to manoeuvre in the usual manner. He destroyed six bombers in 30 minutes. Then, after landing and refuelling, he shot down a seventh on his return flight. Soon after their encounter with the night fighters, bombers were falling from the sky at the rate of one a minute. One pilot counted 20 burning aircraft and other pilots simply stopped counting.

Tom Hall's crew was on its second operation, the first had been a shaky-do to Berlin a week earlier when strong tailwinds pushed them over the target early. Hall orbited through flak and fighters in order to bomb on time. By the time he got the Lancaster back to England it was written off. On his second operation, Hall's machine was hit again. He gave orders to bail out, but the machine was soon diving into a spin. It blew up and only two members of the crew survived after an operational career of only five days.

F/O J.D. Laidlaw's Halifax took a mortal burst from a night fighter, but before he died, Laidlaw ordered his crew to jump. The flight engineer was dead and a seriously wounded navigator blocked the front exit. Three men escaped through the rear hatch, but Australian F/O Martin Corocan refused to leave the navigator and died with him.

At the second turning point, fighter activity slackened, as the enemy seemed to suspect the target was further east. But the short leg to Nuremberg soon became cluttered with confusion, wild wind drift, and resultant bombing errors. The target area was obscured by eight-tenths cloud. One group of aircraft, fed wrong winds by weather broadcasts, turned early and bombed Schweinfurt instead of Nuremberg. Others bombed adjacent centres, but the concentration of bombs on Nuremberg only half destroyed one factory and did minor damage to a second.

On the homeward leg, F/O Jim Moffat heard his pilot, Sqd/Ldr George "Turkey" Laird, yell. Something ripped the top turret off their Halifax and sliced through the fuselage and port rudder a few feet from Moffat's head. A Lancaster had collided with their Halifax. Moffat got out of the rear turret, but the escape hatch was jammed and he was literally sucked through a gash in the fuselage. Moffat fell clear, but 14 men in the two crews perished as the two bombers crashed into Belgium.

Almost 700 airmen were lost that night. Moffat, of Lachine, Que., became one of 15 veterans of the Nuremberg raid who lived out the war as an evader, but 545 were killed and 152 became prisoners of war. Of these 109 were Canadians. German casualties in the Nuremberg area were 69. It was the last target in the four-month long Battle of Berlin during which Harris lost 3,750 aircrew, of this number about 1,300 were from Six Group. Harris had defied the RAF commander Chief of Air Staff Charles Portal in the selection of targets as he tried to bring about Germany's collapse before the invasion, but by April 1944, firmer hands at Supreme Headquarters of the Allied Expeditionary Force took over to divert Harris from his private war.

*The final moment before an operation featured wild jokes and wild bids at a poker game known as "Seven-Toed Pete."* (DND)

**ABOVE:** *Photograph of three German soldiers courtesy of Don MacDonald.*

**OPPOSITE PAGE:** *Evader Don MacDonald (left) and two Americans enjoy a brief liberation at a safe house in Belgium. On the same roll of film, their host got a shot of three Germans across the street. (COURTESY DON MACDONALD)*

*In occupied Europe a silent army of citizens risked all by....*

#  MENDING BROKEN WINGS

**BY THE SUMMER OF 1944** thousands of men were climbing into aircraft and performing distinguished acts of bravery as a routine function. One scene that still haunts survivors of the air war is hearing the rattle of wind on silk as they fall through the darkness while overhead their pilot struggles to keep a bomber aloft long enough for the crew to escape. Such a scene often ended with an explosion taking the pilot's life and the sacrifice usually went unrecognized except by the men whose lives were saved.

Ian Bazelgette was such a pilot. But unlike others, his sacrifice was recognized with the Victoria Cross and he unofficially came to represent the many who died at the controls so that their crew could escape. Although a mountain is named after him in Jasper, Alta., Bazelgette is seldom remembered when Canadians think of VC winners. The reason is that the Calgary-born Bazelgette was living in England when war was declared. He joined the army and then transferred to the RAF where he became a pilot. He flew Wellingtons and Lancasters to complete a tour with #115 Squadron, a group with one of the finest records in Bomber Command. While completing his tour, he won the DFC.

He then did a tour as an instructor and was later posted to a new Pathfinder squadron as a flight leader. Sqd/Ldr Bazelgette flew out of Downham Market on the night of August 4, 1944. He was part of a raid on flying-bomb storage sites at Bois de Cassan and Trossy St. Maxim. This came at the time British and Canadian troops were fighting towards Falaise and these weapons threatened British ports.

The role of #635 Squadron was to mark the path for the main bomber force. Bazelgette's Lancaster was hit on approach and both starboard engines were knocked out. Fire ate along the starboard wing and into the fuselage where smoke and acrid fumes overcame the mid-upper gunner. The bomb-aimer had an arm blown off, but Bazelgette went on through heavy flak to bomb and mark the target. Once the bombs were gone, the flaming aircraft flew out of control and Bazelgette had just managed to right the machine when a port engine packed up. He then ordered the crew to jump as the machine fell to 1,000 feet. But he refused to abandon the two wounded men. Four men jumped and the Lancaster spiralled down towards a landing. The pilot made a good approach and was very close to touchdown when the bomber exploded. The remains of the crew were buried at Senantes.

While Ian Bazelgette represented a number of pilots who died in order that their crew had a chance of survival, David Hornell represented another group of historically unrecognized airmen. Coastal Command, by definition, ensured that personnel would be posted to some isolated rock in the sea where aircrew endured the tedium of nothingness on patrols sometimes running to almost 16 hours. Although monotony characterized many Coastal Command patrols, their aircraft were major instruments in Britain's survival during the U-boat campaign sinking 212 enemy subs and seriously damaging an additional 120. But it came at a cost of 1,777 aircraft.

David Hornell of Mimico, Ont., was pilot of a Canso flying boat returning to Wick, Scotland, after a 10-hour patrol on June 10, 1944. They spotted a German submarine on the surface and attacked. Flak from the sub damaged the Canso's starboard wing. Fire broke out in the starboard engine, but Hornell attacked again straddling the sub with two depth charges sending it to the bottom. The engine fell off as fire devoured the wing and Hornell fought to get the machine into the wind but was forced to ditch in a heavy swell.

All eight members managed to escape ash the flying boat quickly sank, but only one dinghy was serviceable. This meant the crew had to take shifts hanging overboard. Winds mounted and high waves tossed the dinghy about as two members of the crew died. Hornell had spent a good deal of time in the water and was very weak some 16 hours later when a rescue lifeboat was dropped from an aircraft. It landed some distance from the dinghy and Hornell tried to swim out to it, but his crew restrained him. Six hours later, the crew was rescued, but Hornell was unconscious and died shortly afterwards. He was later awarded a posthumous Victoria Cross. The day after Hornell's death, Andy Mynarski of the Moose Squadron took off on a flight that would give new meaning to courage and devotion to others.

## BRIGHT COURAGE: BLACK MONDAY

Within 10 nights of the Nuremberg disaster, RAF crews hit the first railway targets. Throughout the month of April 1944, casualty rates dropped and crews enjoyed the luxury of short trips. On the night before the Longest Day, Bomber Command flew 1,200 sorties against targets in France and attacks on rail and road communications, ports and the oil industry continued. On the night of June 12th, Bomber Command selected six rail centres for attack. The Canadians hit Cambrai and Amiens and the worst of the old days was suddenly back as Six Group lost 15 aircraft or over 100 men. The night became known as Black Monday, but it also became a symbol of the strong bond of fellowship that had developed with Six Group crews.

The Cambrai bombers struck from a relatively low and dangerous height. F/O L.R. Lauzon of Toronto had just turned off the target when flak ripped through the Halifax starting his fuselage ablaze. Lauzon ordered the crew to bail out and fought the controls while they did. He was about to jump when mid-upper gunner Sgt C. Christoff fought his way forward with a smouldering parachute in his arms. Luzon offered the gunner his own chute hoping to somehow land the machine, which was now screaming earthward. Christoff of Ona, Ont., refused the chute and decided to stay with his skipper. He grabbed a fire extinguisher and fought the blaze while Lauzon actually managed a landing. They got clear of the aircraft, but the Germans picked up Lauzon while Christoff became an evader.

Meanwhile in another aircraft, Jim Kelly of Winnipeg sat at his wireless station and tried to think happy thoughts as they approached the coast. The mid-upper gunner Andy Mynarski, who was his buddy from Winnipeg, had just been commissioned, which called for a party when they got the chance for a stand-down.

Kelly's reverie was interrupted when the tail-gunner Pat Brophy of Port Arthur, Ont., reported flak as they approached the coast. Although the last few weeks had been relatively good ones this was their 13th operation and they would be heading over the marshalling yard at Cambrai on June 13th.

Up in the cockpit F/O Art de Breyne, of St. Lambert, Que., marvelled at the gentle touch of the new Lancaster with its light fuel load. As he crossed the coast, he prepared to let down to 2,000 feet. That was something else that bothered Kelly. A Lancaster at 2,000 feet was a sitting duck for light, medium, and heavy flak and even rifle fire. Suddenly, the interior of the aircraft was swept by a glare and de Breyne threw the bomber into a dive, almost throwing Kelly off his seat. The pilot hauled back on the controls and the Lanc went into a gut-wrenching climb, but they escaped the cone of searchlights. They were on their descent to the target when Brophy yelled into the intercom: "Bogey astern!" De Breyne threw the bomber into a corkscrew, but the Ju-88 caught them from below. Brophy opened up with four machine guns and the night-fighter responded with cannons knocking out the port engine and setting the wing on fire. Cannon fire then smashed into the fuselage that linked Brophy and the rest of the crew and soon burning hydraulic oil made it a corridor of flame.

As the aircraft plunged, the crew listened for orders, but the intercom was dead. Then the red light in both turrets blinked "dit da da dit," meaning "P" for parachute. Art de Breyne fought to keep the machine out of a death dive as bomb-aimer Jack Friday of Port Arthur yanked at the forward escape hatch. When it opened, the updraft smashed it against his head and knocked him unconscious.

Roy Vigars of Surrey, B.C., struggled to the hatch and pushed Friday through while holding the D-ring of his parachute. Vigars then fought his own war with the hatch that again jammed and the flight engineer kicked at it for an eternity as navigator Bob Bodie watched from behind de Breyne. Vigar finally kicked the hatch free and jumped while Bodie of Vancouver and Jim Kelly quickly followed.

Four members of his crew had escaped through the forward hatch and this gave the pilot hope that his gunners might also have escaped through the rear hatch. But the hydraulics that controlled the rear turret were shot away. Brophy was locked in at an angle where he couldn't get out or even reach his parachute in the aircraft. He pried open the doors far enough to get his parachute and tried to hand-crank the turret to a beam position. Then the crank handle broke as the flames swept down the fuselage towards him. Mynarski climbed down from the mid-upper and struggled to the escape hatch. He was about to jump when he looked back, saw Brophy through the flames and read the situation. He crawled towards him on hands and knees through pools of flaming oil, his uniform and parachute burning.

Brophy later told David MacDonald of *Reader's Digest* that he screamed, "Go back, Andy! Get out! Andy grabbed a fire axe and smashed at the turret. He tore at the doors with bare hands, now a mass of flames from the waist down. When I waved him away again he hung his head and nodded as though he was ashamed to leave."

Mynarski jumped and Brophy, the last occupant, rode the burning bomber and five tons of bombs on the short trip to the ground. Its flaming port wing hit a tree and snapped the turret doors open and hurled Brophy to safety. Jim Kelly was among those who survived. While he was hiding out, a Frenchman reported finding a parachutist who died of burns shortly after landing that night. Painted across the front of his helmet was the name "Andy." Months later, when Brophy documented the story of what happened, Andrew Mynarski became one of the few to get a Victoria Cross on the testimony of a single witness.

Kelly recalled being second last man out of the doomed aircraft, "the big tail wheel swished by my head and in no time I landed hard on my back." He crawled into the darkness, away from Amiens that was burning in a distance, and lay in a hedge as he tried to clear his head. "About four hours later, I saw a figure ... no helmet ... no rifle ... so I took a chance and called out. It was Bob Bodie."[46]

They prowled the countryside for two days and on the third awoke from a sleep to find a young boy looking at them. They thumbed through a phrase book without success and were discussing what to do next when suddenly the boy bolted. He returned that night with his mother who brought wine, but regarded the Canadians with suspicion. Later, they learned that the boy had heard them say "yeah" and interpreted it as the German "ja."

Finally, the mother told them to stay put and a few hours later two armed men arrived to take them to Varennes. Here the mother and father who were still suspicious that the evaders might be Nazi plants interrogated them at length. But the Canadians were gradually accepted as evaders. A lack of food became a problem a few weeks later. Kelly and Bodie were then moved to another safe house by Collette, a courier who soon had them en route to a third safe house.

Things went well for two days at the third house, but when shooting broke out in the streets and Germans rapped at the door the evaders headed for the attic. The excitement had merely been a German military exercise, but the couple that owned the house had but one word for the Canadians: "Allez!"

Collette once again took charge and as the Gestapo in Varennes closed on safe houses, the Canadians became part of about a dozen airmen who took refuge in a field. After a week, the two became guests of a family of seven whose enthusiasm for harbouring evaders exceeded their sense of security. They did everything but sell tickets as the evaders became instant celebrities and had a constant stream of visitors. One was a mysterious priest who asked: "How would you like to be in London tonight?"

The priest didn't have to wait for an answer, but once outside he made a quick confession, "I'm sorry but it was the only way I could get you out of there. The whole village is talking about you." The priest was actually a member of the British Special Operations Executive (SOE) who had been dropped into France to organize underground activity. Once again Collette took them to a safe house.

This time it was a comfortable walled Chateau owned by Madame Jeanne Secant, a widow with two small daughters. For six weeks the Canadians lived in single rooms and relative luxury. Then German troops appeared at the door, searching for accommodations in the 20-room chateau. Madame Secant argued, but the Germans were insistent. Then she sighed and waved towards the interior where her daughters languished.

"Very well," she said, "if you don't mind diphtheria."

That particular group of enemy troops moved quickly down the road, but soon others came to occupy the Chateau. The SS pounded at the door one night and there was little negotiation. Kelly and Bodie jumped out of bed and rushed to

Madame's bathroom, thinking that Madame would preserve her adjoining room and that the bathroom provided a haven. In their haste they both ran naked to the bathroom and climbed into a clothes closet. "I can't describe how we felt while this was happening," Kelly said. "It was as if we were running on empty."

Early next morning Madame Secant came up with clothing. Heavy footsteps on the stairs sent the evaders back into the closet and the SS commander stomped in and glared at Madame as the battle for the bathroom was engaged. They argued but the German showed no intention of leaving. Then in a brilliant act of defiance, Madame Secant dropped her drawers and mounted the bidet with a gesture of surrender. The SS officer suddenly stomped out. Madame Secant then got the evaders to the local cemetery where a friendly gendarme picked them up. From there the "priest" commandeered a car and got them to Paris where they were later flown to England.

At first glance, a man fighting flames in a dying bomber while trying to save a friend, and a lady, dropping her drawers and risking death to save men she hardly knew may have had little in common. But both represent the epitome of courage. Although Madame Secant acted individually, she was one of thousands of helpers who risked all to help Allied airmen.

## THE SILENT ARMY

Jim Moffat, landed in the dark as 14 men died in the twisted remains of two bombers. He lay under a hedge until daylight when he approached a youth and asked if he was in France. "Nien!" was the reply prompting Moffat to put considerable distance between him and the young man. Later, in the village of Halanzy, a postman circled on a bicycle while another man told him to get behind the hedge. Moffat crawled behind the hedge and waited. The man later returned and took Moffat to a tavern where his uniform was burned. He was then taken to the home of Vital and Marie-Claire Paul where he spent the night. Then he was smuggled to the home of Vital's brother at Etalle. The brother Albert was head of the resistance in Etalle and the SS constantly raided the village houses. For six weeks, Jim and another RAF evader, Bill Jones, lived in a crawl space over the garage attic. One night Albert took them into the woods to show them an arms shipment that the RAF had made. He was elated because the .38 revolvers were made in Canada, but the inevitable result of the airdrop was Albert's wife's scream of terror at daybreak as the SS crashed into the house.

Moffat jumped out a rear window and ran barefoot into the breaking day. He then lost his pants on barbed wire as a dog barked in pursuit. Moffat crashed his way into a clump of bushes and pain from gashes in his arms and chest told him it was a thorn-bush. He stopped breathing as German boots and a German shepherd dog rushed by. The dog was on the scent of Albert Paul or the other evader, Bill Jones. Albert was captured and shot, but Moffat remained a fugitive for some six months. One night he stumbled onto an encampment in the woods that was occupied by 20 dead members of the underground. Later, he joined a second underground group on raids after the invasion. The climax was a standoff of sorts. Moffat and 17 others attacked the village of Quincy, which they thought was occupied by only 25 Germans. In reality, it was defended by 250 enemy troops who, luckily for the small underground group, withdrew the next day as the Yanks appeared.

A silent army of some 12,000 citizens rescued some 3,600 Allied airmen in northwest Europe. They were officially known as "helpers" – a name that does not begin to convey the measure of their courage or the magnitude of their sacrifice. Five hundred were shot, thousands were arrested and hundreds vanished in concentration camps. In short, these people risked it all to give downed airmen a chance to fly again. Today surviving helpers or their descendants treasure faded certificates that proclaim they were once "Helpers of Broken Allied Wings."

It started shortly after the evacuation of 338,000 Allied troops from Dunkirk as civilians helped stranded soldiers escape. Fifi Fraipont was such a person and the British later contacted her seeking permission to use her home as a safe house for downed airmen. She agreed and her home near the Dutch border became sanctuary for a stream of evaders. When Fifi asked her parents in Liege to take an airman they did so, but the Gestapo soon raided their home and Fifi's parents were sent to a concentration camp. In a sense, Fifi's father was fortunate because the penalty for a man harbouring an evader was death.

The severe penalties however failed to prevent the eventual establishment of safe houses from Denmark to the Pyrenees. Couriers provided an unofficial link as escape lines developed. Emmy van Traak was 15 when she became a courier and 19 when captured. Leonce Jacquet was 17 when his uncle took him to fetch a Canadian airman in a village near Liège. Don MacDonald of Goderich, Ont., had been near the end of his tour. "After Berlin, Stuttgart, Frankfurt and Schweinfurt I thought Montzen would be a piece of cake," he recalled. But bombers fell from the sky on the way in and as pilot Johnny Burrows started his bomb run, cannon shells from a night-fighter ripped their aircraft. Although Burrows completed the run, both he and crewman Paul Driver died. Something hit MacDonald's legs rendering them numb.

Another fighter soon jumped them and this time their Halifax burned. Survivors jumped and MacDonald blacked out when he hit the ground. During the following days, he became a parcel that was passed from house to house. Leonce later recalled one such exchange: "We saw Donald and we had to take a tram, but the following agreement was reached between us. We must not speak to Donald and we had to do as if we didn't know him. The street was light and I could see far. At about 500 metres ahead the Germans were checking everybody at the tram. So we walked for a quarter of an hour. My uncle in front, Donald at a certain distance, and I behind."

Spitfire pilot Ray Sherk was originally forced down behind German lines at El Alamein. He was captured and sent to Italy where he spent 13 months in an Italian POW camp. He later escaped as Italy capitulated, but was recaptured by the Germans. Six weeks later, he escaped again and went back for a second tour in northwest Europe providing fighter-cover for B-17s. On a relatively quiet Sunday morning, he switched over from his drop tanks and his engine cut out. Sherk was forced to jump and came down near a church at Beaumont-Hamel Park, where the Newfoundland Regiment was wiped out in 1916. Louis Serre appeared to guide him through the maze of WWI trenches to a farmhouse.

Minutes later, Sherk was disguised as a farm labourer, but the German dragnet was closing in. Sherk also became a parcel as Louis' wife Jeanne arranged for identity papers and shipped him off to a safe house. Although they were not part of a regular escape group, the Serres arranged for Sherk's gradual escape into Spain.

There was an element of risk in the enthusiasm with which young schoolkids bragged about having an airman at home. Don Forsyth of Ottawa, later recalled his concern over the appeal the revolver he was wearing had for the young son at his safe house. Forsyth looked out the window one day to see the boy facing three playmates while fanning an imaginary six-gun. "Bang! Bang! I'm a Canadian cowboy," he shouted.

As the number of safe houses increased many were linked in what became formal escape lines with collection centres from The Hague down to the Spanish border. But there were always safe houses that evolved in a burst of emotion as downed, exhausted airmen sought shelter and became pawns in a deadly game of chess.

Andrée de Jongh had been hiding Allied soldiers and airmen since the fall of Dunkirk. In August 1941, the 24-year-old known as "Dedee" delivered a British soldier to the British Consulate in Bilbao, Spain. The thought of the young woman having made the trip across the Pyrenees, where only the hardiest of smugglers survived, stunned the Consul. But Dedee had not come to talk about her journey and soon got down to business. Forced to leave Brussels, she moved to Paris and had her father, Frederic De Jongh, take over the Brussels link of what had become the Comet Escape Line. Now she wanted to expand the line to Spain, but needed financial help from the British. She knew precisely what it cost to house, feed and transport an evader and soon worked out a deal with the British. Although the RAF's bombing campaign got off to a spluttering start, the loss of trained aircrew was a concern and MI9 (Military Intelligence) agreed to provide funds for housing and feeding evaders en route to the frontier and to pay for guides for the trip over the Pyrenees. Dedee demanded cash on delivery and no interference with the operation of her line.

During one three-month period, Dedee personally delivered 54 downed airmen across the Pyrenees. For over a year, the Gestapo searched for her and her father had a price of five million Belgian francs on his head. He left Brussels on April 30, 1942 and fled to Paris. Three days later three principals in the Brussels' operation were arrested. Baron Jean Greindl then took over the Brussels link and saved the branch from extinction. Dedee made another 18 trips over the Pyrenees with some 118 evaders.

Then on the Spanish side the evaders would wait for a car from the British Embassy while Dedee would turn and start back over the mountains. Although Dedee's Comet Line liberated some 1,000 evaders, traitors and the Gestapo eventually closed in on them. Her father was arrested and shot along with some 25 key members of the line while Dedee and dozens of others were sent to concentration camps. After the war, Dedee's life was remarkably similar to that of Mother Theresa. She became a missionary and served in leper colonies in the Belgian Congo and Ethiopia.

Albert Guerisse was a Belgian army surgeon who escaped to England after Dunkirk. He volunteered for duty with the SOE and while in France was recruited by MI9. Soon Guerisse was working on escape operations and took over the Marseilles section of what grew to be the substantial O'Leary Line. Guerisse adopted the cover name of Pat O'Leary, an improbable French Canadian. Although the O'Leary Line moved 600 evaders to England, both it and the Comet Line became cursed with infiltration from rogues, traitors and an Englishman named Harold Cole. A small time crook in England prior to the war, Cole somehow ended up with MI9. O'Leary became suspicious of Cole and his high living as well as his propensity to pick up and discard women. Cole was apprehended for misappropriation of MI9 funds, but escaped and later planted several spies in the line. He provided the Germans with enough information to infiltrate and virtually smash the O'Leary Line. O'Leary was arrested in March 1943 and sent to Dachau concentration camp.

Although Cole was the primary traitor, Roger Leneveu or "Roger Le Legionnaire" was also instrumental in the penetration of the O'Leary Line while Prosper Desitter and Jacques Desoubrie were responsible for the destruction of the Comet Line in Paris. Although all were eventually shot, their actions resulted in the death of at least 150 patriots.

In the months that followed, both the RAF and U.S. 8th Air Force suffered particularly heavy losses and the number of evaders rose sharply. The RAF opened its Battle of Berlin in late August and lost some 875 men over a period of 12 days. Long-range daylight bombing without adequate fighter protection to the target brought even heavier losses for the 8th Air Force. In one six day period in October 1943, it lost 1,480 airmen.

MI9 sought a cross-Channel route, but the first attempt failed and on November 30, 1943, Canadians Lucien Dumais and Ray LaBrosse landed south of Paris to salvage the operation. Both had been captured at Dieppe and escaped. Now in the service of MI9, their task was to establish contact in Paris and seek a link on the coast of Brittany. Soon a line ran from Paris to an isolated house at Plouha on the Brittany coast. The first successful boat evacuation from *La Maison d'Alphonse* occurred late in January 1944. The line drew on numerous safe houses and the colonies of airmen who were now being sheltered in three wooded areas near Rennes in the Ardennes and in the forest of Freteval.

The Shelburne Line evacuated 365 evaders and the security and discipline Dumais and LaBrosse imposed was responsible for much of the success in the Bonapart section of the line. The courage of patriots like Francois Kerambrun was also a key factor. Kerambrun was a driver, the last link between a chain of safe houses and *La Maison d'Alphonse*. On one occasion, Kerambrun piled 20 American evaders into his truck in broad daylight. It was the alternative to being caught after curfew and Kerambrun's cover story was that he was taking workmen to do a rush job.

His cover story was put to a severe test when a truck loaded with evaders was impaled on the spike of a tank trap. Kerambrun had some 15 men out heaving-ho when two gendarmes approached. When the cover story suddenly became implausible he decided to tell the truth and trust to their patriotism ... or kill the gendarmes. Fortunately, they were patriotic.

Some 1,975 Commonwealth airmen became evaders and many of the Canadians have made at least one pilgrimage to Europe, seeking the place where a look or a whispered word changed their lives. Above all, they returned seeking the ordinary people whose extraordinary courage brought about that change. The RAF Escape and Evasion Society was formed in 1945 to remember and aid helpers that suffered long-term effects from imprisonment while mending broken wings for some 3,000 Allied airmen. The Canadian branch of the RAF Escape and Evasion Society has had over 200 helpers as guests. Time has burnished the bond between helper and evader. A Belgian guest at the Society's annual meeting in Brockville, Ont., in 1997 started a run on Kleenex when he said, "I don't forget those men who came to us and are unfortunately not among us."

As recently as June 2002, the link between evader and helper was reinforced when Ken Woodhouse of Saskatoon returned to Paris where a plaque was being unveiled in a high school. It honoured Maurice and Marguerite Cavalier, two helpers who aided Ken when his aircraft developed engine failure near Paris. The Cavaliers lived in the school and helped several airmen before the Gestapo arrested Maurice. Marguerite insisted on going with her husband who later died in a work camp. Addressing a class at the high school, Ken Woodhouse reminded the students of what they owe the Cavaliers. He finished: "No greater love has any man than to lay down his life for his friends. But he did that for me ... and I was a stranger!"

## BEHIND THE WIRE

"Abandon aircraft! Jump! Jump!" These were the last words some 2,500 Canadian airmen heard or uttered in a doomed aircraft over Hitler's Europe. Pilots of single-engined aircraft just jumped. The lucky ones ended up as prisoners of war or *Kriegsgefangener* or as they defiantly and proudly called themselves just plain "Kriegies." Tony Little of Ottawa, heard those fateful words from his pilot as fire ate away the wing of their Halifax one night in January 1945. He jumped and landed hard and spent hours drifting in and out of focus with a concussion. He later recalled seeing a pigpen, a house, and a jail with a helmeted guard seemingly 12 feet tall. The second time he saw the guard, Little had recovered somewhat and the guard had shrunk to human proportions. It was the first day of Tony Little's life as a Kriegie.

Pilot Sgt. Gilles Lamontagne screamed those words the evening a night-fighter attacked his aircraft. The cockpit was burning and the third attack set the entire Halifax ablaze and Lamontagne joined the fraternity of Kriegies. He later went on to become mayor of Quebec City for 12 years, defence minister and lieutenant-governor of Quebec. A former minister of Veterans Affairs, Roger Teillet, was also a Kriegie as was Bruce Brittain, a former deputy minister. They all fell from the sky and went on to the life of the Kriegie. Each later became proud members of one of the most exclusive clubs in Canada: the RCAF POW Association.

Today DND is concerned with post traumatic stress disorder and understandably so. But throughout our history any Canadian engaged in combat was subject to stress. For most bomber crewmen there was a terrible sameness to it all - night, cold, cramped quarters, darkness, blinding light, an explosion, the unmistakable stench of cordite, fire, a leap into darkness and the terror of being alone in hostile country. Many were not quite sure whether they were victims of flak or night-fighters, but in a matter of seconds - minutes at most - they were transported from the familiar surroundings of a bomber to the loneliness and terror of being a hunted animal in enemy territory.

S. Leslie, of Vancouver, was a pilot of a Halifax attacked by a night-fighter while bombing marshalling yards at St. Elaine. The bomber began to burn and the

enemy was raking them on another pass from below. Leslie gave orders to abandon aircraft and had just released the hatch over his head when the Halifax exploded. He was blown clear, the only member of the crew to survive.

Ed Rae's pilot gave orders to abandon aircraft and Rae moved back from the
rear turret to the escape hatch. The aircraft was filled with flame, smoke and
explosions. A burning city moved across the open escape hatch and Rae paused.
He decided to wait until the bomber landed and then he'd simply walk away. But
then he said he saw his mother through the smoke who asked, "Eddie are you just
going to stand there looking stupid?" It was enough to send Ed Rae through the
hatch.

Jim Finnie of Ottawa, moved from the rear turret of his doomed Halifax to
find the mid-upper gunner struggling with a popped parachute. Finnie told him
to grab silk and they went through the hatch together and miraculously the mid-
upper's chute was not tangled and they floated down to captivity with a strange
sense of relief. Floating down was a nice interlude, according to one Kriegie who
clung to his parachute ring because he heard it was worth 20 quid on the black
market.

The experience of fighter pilots was slightly different. They usually went down
in daylight and often from low level. Don Morrison flew fighter cover for the
American B-17s that hit the Luftwaffe drome at Abbeville on the day of the
Dieppe raid. On the way home his section of Spitfires peeled off towards Dieppe
where he shot down a FW 190 whose exploded debris knocked out Morrison's
Spitfire. He jumped and was rescued. The day's action brought his score to six
enemy aircraft destroyed and five probables. Less than three months later he was
shot down over St. Omer. His left leg was blown off and remained in the aircraft
as he finally fought clear. He had no recollection of landing and was unconscious
for 10 days.

Phase two of the Kriegie's trauma came when they touched ground or water.
Stan Croft didn't get to use his parachute. Something hit the starboard engine
flipped the bomber over on its back and it plunged into the water. Croft was
knocked unconscious, but came to in the water. A Dutch fisherman picked up
Croft and his pilot, but their rescuer was later forced to surrender them to Germans.

Ed Rae lay on his back for some time feeling very alone. His crew was scattered
and he had no idea where he was. He spent the night in a haystack and the next
day stole a bike, which he rode until it got a flat tire. He abandoned the bike and
in a small village heard footsteps behind him. Then a guttural voice ordered:
"Come!"

Gib McElroy of Ottawa, evaded capture for three days after jumping. At this
stage of the war, just before D-Day, they had been told not to contact the under-

ground; the underground would contact them. On the third day at dusk, lonely and a little afraid the 19-year-old decided to try the clergy for help. As he walked towards the church, he heard someone behind him ask: " English?"

"Canadian!" McElroy replied as he turned and faced the gun of a collaborator.

When Leslie became an evader. The Belgian underground worked him into their system and he was moved from place to place for weeks. They provided him with civilian clothing and identification. But a mole was at work. One night as he was sent to a safe house the escape line was decimated. Leslie remained there unattended as that particular cell in the line collapsed. Three days later, he established contact with the escape line and was sent to Namur in the Ardennes.

He was apprehended in a small village and became prisoner first of the Luftwaffe and then the Gestapo - the two organizations that waged war for the souls, minds, and bodies of Allied airmen. Leslie was taken to Gestapo headquarters at St. Giles prison in Brussels where he was grilled repeatedly for weeks. As the British closed on Brussels, the Gestapo became preoccupied with escape. Prisoners were loaded onto a train, which, thanks to Belgian crews, suffered numerous delays in getting out of the station. Leslie escaped at the outskirts of Brussels and was one of the first POWs to enjoy the sight of the mighty Gestapo running for the Fatherland.

Most Kriegies went through a sieve. After landing, if not immediately apprehended by the military, they ended up at the local police station, which turned them over to the military. A few lucky ones chanced upon the underground and their routes were different, but most were pushed through the system to the point of interrogation. Sometimes Luftwaffe interrogations were a piece of cake. They were creative and relied on the bond between airmen where the enemy would try to engage prisoners in "shop talk." But sometimes it boomeranged. One Kriegie ended his session with information that the Germans had a flying bomb.

From interrogation, Kriegies went to a *Dulag* - a holding area for the *Stalags* or prison camps. Here the struggle for survival took on a different tone. Some 10,000 British and Commonwealth airmen were prisoners of war, but only about 30 actually escaped. Yet this was the motivating force that sustained most Kriegies. However, it would be wrong to suggest that every POW was filled with an inordinate drive to escape. First, the chances of escape diminished dramatically once a prisoner reached a Stalag. But here the concept of escape became a way of twigging the Hun's nose and keeping him occupied.

For instance at Barth, a camp on the Baltic, 53 tunnels were dug in less than two years, but only four men escaped and only one reached England. However, tunnel digging remained the Kriegies number one sport. Each camp had an escape committee that co-ordinated tunnel jobs and brought the amazing resources of the POW community to bear on a project.

The most famous escape attempt occurred at Stalag Luft 3 in Sagan where 600 Kriegies were gainfully employed for months. Several Canadians were key members of the well-organized committee. Although the movie *The Great Escape* was disturbingly accurate in some respects, it had an identity crisis when it portrayed the work of Canadians such as Barry Davidson.

Davidson, of Calgary, was shot down early in the war and had spent almost three years behind the wire when the Sagan escape was planned in 1943. But he doesn't appear in the film. Instead, James Garner played the role of a Yankee called Scrounger, which was actually Davidson's role. Davidson had cultivated German ferrets and was able to have ink maps and other items smuggled in.

Keith Ogilvie of Ottawa acquired a ferret's wallet while both of them watched a baseball game, giving the committee access to identity documents. He later returned the wallet and the grateful guard became a source of many gifts.

A tailor shop was set up, false identity cards run off and photographs taken. While these preparations were underway Wally Floody of Toronto, "The Tunnel King," took charge of tunnelling 240 feet beyond the wire. Seventy-six escaped and 73 were recaptured and 50 were shot including Canadians James Wernham, George Wiley, Patrick Langford, George McGill, Henry Birkland and Gordon Kidder.

The toughest battle Kriegies had to fight was with themselves and putting time to good use. Barry Davidson helped organize hockey games on rinks flooded by buckets. Then there was theatre. Art Crichton fronted the sweetest band west of the Elbe. Ken Hyde embarked on a career as a photographer, a strange choice considering the restriction of cameras. Yet he compiled a remarkable array of photographs and each represented a personal victory against the Hun.

Books took on a new meaning for active young men and Canadian Legion Educational Services sent over 60,000 textbooks and 1,900 university courses through the Red Cross. One Kriegie decided on theology. When the textbook finally arrived, he leafed through it with a deepening frown because it contained nothing but religion. But sometimes it worked. The former brew-master at Stalag 3 became a bishop in later life.

By January 1945, the Russians started a drive on a 100-mile front and 10,000 POWs and thousands of civilians started a withdrawal in -20 degree temperature. It became a death march for captive and captor alike. Although camps like Stalag 3 had a store of Red Cross parcels, the men were forced to leave with what they could carry either on their backs or on homemade sleds. Soon exposure took its toll and the rigours of the march hit the guards hardest because they were older. The weakest rode in Kriegie sleds. Some even gave their weapons to Kriegies to carry in a strange juxtaposition of roles.

Several camps were involved and the grim episode has never been adequately documented because of the confusion. Some Kriegies were loaded onto boxcars, 65 to a car becoming a tangle of arms and legs where there was no food or sanitation and dysentery was common. On at least one occasion the doors remained locked for three days. This was the point when the last reserves of courage began to slip away. One man later recalled eating a handful of oats like a horse and then sobbing on a comrade's shoulder. Some fell into Russian hands and were not released until three months after VE-Day. There is suspicion that some were never released.

## THE DEVIL'S DUES

When they cleared the trees from the mountain five miles from Weimar, the Nazis left one standing. It was the tree under which the 19th century German intellect Johann Wolfgang von Goethe contemplated the human condition. The 40-hectare site upon which the Nazis built also dealt with the human condition, but the sign over the front gate at Buchenwald urged all to "Give the devil his due."

It started as a work camp for Jews and political undesirables. Commandant Karl Koch contracted prison labour out to private industry and kept the money and died a very rich man when the SS finally caught up with him. His wife Ilse, the "red witch/bitch of Buchenwald," was a sexual pervert who also had eyes for the boys in order to make lampshades out of their skin.

By 1942 the devil's dues at Buchenwald were demanding medical experiments on helpless victims. Inmates were injected with various diseases and doctors watched and took notes as inmates deteriorated and died. A cure for homosexuality also failed. Buchenwald's three crematoriums could process 400 bodies a day and during the war the camp claimed 60,000 lives from various causes. Three of these were Canadian.

Buchenwald and other concentration camps were secretive, end-of-the line camps for Jews, political prisoners, various underground criminals and homosexuals. Canada's first tragic link with Buchenwald probably came when Frank Pickersgill and John Macalister, two Hamilton-born agents with the SOE, were captured. They parachuted north of Valencay, France, in June 1943. Pickersgill, brother of Senator Jack Pickersgill, was ordered to establish an underground cell, but the Germans had penetrated the network. A few days after landing, the Gestapo captured Pickersgill and Macalister after they were betrayed. The two underwent 14 months of interrogation and torture.

While they languished in a Polish concentration camp, the enemy set up a phoney cell in Pickersgill's name. They called up 15 equipment drops from the British, including $40,000 and about a dozen agents - all of whom fell into the arms of the SS. Among these was Canadian Romeo Sabourin who lied about his age to get into the Fusiliers de Montreal. He completed SOE training in 1944 as a wireless operator and literally jumped into the guns of the SS. Wounded after a gunfight, he was then taken prisoner. It took British intelligence at SOE a full year to suspect something was amiss. When they did, they proposed to the German who had been masquerading as Pickersgill that the SOE should send an agent over to have a chat with the Canadian. The chat would take place by radiophone from the ground to an aircraft circling overhead.

Pickersgill was brought to Paris from Ratvitch, and after repeated offers of good things from the SS, he repeatedly refused to co-operate. Finally, he attacked a guard with a bottle, knocking him to the floor. He ran downstairs, fought his way through a guards' station and jumped from a second floor window. The SS opened up with Schmeissers machine guns and Pickersgill was hit four times. He ran on but then collapsed. Pickersgill and Macalister, who was then in a Paris prison, became part of the manifest of some 37 agents bound for Buchenwald in mid-August 1944.

The first Canadian to actually end up in Buchenwald was George Rodrigues, a member of the Corps of Signals who transferred to MI9 to work in a British escape organization. Rodrigues jumped into France in August 1943, and worked for two months before being arrested. After prolonged torture, he was sent to Buchenwald and remained there until the camp was evacuated in the final days of the war. He died of malnutrition and tuberculosis three weeks after VE-Day. All the Canadians in the SOE knew the price of capture and several like Gustave and Bieler paid that price.

A month before D-Day, Hitler passed an edict which said enemy airmen would be shot without a court martial if they fired on German airmen who had baled out; if they attacked aircraft which made emergency landings; or if they attacked public transport or strafed civilians. This came during the period when Bomber Command was attacking transportation in occupied Europe. Technicalities such as the Geneva Convention, which discouraged shooting prisoners of war, were overcome by declaring airmen criminals rather than prisoners of war. This opened the route to firing squads or gas ovens for allied airmen.

Cal Willis of Ottawa, was a bomb-aimer on a Halifax which fell to night-fighters over a target southwest of Paris. He jumped and seconds later the aircraft exploded, killing five members of the crew. A tree broke his fall and he hung suspended three feet from the ground. After disengaging, he stumbled into a field where he fell asleep and was awakened by a farmer who put him in touch with the Resistance. They took Willis to a safe house where he joined his navigator Ernie Shepherd. "The place was full of spies and we listened to the BBC that night and everybody got excited,"[47] Willis recalled. A coded message following the news announced an invasion within 48 hours.

The downside was that the Resistance people suddenly went about other priorities such as blowing up bridges. Willis and Shepherd were driven to Dourdan and deposited in a second house. A couple of days later, 12 cars and 50 Gestapo screeched into the yard. Willis and Shepherd were captured and the convoy moved towards Paris. They were grilled for some time at Gestapo headquarters and then ended in Fresnes prison, which, among other things, was a clearinghouse for downed airmen en route to captivity. Two months later, Willis and Shepherd were stuffed into a cattle car with some 90 assorted prisoners. It was standing room only with a can in the middle of the car as the only hint of sanitation. Willis shrugged off the toilet facilities, saying: "They didn't feed us enough to induce much action anyway."

The only break in the six-day trip was when bombing blocked the entrance to a tunnel and passengers had to walk around to a second train waiting at the other end. Upon arrival at Buchenwald, they were stripped and moved into a large room. The doors were locked and they waited in terror for gas to hiss from the overhead jets. Instead, all they got was a shower.

This was typical of the subtle cruelty of the place where men and women shuffled by like walking dead. Names were called, and pathetic groups moved towards a crematorium. Willis later recalled the insistence of doomed men who clung to the hope they would be shot instead of being hung or sent to the gas chamber.

Bill Gibson of Halifax, was shot down early in July while bombing marshalling yards south of Paris. Gibson and his pilot jumped and were picked up by the Resistance. After about two weeks, a collaborator turned them in to the Gestapo. At Fresnes prison Gibson spent 32 days in solitary. Then, like Cal Willis, he was bound for Buchenwald on August 19th. They were two of 27 RCAF airmen held at Buchenwald, part of 167 Allied airmen who became victims of Hitler's edict. Eleven days before the airmen arrived at Buchenwald, 37 male and female agents were rounded up in Paris prisons. Among them were Frank Pickersgill, John Macalister and Romeo Sabourin.

At Buchenwald, they awaited death from disease or execution. Hundreds of prisoners died each day and the dead piled up undisturbed as fellow prisoners drew their meagre rations. Eventually, the dead were thrown outside like cordwood. The day after the airmen arrived, the Americans bombed a factory near the camp. The prisoners were forced to lie on the ground with machine guns at their heads and were ordered not to move. The bombing was precise, but shrapnel hit two prisoners.

Fifteen of Pickersgill's group were executed on September 6th and three days later the three Canadians became part of a second group marked for death. They formed up when summoned and then tried to make like defiant guardsmen. Pickersgill at the head of a file still suffered from four open wounds, malnutrition and brutal beatings. He staggered as he moved off. His broken body and defiant voice led the others in song as they marched across the compound. They sang "Madelon" for the French at Pickersgill's side, "Alouette" for Romeo Sabourin and "Tipperary." That night they were beaten and sent to the bunker adjacent to the crematorium. There were no last rites, but a Roman Catholic priest prayed outside the bunker all night. The next morning, he heard scuffling and defiant noises from the crematorium and later the cries of men being hung on hooks while being strangled. That night the chimney belched its smoke, rendering the devil his due.

The 27 Canadian airmen consigned to Buchenwald were spared the fate of the SOE agents, but for up to three months they were subject to life and death in hell itself. Inmates slept on shelves, six abreast in layers of four. Day began at 4 a.m. with a cumbersome process where prisoners stood in the yard for up to five hours while being counted. Breakfast consisted mostly of acorn coffee and usually a second roll-call followed. "The Germans were notorious counters," Willis recalled. There was little food and no exercise and Willis lost 40 pounds in the three months before they were transferred to Stalag Luft 3. The experience of the RCAF veterans who survived Buchenwald took a sad turn following the war. The German government paid compensation to 11 nations whose men were held in the death camp, but Canada was not included. Britain's share was soon gobbled up and members of the RCAF, RNZAF and RAAF did not receive a cent. Restitution was finally awarded to surviving Canadians by 2005 and Cal Willis invited the author to lunch with the German government finally picking up the tab.

**ABOVE:** *The massive raid destroyed or damaged some 300 Allied planes, mostly on the ground, but the raid broke the back of the Luftwaffe, which lost 214 aircrew who were at this point irreplaceable. (PMR 74-318)*

**OPPOSITE PAGE:** *Mitchells of 180 Squadron were out on an operation in the Ardennes the morning an estimated 800 enemy aircraft struck 16 Allied bases. (PL-30294)*

# ❦ SECOND TAF: THE SOLDIER'S FRIEND

*The bomb-line for the B-17s was a matter of yards and Canadian troops were on the other side of it, including one pilot's brother.*

*AFTER THE BATTLE OF BRITAIN* the emphasis in the air war shifted to bombers, and the hope that 4,000 of these planes would bring about the German surrender. For a period, fighters and fighter-bombers were relegated to sweeps over occupied Europe but a few leaders remembered the work of the Desert Air Force and the lessons of North Africa. In the summer of 1943, Canadian Spitfire Wing #126 was formed and it soon became part of the 2nd Tactical Air Force (2nd TAF). With the invasion of Europe, it would be part of the historic struggle where air power tilted the scales in the land battle for Europe.

The first elements of #126 Wing reached Ver-sur-Mer the day after D-Day, but pilots from five Spitfire squadrons were still flying from England. D-Day had been a disappointment for Allied fighters, but W/Com George Keefer of Charlottetown, got a Ju-88 the next day while Sqd/Ldr Greg Cameron, of Toronto, got two. Four days after the assault on the beaches, 128 sorties were flown from the field known as B3.

Montgomery called on Bomber Command prior to an attack on July 8th. Some 450 heavies hit the outskirts of Caen just before midnight the night before. By the time the Canadian troops attacked the following morning, the enemy had fully recovered and the operation became a stalemate two days later. Neither Montgomery nor Harris had addressed the problem of timing the bombing to coincide with the ground attack.

Some 11 days later, Montgomery again called upon Bomber Harris, who resented the intrusion into his plan to bomb Germany into submission. Montgomery wanted help and implied that Operation GOODWOOD would be a breakout. Some 2,000 bombers again hit the outskirts of Caen, but once again Montgomery let the attack falter, and most of the Allied commanders were livid at Montgomery's failure and apparent deception. The Americans to the west had fought their way some 80 kilometre's inland and Flying Fortresses were used on enemy troops and, unfortunately, the Allies as well. On the first day of the American assault, bombings killed 25 American troops and wounded 115. The following day, 1,800 B-17s wheeled towards the men on the ground, killing 150 and wounding 490 as the tragic summer of friendly fire became a reality.

The Germans counterattacked in force after the Americans took Avranches, an advance of some 100 kilometres from Cherbourg. In a summer that had seen little but a battle of egos in the British sector, air power was about to take on a new dimension. Typhoons of 2nd TAF began taking on enemy tanks while American fighters concentrated on possible fighters. Rocket projectiles pinpointed quickly moving targets and communications remained open throughout the afternoon. By evening the enemy was on the defensive.

That night Bomber Command was brought in to again support the Canadians south of Caen. Although bombing was good, dust and smoke built up to such an extent that one-third of the bombers were ordered to abort. Two days later, some 500 U.S. heavies bombed short while attempting to assist the Canadians and Poles. Richard Bison of the North Shore regiment was one of 300 casualties. The images of that day still haunt him: "They flew across our flank and seemed to leave something behind. Then we saw but couldn't believe it. Bombs! Hundreds of bombs sliding across the sky right at us."[48]

One week later on August 14th, Bomber Command inflicted more casualties on Canadian and Polish troops. Some 300 men were killed, wounded or missing. This time the tragedy deepened because 44 of the 77 erring aircraft were Canadian. Confusion over smoke signals was key to the disaster and Harris divested himself of responsibility by blaming his crews and hinting that the army was at fault. The fact is that Bomber Command was apparently ignorant of a five month-old standing order from the Supreme Headquarters Allied Expeditionary Force that proclaimed yellow smoke, flares and panels should be used for identification purposes between air and ground units. Yellow was not to be used for any other purpose. This order got to all services involved in the invasion, but according to Harris, it never reached Bomber Command. The bombers used yellow target markers while the men on the ground used yellow flares for identification. The closer the first wave of bombers got to the troops, the more smoke the army sent up to identify their positions. On at least four occasions, these troops were bombed.

In a 12-page document, Harris responded to criticism, insisting that no one had told Bomber Command about the standing order. His senior staff officer had assured him that there would be no possibility of conflicting pyrotechnics. One Auster pilot gallantly flew his small observation aircraft into the bomber stream firing red flares in an unsuccessful attempt to divert the bombers. Instead of recommending the army pilot for an award, Harris not only accused him of compounding the confusion, but also ranted for some length about how such a sensational story could be released to the press.

He then called for an investigation and went to great lengths to spread the blame to his #6 Group crews. He observed: "Air bombers as a whole are by no means of outstanding intelligence. They are in the main selected as such because, although passing other standards for aircrew, they are the least likely to make efficient pilots or navigators."[49] Harris also took action against crews who did not follow a timed run from Caen. This included revoking any acting rank for squadron and flight leaders and banning all crews to other squadrons. While communications between Bomber Command and the army hit a nadir, things were improving for the 2nd TAF. Air Marshal Arthur Coningham's voice became one of many critical of Montgomery's conduct of the war. He is alleged to have despised Montgomery to such an extent that he refused to operate on the same continent with him. However, Coningham was extremely fortunate to have A/V/M Harry Broadhurst as his deputy in France. Broadhurst did a masterful job of keeping army-TAF communications open.

Broadhurst and his men worked and lived close to the army. This gave them a new perspective on the war and what was required of them. What evolved was a pattern where on any given night RAF and army officers met to study bombing objectives for the following day, often based on photos Spitfires brought back. A general program for the day would be established with the understanding that a considerable amount of freelance air support would be required during the day. After initial objectives were hit, the taxi rank on fighter bases came into play to support army needs. Instead of calling up a cab, the army called up a Typhoon. On the key issue of communications, it was impossible for the army to contact Bomber Command once a mission was mounted, but 2nd TAF had a mechanism in place whereby an order from brigade level could scrub a mission.

General Patton's American tanks continued their swing until they were within

20 miles of linking up with the Canadians and Poles who had encountered stiff resistance south of Caen. As they struggled southward, Montgomery ordered Patton to stand at Argentan. He wanted no American troops on his designated battleground. Meanwhile, as the retreating Germans were compressed into a narrowing gap, the whole area became a massive killing ground as Mitchells, Mosquitos, Typhoons, Spitfires and Thunderbolts brought traffic to a standstill. The day before the gap was closed on August 19th, 2nd TAF claimed 3,000 vehicles. For miles the stench of burning flesh and a pall of oily smoke marked the remains of some 10,000 dead as Allied troops rounded up 50,000 prisoners. Air power had truly become a key component in the land battle, but at a high cost.

As the war moved inland, 2nd TAF continued to hammer tactical targets. The campaign moved north to the days before the Rhine crossing. One B-25 captain huddled with his crew before takeoff. He made a few quick calculations, "Let's think about where those buggers drop," he urged, "My brother will probably be 1,000 yards away."


## THEIR FINEST HOUR

Winston Churchill notwithstanding, the finest hour for Canadian fighter pilots was not the Battle of Britain. Canadians served with great distinction in Malta and North Africa and in the three months following D-Day, nine squadrons of Canadian Spitfire wings accounted for 239 enemy aircraft. Along with three Canadian Typhoon squadrons, the Spitfires were also a major factor in the 2nd TAF's claim of over 3,000 vehicles destroyed in one day in the Falaise Gap.

When the Spitfire wings moved up to Belgium the tempo of the air war had slowed, but this changed shortly after Operation MARKET GARDEN. In an explosion of air combat, the Canadians accounted for at least 95 enemy aircraft in less than a week. MARKET GARDEN was a combined British-U.S. plan to seize several bridges across the Maas, the Waal and Lower Rhine. American airdrops and landings from Eindhoven north to Nijmegen secured a 40-mile corridor, but the British operation in the Arnhem area was a disaster.

Two Canadian Spitfire wings were drawn into a massive battle with the Luftwaffe over this disputed corridor particularly in the Eindhoven area. A third wing had been disbanded and squadrons were reassigned to the remaining Canadian wings and an RAF wing, while three squadrons of Typhoons were then active in the theatre. #126 Wing was based at Le Coulet near Louvain and #127 Wing was about to move from near Brussels to Grave, Holland by September. General der Flieger Galland, the Luftwaffe's fighter chief, later explained that the resurgence of German air power, which manifested itself on September 25th, was the result of receiving more than 3,000 single-engine planes in a month.[50]

Perhaps the most telling comment on four years of RAF strategic bombing was the fact that over 4,000 aircraft were produced that month in Germany. Many of the German fighters went against American heavies where within a week they destroyed 105 bombers. But 200 fighters were diverted to the Nijmegen area and on September 25th the two irresistible forces met.

On the third patrol of the day, a squadron of Spitfires from #126 Wing ran into a pack of hostiles attacking the bridge at Nijmegen When the Canadians attacked, the Me-109s jettisoned their bombs and the top cover fighters also challenged the Spitfires. F/Lt George Johnson of Oakville, Ont., got two and damaged one, while F/Lt Russ Bouskill of Toronto got a FW 190 and damaged a Me. On the next patrol that day by #412 Squadron, F/Lt Don Laubmann, of Provost, Alta, a skilled and patient veteran who had nursed five victories for the year, added one and within the next six days would add eight more. By the last patrol of the day, #126 Wing accounted for five enemy aircraft.

Nine aircraft from #127 Wing ran into 30 enemy fighters and F/O D. Kimball of St George, N.B., brought down two. Other claims include one destroyed and four damaged. F/Lt. John Mitchner of Saskatoon scored a double and the wing ended the day with seven victories and five losses. The Silver Foxes, a Canadian squadron, had gone to an RAF wing, scored three additional victories on the opening day of the great air battle. Don Laubmann got three the next day while F/Lt. Rod Smith of Regina, added two and F/Lt. Bill Banks and F/O Phil Charron both of Ottawa brought the count up to seven for #412 Squadron. Charron flew one of four Spitfires that 40 enemy fighters attacked and was the only survivor.

The Canadians accounted for 35 machines on the third day, but lost Wally McLeod, the top-scoring RCAF pilot. With 21 victories, Sqd/Ldr McLeod of Edmonton was driven by a desire to be top gun. Like Beurling, McLeod was an incredible shot having destroyed a FW 190 with 13 rounds from each of his twin cannons. W/Com Johnny Johnson was flying with McLeod's squadron when they vectored onto the Emerich area. They spotted nine 109s some 4,000 feet below them and attacked line astern. Johnson saw the leader of the MEs pull up in an Immelmann gaining altitude. He warned McLeod as he closed on his own target. After sending down the flamer, Johnson called repeatedly for McLeod but there was no answer.

Action diminished on day four with the Canadian wings counting two destroyed and four damaged. F/Lt. Johnny McColl of Stoney Creek, Ont., had a brief encounter with a jet and while he scored hits on a Me-262, it pulled up and left him standing still. Although it had a 100 m.p.h. edge on the Spitfire, the 262 had a history of delays in becoming operational. Hitler insisted the natural fighter become a blitz bomber. In August 1944, as the first nine were delivered to the front, two of them broke up upon leaving Germany and two wiped out during landing. McColl's encounter presumably was with one of the five survivors. Within a few weeks Hitler would change his mind about the jet bombers and Galland would take delivery of the first Me-262s to be designated as fighters.

On the morning patrol of the fifth day, Rod Smith led #401 Squadron against 30 Me-109s and scored two victories. F/Lt. Hedley Everard of Simcoe, Ont., also claimed two. Their engagement was a prelude to a day of intense action in which #126 Wing brought its total aircraft destroyed in five days to 48 while #127 Wing tallied 40. Including the six victories of the Silver Foxes and a final victory by the City of Oshawa Squadron, Canadian squadrons reached a total of at least 95 victories in six days. However as Typhoons were also drawn into the combat, the total Canadian victories probably reached 105.

After its September losses, the Luftwaffe brought more jet fighter-bombers into the sector. W/Com Johnny Johnson tangled with one on the morning of October 5th while flying with #127 Wing. According to Johnson, the few rounds he got off were nothing but a gesture of impotence against the jet. Shortly after noon that same day, Rod Smith led #401 Squadron down on an upcoming jet over Nijmegen Several pilots were involved in what followed. Hedley Everard fired a burst from 150 yards. The 262 belched smoke, but accelerated. F/Lt. John MacKay of Cloverdale, B.C., followed it making strikes on the fuselage and wing root. Two other pilots made passes at the jet, which was then on fire. The burning jet tried to ram Rod Smith who fired two bursts at it as it overflew him and crashed two miles outside of Nijmegen

F/Lt Richard "Dick" Audet of Lethbridge, Alta. had been doomed to fly a drogue for eight months before getting into action. Aerial combat eluded him until late December when he led a section from #411 Squadron on patrol in the Osnabruck area. Alerted by control, they turned towards the Rhine and ran into a flight of enemy fighters. Audet dove on a dozen enemy fighters and within 10 minutes was an ace, the only RCAF pilot to destroy five enemies in one sortie. He added six other victories before his death from flak while strafing a train.

The quality of German fighters during this campaign was very high and the performance of the Canadians contributed to the demise of the Luftwaffe. Although the German fighter arm grew stronger in terms of machines it never did recover from the loss of experienced pilots. Its deathblow would come on January 1st, but perhaps its most critical hour was the finest hour for the Canadians of #126 and #127 Wings.

## THE GREAT BLOW

Nineteen-forty-five was less than eight hours old when the Mitchells of #180

Squadron barked surly profanities at the cold Belgian morning. Engines warmed up and the machines rumbled out of dispersal, with their slipstreams blasting snow along the icy perimeter path to the runway. Nose down, like angry hippos, they charged the runway and overflew the inevitable cemetery at its end. For some reason, the RAF always selected runways near graveyards and B-58 near Brussels was no exception.

The medium bombers formed up in boxes of six and climbed to height en route to Dasburg, a target which didn't mean any more to the crews than other targets in the Ardennes where they had been bombing over the past two weeks. As they neared the target, Cosy Cot came over the radio transmission to tell Blanket that its "little friends" would not be with them. There would be no fighter escort for the bombers. If anybody thought about it at all it was to mutter something unflattering about fighter pilots. How come they could get juiced up on New Year's Eve and sleep it off next day?

What the B-25 crews did not know at that moment was that most fighter pilots in Holland, Belgium and France were about to become totally engaged as the Luftwaffe made its last stand. It climaxed a series of events during which the capable and renowned General Adolf Galland had more trouble than usual with Herman Göring and Adolf Hitler.

Göring had fallen under the spell of a lobby that wanted to produce thousands of Heinkel He-162 jets, although Galland considered them inferior to the Me-262. Galland's opposition to production of an inferior aircraft widened the rift between him and Göring. During the summer what was referred to as a "Great Blow" scenario was planned whereby 3,000 fighters would pounce on Allied bombers and destroy up to 500. Galland's pilots sat in their aircraft day after day awaiting word to strike. The plan depended on a concerted strike, but before it went into action Galland was ordered to send his reserves to another location.

Galland was kept in the dark about the Ardennes offensive until two days before it kicked off on December 17th, explaining the lack of air support when *Generalfeldmarschall* Gerd von Rundsledt's Panzers started rolling. However, the revised version of the Great Blow took place on January 1st when the Panzer thrust lost its drive. Over 800 fighters took off from 30 bases. They formed into three groups each led by a Ju-88. Flying at treetop height, they targeted Allied airfields in Holland, Belgium and northern France.

Icy runways at Evere, near Brussels, delayed patrols by four Canadian Spitfire squadrons, although the Mitchells had taken off earlier. After runway sprinkling, F/Lt. Dave Harling led #416 Squadron around the perimeter track, and as he swung onto the runway, enemy fighters were attacking. Harling got off the ground long enough to shoot down one attacker, but he died seconds later as 60 fighters bombed and strafed.

Light anti-aircraft guns around the field soon pumped empty and enemy pilots strafed almost unopposed for 45 minutes. P/O Steve Butte of Waugh, Alta., returned from a weather recce with three pilots and they knocked down six enemy fighters, but had to retire when they ran out of ammunition. Eleven Spits were destroyed, 12 damaged and dozens of assorted aircraft were left burning on the major base.

At Heesch, in the Netherlands, two squadrons were out on fighter sweeps but 10 Spitfires from #401 Squadron managed to get off the ground. In a series of isolated dogfights that followed, F/Lt. Johnny Mackay, who had sent a FW 190 down in flames over the Reichwald Forest, spotted another on the tail of a Tempest. During his attack, he ran out of ammunition, but pursued the enemy who attempted a turn at low level and his port wing dug into a frozen lake. Mackay then sighted a Me-109, which he closed on and dominated without firing a shot. He literally forced the fighter into the ground where it exploded.

F/Lt. Donald "Chunky" Gordon of Edmonton, got two before he was shot down by friendly fire. #126 Wing claimed 19 enemy fighters for a loss of one pilot killed and one wounded. At Eindhoven, 16 Typhoons from #438 and #440 Squadrons were waiting to takeoff when the enemy struck. Two pilots got off but were shot down after bringing down an invader and the other Typhoons were riddled on the ground for 20 minutes.

It was interrupted only when four Typhoon pilots returned from a weather recce. The #439 pilots engaged 15 FW s and destroyed four. Six pilots from #440 Squadron returning from reconnaissance took on 19 hostiles and Sqd/Ldr Gordon Wonnacott of Edmonton, destroyed three and F/O Wally Woloschuk got one and damaged another. The raids inflicted heavy damage on 2nd TAF aircraft. While the official figure of Allied aircraft destroyed usually rounds out at 300, many on the damaged list never recovered. Considering the firepower brought against Allied bases, the loss of life was remarkably small. The Allies were able to replace aircraft, but the Luftwaffe lost 300 fighters, some 214 pilots of whom 59 were experienced flight leaders. "The Great Blow" became the assault that crippled the Luftwaffe.

**OPPOSITE PAGE:** *The politically motivated raid on Dresden killed an estimated 110,000 people. As public opinion stiffened, Winston Churchill censored his command for the raid he insisted upon.* (IWM)

# 🐚 THE CLOSING ACTS

*Bomber Command: More of the same*

**BOMBING OPERATIONS REVERTED TO** the RAF and the United States Army Air Forces (USAAF) in September and the High Command issued another directive that echoed the hopes of the Casablanca conference in 1943. Oil targets and tank and vehicle production would now be primary objectives for both air arms. But Bomber Harris was soon up to his old tricks as he launched the third Battle of the Ruhr.

Duisburg was struck twice within 14 hours and the Battle of the Ruhr was a revisitation of old targets, only this time crews were flying in daylight and could see the damage inflicted, as the war became a more personal thing. Harris maintained his distaste for panacea targets and his object was to flatten any areas that had been built up or had escaped damage in earlier raids. This does not suggest that Harris ignored oil targets. A week into the campaign, Six Group took part in an attack on an oil refinery at Wanne-Eickel where a chemical factory was destroyed. Smoke from the burning factory obscured the daylight target and the oil refinery escaped serious damage.

RAF Marshal Sir Charles Portal had become a convert of the oil campaign and grew increasingly concerned with the low priority Harris was giving it. In mid-January his difference of opinion with Harris came to a head and the latter threatened to resign. Portal backed off and withdrew his objections. American bombers considered oil as a priority target and although Bomber Command continued with area bombing, it did hit a number of oil plants in Western Germany in the process. The Ruhr campaign involved some 14,000 sorties and as Canadian Six Group observed its first anniversary most of the start-up bugs had been overcome. By the end of the war, it would have flown 40,822 sorties at a cost of 4,272 dead, but over 17,000 Canadians died in air action.

Unfortunately, less than three months from victory a pall was thrown over the work of Bomber Command and the sacrifice of more than 55,000 aircrew. Bomber Command became a ploy in Winston Churchill's political one-upmanship and the result was as morally devastating as the bombs that fell on Dresden.


## DEATH OF DRESDEN

The concept of using bombing to break a nation's will died hard. A month after the invasion, the chiefs-of-staff discussed a plan to strike Berlin with a catastrophic blow. The RAF's Sir Charles Portal later sent a revision to the others suggesting that a massive blow at some other city, which had not been extensively damaged, might be more effective in breaking morale. This idea remained on the backburner until the Russian offensive made it suddenly urgent. The rapid advance of Russian troops on Germany's eastern flank had high political ramifications. Britain and the U.S. wanted to encourage their ally while maintaining a degree of control over post-war spoils. One way of doing this was to select cities in the path of the advancing armies to impress the Russians. Just before he left for Yalta for a conference with Roosevelt and Stalin, Prime Minister Churchill ticked off the air minister for not taking action.

Referring to a previous message, Churchill's snarky memo to Sir Archibald Sinclair read: "I did not ask you about plans for harrying the German retreat from Breslau. I asked whether Berlin and no doubt other large cities in East Germany should not now be considered especially attractive targets. Pray report to me tomorrow what is going to be done."[51] Churchill's memo started a stampede at the Air Ministry and Bomber Command. The original Operation THUNDERCLAP was suddenly reborn and Dresden became the city to be sacrificed. Bomber Harris showed little enthusiasm for the target, but when it became official he raised no further objections. According to him, it was considered an important target by much more important people than him.

On February 13th, as crews from different groups sat through briefings, the theme varied from place to place. They all learned that Dresden was the target and the flight would be some 10 hours. But reasons for the operation varied. One group was told Dresden was being bombed because it was a railway centre, while another was assured it was attacking a German army headquarters. Canada's Six Group was told Dresden was an important industrial centre. The spin-doctors had been at work obscuring the fact that Dresden was marked for death because Churchill wanted to impress the Russians.

Dresden had little significant industry and had two previous bombings, which were not extensive. The population of 630,000 had at least doubled with refugees and some 26,000 Allied prisoners of war. In spite of the crowded conditions, residents of the city of old-world charm were beginning to hope that they might be spared. The RAF raid was planned in two waves with a lapse of three hours between each wave. The second blow was intended to catch enemy fighters back at their bases being rearmed and refuelled while fire-fighting crews would still be at work.

By 6 p.m. 244 Lancasters of the first wave were airborne and nine marker Mosquitos took off two hours later. At 10 o'clock the marker leader dropped the first flare on the Sports Stadium at Dresden. Citizens saw the brilliant red markers ring the *Sportzplatz* and within five minutes the first of the Lancasters were dropping 4,000-pound blockbusters followed by 750-pound incendiary containers.

There were neither flak nor fighters and the last bomber left in half an hour, leaving a wedge of flame that the second wave saw from 50 miles away three hours later. When the master bomber of the second wave reached the city a firestorm had started. Super heated air above the flames sucked cold air in from the sides setting up tornado-like conditions. At nearby Klotzche airfield, pilots of 18 Me-110 night-fighters sat in cockpits and waited for orders to scramble. But none came because the station commander was expecting a flight of transport aircraft from besieged Breslau. In a bizarre sequence, the drome's perimeter lights flashed on and off repeatedly while a Lancaster dropped a flare. This spooked ground crews who bolted for cover, leaving the start-up equipment unattended and the night-fighters on the ground.

The bombing went on with a terrible precision. Some crews felt guilty because there was neither flak nor fighters and as they poured their incendiaries into 40 square miles of flame, they created a beacon of terror that could be seen for 150 to 200 miles. As weary crews flew over East Anglia, American crews stood at their aircraft waiting for a weather update. By 8 a.m. some 450 Flying Fortresses took off for the third blow at Dresden. At noon they struck the devastated city again and this time long-range Mustang fighters strafed citizens. In view of the number of transients in the city, an accurate casualty count has never been determined but estimates ran as high as 150,000 dead. This was almost twice the number of dead at Hiroshima and the bombing created a strong backlash in London, Washington and around the world.

The Bishop of Chichester was a highly vocal critic of area bombing and a bitter debate erupted in the House of Commons. Sir Archibald Sinclair – the man who had been chastised by Churchill – abruptly left the House as a member delivered a devastating attack on the policy of area bombing. As criticism continued, Churchill – the man who demanded the raid – told the chiefs-of-staff, "It seems to me that the moment has come when the question of bombing German cities simply for the sake of increasing terror, though under other pretexts should be reviewed. ... The destruction of Dresden remains a serious query against the conduct of Allied bombing."[52]

Five weeks later, Churchill made his victory speech, but he had completely abandoned Bomber Command and the gallant 55,000 airmen who had died in pursuit of victory. In 1946 Harris left England unhonoured and unrecognized and it was not until 1953 that the government lifted the curse on Bomber Command and awarded Harris a baronetcy.

In comparing precision bombing to area bombing, many analysts felt that the latter failed to substantially diminish German war production. War production in the Reich actually increased between 1942 and the summer of 1944 although miles of real estate had been flattened. The Germans were quick to rebuild and decentralize production and this tied up some 500,000 to 800,000 labourers and almost a million men were needed to man flak guns. Although revered by former Bomber Command crews, Harris became the focus of criticism by historical revisionists. He was a stubborn, egotistical man who sometimes made faulty decisions as in the case of the Nuremberg raid. But he built up a force that put a difficult policy into action and while critics of area bombing point to its failure to bring Germany to its knees, many fail to consider the outcome had it not been implemented.

Sir Arthur Harris ended the war on a low note, just as his American friend Brig-Gen. Ira Eaker had been shoved offstage to the Mediterranean. However, Eaker fared much better than Harris in peacetime and later held many respected posts including president of the U.S. Strategic Institute. Eaker had an opportunity to talk to Albert Speer after the war and asked Hitler's former armament minister which type of bombing had been more devastating. Speer's reply spoke volumes for the work of the odd couple.

"It was a combination," he said.


## MANNA FROM HELL

The danger of widespread starvation in the cities of Western Holland became more acute as the war wound down. It led to critical food drops by Allied aircraft. Paul Burden of Fredericton later described what this meant to the crews.

"While my Pathfinder squadron started the month of April with raids on German targets, we ended up flying Operation MANNA. A truce had been arranged with the German commander in Holland allowing the RAF and the United States Air Force to fly food to the Dutch people.

"For our Dutch allies, it was manna from heaven. But my first operation turned out to be manna from a personal hell. With 38 operations in my book and sensing the end of it all, I was not disturbed when my name was not on the battle order for #405 Squadron for April 30th. I stood in the mess pondering the battle order, wondering if it was all going to end by simply not having your name posted on the bulletin board.

"Then Charlie rushed up well beyond the brink of despair. Charlie belonged to Meathead's crew. 'Paul,' he gasped, 'we need a driver. God do we need a driver!' My friend Meathead had expired from bottle fatigue. He was on the battle order and his aircraft awaited out at dispersal.

"Pencils always came out when a squadron prepared for an operation. A million clerks with sharp pencils figured out the cost of your flying gear, your parachute, and your sidearms ... whatever you drew and signed for before a flight. So in response to Charlie, I casually made my way out to V-Victor without any of that high tech flying stuff.

"I fired up the Lanc in routine fashion. The only abnormality was the near-body lying on the floor in the area normally occupied by the flight engineer. We warmed up and then the navigator reported the Gee wasn't working. Gee was some kind of electronic device the knowledge of which enabled navigators to assume a fleeting degree of superiority over pilots.

"In retrospect, the Gee failure was a mere bagatelle because any navigator who couldn't find Amsterdam or the Hague on a clear day would get lost on the way to the men's room and had no business on a Pathfinder squadron. The other curious aspect of the flight was that radio silence was being observed although the flight had been planned with the Germans. In fact, a bunch of them were sitting in the bleachers waiting for us to appear at a racetrack near The Hague.

"But old habits die hard, and we observed radio silence and shot off a red flare to indicate a malfunction. Pip-Squeak came careening down the perimeter track in a battered Austin to investigate the Gee failure, and this brought us face to face with another crisis.

"As Pip-Squeak approached, I embraced the floorboards and the crew propped Meathead into the pilot's seat, coaching him. Meathead's lips were blue as he looked down at Pip Squeak and labouriously formed the words: 'Gee U.S.' Pip Squeak yelled up: 'Take X-Ray the spare kite!' Then he crunched gears on the Austin and was gone.

"Meathead's crew managed to trundle him down the taxiway while I darted behind parked aircraft like an Indian stalking a wagon train. Soon we were all assembled in X-Ray. Once again, I fired up and then we took off. It was all done observing proper radio silence. The approach to the coast in daylight brought a strange lack of flak.

"Meathead and I had shared many operations together and I was overcome by the drama of the moment: this was our first flight into peace. I think Meathead was similarly moved because he snorted and rolled over on his shoulder. We found the racetrack and dropped two target indicators at 100 feet as German troops sat in the bleachers waiting for show time. No shots were fired and I was startled at the sight of hundreds of Dutch citizens on the streets and in windows waving flags and bunting.

"This was the first of some 3,000 sorties during which Bomber Command delivered 6,670 tons of food but my memory and the official RCAF record are at odds on this first operation. As we approached our home base at Gransden Lodge, I encountered another problem: the normal request to join the circuit. If I used the RT my voice would be recognized.

"As I approached the base, a wartime career flashed before my eyes with a deep sense of foreboding. The Canadian government had been making seductive sounds to servicemen about gratuities and other goodies. I was 90 seconds away from destroying it all if I spoke. I looked down at the body that was now starting to look like a freshly caught Miramichi salmon twitching in the bottom of a boat.

"Meathead even managed to smile although he still showed signs of acute discomfort. 'Get him awake!' I said. I would be flying the plane but we needed Meathead alert and within reach of a mike or RT as we called it then. We rehearsed it and then Meathead came through as he had done on so many operations. He found the strength to mutter into the microphone: 'Chisel X-Ray to Ardmore...downwind out.'

"I flew the downwind leg. Then Meathead managed: 'Chisel X-Ray funnel!' Ardmore replied: 'Land now.' Which is what we did. Like a bubonic rat, I scurried to my quarters while Meathead's crew celebrated its mission of mercy. Aside from having two pilots for one Lanc, the lack of flak, the Germans in the bleachers and the Dutch people in the streets it was a routine operation.

"When the next battle order was posted, I was officially assigned my first Manna mission. The Yanks called it Chow Hound. When I told my crew about the reaction of the Dutch citizens and what to expect they gathered up all their goodies from parcels and quickly raised scrounging to a fine art as they prepared a special parcel to fit between the guns of the rear turret.

"As we approached our target our air bomber took over the aircraft directing me: 'Left, left steady!' Then we were over the target, hundreds of kids. The bombaimer yelled to the rear gunner: 'Now!' I banked away blinded by tears and a snotty nose as Tomlinson, the rear gunner, reported: 'The parcel hit the ground

...it ricocheted off the wall of that apartment building ... and Jesus Christ, I've never seen so many kids!'

"Our third sortie was to Rotterdam on May 7th. By now, without official blessing we were taking ground crew as spectators. A ladder was placed across the open rear door to provide an excellent view. One of the passengers was Freck, a diminutive of the Women's Auxiliary Air Force who had faithfully brought two buckets of hot water on the handles of her bicycle to our digs each morning for washing and shaving. I like to think that the flight to Rotterdam and the sight of hundreds of happy Dutch people was Freck's great event of WWII.

"Even though Bomber Command and I differ on how many Manna operations I flew, somehow they stuck with me for over half a century, long after the other operations were pushed to the back of my mind."

*Bomber crews found a joyous sense of finality and perhaps atonement in the food drops to the starving Dutch. (IWM)*

**ABOVE:** *A few hours before the atomic bomb fell on Nagasaki, Hammy Gray sank the Japanese cruiser* Amakusa, *but died in the action. He was awarded the Victoria Cross for his actions. (DND)*

**OPPOSITE PAGE:** *Harry Smith celebrated his 21ˢᵗ birthday by flying Liberators over Japanese territory on trips that lasted 10 minutes short of 24 hours. His mission to Khorat, however, lasted 17 days. (COURTESY HARRY SMITH)*

# 🐚 WINGS OVER THE PACIFIC

*HOURS AFTER THE FIRST* bombs fell on Pearl Harbour, some Canadians were in action 5,000 miles to the east as the Japanese assaulted the Malaysian peninsula. Early strikes wiped out 50 ancient RAF aircraft and within 48 hours the ships *The Prince of Wales* and *The Repulse* were sunk. This set the tone for Canada's forgotten war in the Pacific and South-East Asia. At the outset, some 35 Canadian airmen were operating in a vast area and some 350 radar technicians soon joined them. By the end of hostilities over 7,500 Canadian airmen would see service in a war that got no attention at home after the disaster at Hong Kong.

Immediately to the south of Malaya lay the island of Singapore, the so-called British Gibraltar of southeast Asia. Air defences were scattered and un-coordinated and the rivalry between the navy and RAF was so intense that a night-fighter squadron was forbidden to fly over the naval base at Seletar for any reason whatsoever. The patrols and heroism of RAF crews, however, was not enough to stop the Japanese who rolled down Malaya.

Six Canadians were flying with a Catalina squadron out of Seletar on the island of Singapore. On Christmas Eve, P/O D. Babineau was navigating a Catalina in search of Japanese fleets when they were attacked from the air and shot down. The flying-boat burned before life rafts could be deployed and the crew spent 11 hours in the water before a Dutch submarine picked them up. A number of Canadians were with two Hawker Hurricane squadrons that arrived in January, but the reinforcements did little to halt the Japanese surge threatening Sumatra. The early Hurricanes were no match for the Zeros and Sgt R. Mendizabel was badly shot up and wounded. Four days later, Sgt J.P. Fleming took out a Japanese fighter and then went down over Malaya. He was one of the first to evade the Japanese in the jungles of Malaya and six days later made his way back to Seletar. Flying out of Seletar, Sgt R.D. Bonnar, a Canadian navigator with #403 Squadron, later spotted a Japanese fleet and radioed a warning of its estimated time of arrival. Unfortunately, the information was of little use because the British had no defences, although at the fall of Singapore on February 15th 70,000 troops surrendered.

The Japanese also moved north into Burma and targeted Rangoon. The RAF mounted 37 old P-40s against some 400 Japanese machines, and in two enemy raids on Rangoon, they somehow managed to score 36 victories. During a brief lull, a squadron of Blenheims and 30 Hurricanes were added to the defences of Rangoon. In late February, the Japanese lost 61 fighters in two raids. But the aerial victories bought little time as the Japanese army rolled northward and Rangoon fell on March 6th.

By this time, the second British line of defence on Sumatra and Java was collapsing. As Java fell on March 8th, Mendizabel saw the last aircraft leave. Taking care to avoid Japanese patrols, Mendizabel and four other pilots reconstructed an aircraft out of scrap and a bunch of long-dead Lockheed trainers. They then flew an incredible 2,600 miles south to Ceylon.

While the British were fully engaged in North Africa, the first Japanese bombs fell on Malaya. Canadian Coastal Command #413 Squadron arrived in southeast Asia almost four months after that attack. The ground crew of #413 Squadron was still on the boat from Scotland and only two Catalina's were serviceable when the alarm went up in Ceylon. A Japanese task force was reported to be breaking across the Pacific. In three months, the Japanese had taken Hong Kong, Singapore and Malaya and had invaded the Philippines, Burma, Java, Borneo and Sumatra. Now two large task forces steamed into the Indian Ocean. The British under Admiral

Sir James Somerville had tried to establish a presence in Ceylon. It consisted of five WWI battleships, 23 other ships and the most promising features, aircraft carriers *Indomitable* and *Formidable* and the light carrier *Hermes*. But all they had to launch were 57 obsolete strike planes and 36 fighters from another age.

The British intercepted a message that Japanese Vice Admiral Chuichi Nagumo's task force was heading for Ceylon while a second force was heading for the Bay of Bengal. On April 4, 1942, Sqd/Ldr Len Birchall's Catalina was one of two that took off from Koggala to seek the enemy. By daybreak, he was 250 miles southeast of Ceylon and his crew spent the next 12 hours droning at 90 m.p.h. in a monotonous search. The Catalina had excellent range so they had lots of time as

P/O Bart Onyette watched the rising moon while waiting to get an astro fix. It put the lone Catalina some 350 miles south of Ceylon, and Birchall, of St. Catharines, Ont., was about to call it a day when a dot appeared on the horizon. As they flew closer the dots multiplied and became an enemy fleet. They identified most of a force of five aircraft carriers containing 360 aircraft, four battleships, three cruisers, 11 destroyers and seven submarines. Carrier-based fighters attacked as Sgt F.G. Phillips transmitted a message and on the third transmission canon fire smashed the wireless and Phillips was seriously wounded. Internal tanks burst into flames and the crew fought fires until the flying boat began to break up. They were too low to jump, but Birchall got the machine down before the tail fell off.

Eight of the nine-man crew managed to get out of the aircraft that was still under intense fire. One air gunner whose leg had been severed went down with the plane. Two were unconscious and were pulled through burning gasoline. The injured men wore life jackets and as enemy fighters continued to strafe, the others were able to dive under water, but the men with life jackets were killed. By the time they were picked up by a Japanese destroyer three of the six survivors were seriously wounded.

On board the destroyer, they were beaten and interrogated, but insisted they had not sent out a message. Things did not improve when the Japanese intercepted a message from Koggala asking Phillips to repeat his last communiqué. Birchall's message had a definite effect on Ceylon. Merchantmen from Colombo harbour fled to sea hoping to escape detection. Somerville's task force meanwhile took the somewhat un-Nelsonian route to Addu Atoll where it refuelled and hid some 600 miles southwest of Ceylon.

Nagumo sent 91 bombers and 36 fighters against Colombo the next day and the force was met by 42 land-based Hurricanes. Of this number 19 were lost to the enemy's seven. One destroyer and one armed merchant cruiser were also sunk and shore facilities damaged. Enemy aircraft later found British heavy cruisers *Dorsetshire* and *Cornwall*, which they immediately sank. Four days later, F/Lt R. Thomas in #413's last operational Catalina spotted a second attacking force. He reported the Japanese fleet 200 miles off the port of Trincomalee then went missing. Shipping was again dispersed and the RAF put up 22 fighters and nine Blenheim bombers of which five were shot down. The port was damaged and one merchantman sunk, and the second wave of Nagumo's pilots found the first of Somerville's ships. They sank the *Hermes*, all its aircraft, a destroyer, a corvette and two tankers.

The attack on Ceylon was a raid rather than an invasion and Birchall's warning, for which he was awarded the DFC, saved lives and resources. The Canadian Press dubbed him the "Saviour of Ceylon" and this has led to some misinterpretation. The British did little to save Ceylon but Birchall's heroic action enabled Somerville's five battleships and three aircraft carriers to escape.

Birchall's crew endured three days on the destroyer and then was transferred to the aircraft carrier *Akagi*. The three most seriously injured were sent to sick bay, but the other three became subject to nightly beatings en route to Yokohama. Beatings, starvation, disease and cruelty became part of the lives of all Japanese POWs. Birchall found himself with yet another task in several prison camps. He became the senior officer and, as such, for three and a half years was the key figure in helping others survive.

The work force in a barracks was depleted by jaundice, beri beri, dysentery, starvation and massive boils. On one occasion, the sergeant of the guard ordered all sick out of bed and began to beat their massive boils. Birchall lost his cool and knocked the guard down. Then the storm broke and he was thrown into solitary, beaten and hung up by his thumbs. A kangaroo court in Tokyo ordered that he be shot. Birchall was taken out and endured the charade of the firing squad loading rifles. The execution was delayed because only honourable people deserved to be shot. The Japanese later explained that he would be beheaded. This time he was taken out where he knelt as a sword swished past his head. Then he was thrown into solitary for two weeks.

When finally released after the war, Len Birchall was awarded the Order of the British Empire in recognition of his service to fellow prisoners. His diary, consisting of 22 volumes, was used as evidence in war crime trials after the war.

In the air and on the ground, Birchall set the standard for the RCAF Coastal Command, which at that time was struggling to meet the challenges of a war over another ocean.

~ ~ ~ ~ ~ ~ ~ ~ ~ ~

After inflicting crippling losses on the British, Admiral Nagumo withdrew his fleet presumably because of air losses. Three of his aircraft carriers were sent back to Japan for replacements of crews and aircraft. It was a decision, which might be compared to Göring's decision to launch his aircraft against London during the Battle of Britain instead of pursuing the attack on airfields. Nagumo's lack of action gave the British time to re-organize and belatedly concentrate on the disaster at Rangoon that had fallen about a month earlier. Some 30 Canadians were with RAF units that were withdrawn from Burma and relocated to India, but by the summer of 1942, the Japanese were victims of their own success. They had taken one-third of the earth's surface and it now required defending.

Such defences were spread from the Aleutians to Sumatra and although the Indian Ocean remained a hunting ground, the invasion of India or Australia, to the south, were not high priorities. Most of the Allied ground action was defensive until Lord Louis Mountbatten became head of the South East Asia Command (SEAC) in October 1943. Among other things, he integrated the RAF and USAF operations, which meant some 1,100 aircraft were now being flown by airmen from Britain, Canada, Australia, New Zealand, South Africa, India and the United States. The Allies began striking back after a massive airlift of troops and supplies from India.

One of the first Allied land actions was a push on the Arakan coast of Burma. The air force struck Japanese supply and communications centres at tree-top height helping the army hack out a tenuous footing. However, the monsoons soon washed out the gains, but a new pattern of warfare was developing. British General Orde Wingate's Chindits launched a new type of invasion when seven columns of commandos slashed their way through 1,000 miles of jungle. Every ounce of food and supplies was supplied by air. By the end of 1943, Beaufighters and Hurricanes dominated the 700-mile front that ran down to Burma. But if a pilot went down, he inherited a mess of troubles not found in any other theatre of war. He had to contend with heat, monsoons, hostile natives, the jungle and any number of creatures therein. F/Lt Bob Johnson soon found it out for himself.

The Charlottetown pilot was shot down on a fighter-reconnaissance mission and managed to jump near a Burmese village. During a 24-day trek to freedom, he fled not only from the Burmese and Japanese soldiers, but from the local animal population as well, including a king cobra that slid over his body while he tried to sleep. At one point, Johnson met a Japanese soldier at arms length on a narrow trail and there were 20 more behind him. He lowered his head and grunted as he walked past a squad of enemy troops. Then he cut for the hills where after 23 days he managed to contact an Indian unit.

When the enemy attempted the invasion of India, they laid siege to Kohima and Imphal, two small but critical points along the border. The 80-day siege was finally broken by starvation and disease among the attacking forces. Low morale was also a factor. Regular airlifts supplied that Allied troops while the enemy starved for food and ordinance. As one Japanese prisoner put it: "It broke our hearts to see the stuff dropping on British troops day after day, while we got nothing."[41] The supply line from India also dropped agents who sought allies, and formed underground units. F/O Harry Smith of Winnipeg flew 25 such missions.

## WHEN CAVU BROUGHT SNAFU IN SIAM

Another circuit or two and F/O Harry Smith could have logged 24 hours for the 3,000 mile flight to Singapore on May 26, 1945. Next day Harry Smith's B-24 crew at Jessore, India, was briefed for its 25th mission, an airdrop some 600 miles behind Japanese lines in Siam. Harry finished reading *You Only Die Once* and later sat through the station movie *For Whom the Bell Tolls*. He had just celebrated his 21st birthday and wondered if somebody up there was trying to tell him something as they made their way out to P-Peter, his aircraft, just before midnight.

The Liberator nudged the end of the runway. Smith still fretted about the late takeoff. After dropping three members of the American Office of Strategic Services (OSS) and their cargo near Khorat, Siam, they would face daylight and 600 miles of hostile sky on the return flight. As Smith of Winnipeg tripped the brakes and sent the heavy Liberator charging down the runway, Bill Pugh's concerns were more immediate. The dispatcher wireless operator contemplated the chances of getting a load of more than 64,000 pounds airborne before reaching the trees at the end of the runway. He later allowed as to how there was a high incidence of sweat on takeoff as four members of the OSS, in addition to a crew of 10 waited for the wheels to stop rumbling. The fourth member of the OSS was an observer who would not be jumping with the others.

Tension faded when the heavily laden #358 Squadron Special Duties aircraft embraced the night sky. Within half an hour, navigator Lofty Brenchley confirmed they were on course and the Yanks were asleep amid an amazing litter of gear. Earlier, co-pilot Bob Poole was placing bets they wouldn't get out the escape hatch with the gear on, but as P-Peter droned over the Bay of Bengal, the routine over the drop zone seemed worlds away.

They made the Siam coast by 6:30 a.m. and the sun exploded in a cloudless sky. Smith was on his descent to the drop zone. "For the first time in a year and a half the sky was completely clear," he recalled. "Ceiling and visibility unlimited. Wall to wall CAVU! No hiding place today!" But CAVU soon turned into SNAFU as bomb-aimer Jack Draper called: "Enemy fighters at two o'clock." Nine Japanese Oscars were closing fast.

"Three set up a race track for head-on attacks; three did the same on the starboard quarter and three strafed from below and above. I began violent evasive manoeuvres and dove for the deck," Smith said. "The frontal attacks were devastating. We were systematically being shot to pieces. Our navigator Lofty Brenchley was killed in one of the first attacks. Bill "Pinky" Pinckney, the mid-upper, fired steady bursts until he too was hit." Wireless operator Bill Pugh was blown from his station as explosions destroyed all radio equipment. Pinky Pinckney in the mid-upper was badly wounded but still firing. Timber Woods another wireless operator was injured about the face and arms.

According to Pugh: "Jack Draper came up from his position in the nose in a bad way – he was injured but no one could tell how badly – and said that Lofty Parsons had been killed and it was a big mess down there." Smith was unable to raise Draper on the intercom and ordered co-pilot Bob Poole to jettison the containers. Poole gripped the toggle between the seats and only five containers had fallen free when he was mortally hit in the chest. Smith called for crash positions as airspeed bled off and the jungle rushed up. "The only hope of survival was to try the treetop landing technique used by bush pilots back home," he recalled. "I lowered the flaps to reduce airspeed and dropped the undercarriage to absorb some of the energy of the impact."

When trees scraped the belly of the aircraft he put both feet on the instrument panel and hauled back on the control column. Ramsay Roe had completed 300 operational hours and was flying one last trip to screen newcomer Lofty Parsons. The gunner/dispatcher wrote: "The alarm bell sounded ... the noise of the crashing plane was beyond description ... caused by the continuing fighter bombardment, exploding ammunition and oxygen canisters and the sound of the plane's wings shearing off."

Smith remembered: "The wings with their load of fuel sheared off right away: good riddance, I thought." Roe said he was not sure what happened after impact, but he remembered seeing the aircraft burning, ammunition exploding and a profusion of table tennis balls, which had been in the wings to provide floatation. Suddenly, it became very important to collect the table tennis balls, which he was scooping up when the look on the other faces brought him back to reality.

Bob Poole, Jack Draper, Bill Pinckney and Lofty Benchley were dead. Harry Smith lost blood from a serious head wound; Taffy Parsons had a bullet in his foot and Timber Woods had shrapnel up his nose and arms while Bill Pugh and Ramsay Roe also had shrapnel wounds. Curley Copley was relatively unscathed. Among the OSS agents, Cpl. Naparolski was mortally wounded, Maj. Gildee had a broken collarbone, Sgt. McCarthy suffered a fractured back, and Lt. Reid had severe burns to his left thigh. Pugh spoke for all when he later wrote: "Those of us who did survive owe our lives to Smithy for his courageous and skilful piloting against overwhelming odds of nine to one."

Naparolski couldn't be moved and to the dismay of his crew, Smith decided to stay with him and send the others off under Maj. Gildee's direction. He gave Gildee his revolver, a map, and a compass and told him to move south because there were 300,000 Japanese to the north who were fleeing Burma. Naparolski died minutes after the others departed. Smith had lost a lot of blood and was sitting against a tree about two hours later when he heard voices. He gripped his Sten submachine gun, but the voices belonged to natives who the main party had sent back. At the village, the natives brought a mirror to Smith who for the first time, saw the extent of his head wound.

"I got the flap of scalp more or less in place and wrapped it in a bandage. By evening we were all reunited at a village similar to something out of *National*

*Geographic,*" he recalled in a submission to a publication by the Pilots and Observers Association. Next morning, a Thai police lieutenant rode up warning of the approach of the Japanese. His patrol took them by bullock cart to a nearby stream where they hid and had their last K-ration and cigarette. All they were left with was a book of matches that read: "Jolly good luck to you wherever you are from Dromedary Foods." A further two days travel and the group boarded a boat for a four-day trip to Bangkok where 15,000 Japanese manned the local garrison. They got to Thai police headquarters in an ancient bus and were bedded down in a cell-like dorm.

The Thai police and armed forces acted as an underground in an occupied country and it immediately became imperative to them that the Japanese not learn of the attempted OSS drop.

During the night a plan was devised to get the OSS agents and Smith, as captain of the aircraft, out of reach. There was room for one more airman and Smith chose Curley Copley because of his long service.

Smith woke Timber Woods and told him of the plan, instructing him to tell Japanese interrogators that the Liberator had been on a meteorological flight. The OSS would keep tabs on those who were being left behind as internees of the Thai. Then Smith, Copley and the three OSS agents were taken to OSS headquarters, which happened to be in the palace of the Regent of Siam. After a few days of lavish living, they noticed the palace was under observation. By midnight the next day, the party moved out. Halfway up a hill in the heart of Bangkok during curfew, their ancient bus started backfiring and drew the attention of a Japanese patrol.

The Thai driver explained to the enemy that he was taking prisoners to jail and while he talked, the bus was ready for acceleration as five breach blocks clicked behind the straw curtain of the bus. The group later returned to the palace, but hit a home run the next night, arriving at a tiny airfield where they were flown out in two small aircraft. For Smith and Copley it was the first leg of a journey back to Calcutta.

The Japanese interrogated Timber Woods, but they soon had bigger problems than the downed crew. A flight of bombers approached the compound and demolished a nearby railway station and freight yard. Pugh recalled: "Then it happened – word spread around the camp like wildfire – the Americans had bombed Hiroshima in Japan with what they were calling an atom bomb that literally destroyed the city – one bomb!"

By mid-September, crew survivors were in Bombay. Harry Smith had been awarded the DFC and a reunion was held at the Taj Mahal hotel. Roe maintained that "Never was a DFC, with which he was awarded, more deserved."

Bill Pugh noted: "It was truly a wonderful reunion but touched with immense sadness over the loss of our fellow crew members and this, I think, caused us all to drown our sorrows a little."[42]


## CROSSING THE IRRAWADDY:

The airlifts across the Burma road to China and the Ledo road to India as well as airdrops to isolated British units gave the Allies a new offensive power. By the end of 1944, they were pushing into Burma. Additional fighters and bombers won superiority in the air and as the war wound down, the Japanese left well over 100,000 dead in Burma. A Canadian airman played a most unusual role in the final British push to Mandalay and Rangoon.

F/Lt Harry Avery of Ottawa was an ardent swimmer who, when not supervising the installation of radar sets on bombers, was swimming in the Bristol Channel. One day, the adjutant's assistant proudly told him that she had put him down for something. "We volunteered you for a special unit," she beamed. Two weeks later, Avery was on his way to Portsmouth undergoing tests for Mountbatten's Sea Reconnaissance Unit.

In mid-February 1945, Avery was a leader of one of four sections of frogmen who first scouted enemy shore where four units would be crossing the Irrawaddy. Then they later led the attack and engaged in traffic control approaching enemy shore. After the highly successful operation, Avery was briefed for another mission where they would slip into Singapore and infiltrate enemy shipping. The operation was scrubbed when the atomic bomb fell on Hiroshima. Three days after it was dropped, Lt. Hammy Gray of the Fleet Air Arm prepared for another ramrod.


## HAMMY GRAY'S LAST RAMROD

For four years Robert Hampton Gray played the old service game of hurry up and wait. A native of Nelson, B.C., he left the University of British Columbia in 1940 to join the Royal Canadian Volunteer Service (RCNVR) and later transferred to the Fleet Air Arm. Although his brother John was killed returning from a mine-laying mission early in 1942, the closest Hammy got to action was flying ancient Skuas out to sea to test radios. There was a brief tour in the Mediterranean and a period in South Africa where the mild-mannered pilot distinguished himself by reporting from a Christmas party with a black eye.

Back in England, he missed action on D-Day and it seemed that the war might run its course without him. But during the years of frustration, Gray showed promise at administrative duties and, when posted to #1841 Squadron aboard the *Formidable*, he was made senior pilot. On August 22, 1944, Hammy Gray finally flew out to action – well, near action. An air strike of Barracudas and Corsairs set out for the German Battleship *Tirpitz* that was holed up in a Norwegian fjord Kåfjord, but the first mission was aborted because of weather. Two days later, the *Formidable* launched 18 Corsairs and 16 Barracudas. Gray led a flight of Corsairs down into Kåfjord where numerous destroyers and shore-based flak batteries surrounded the *Tirpitz*.

At low level, the Corsairs endured intense flak, but they drew away fire from the Barracudas, which bombed without success. Seven Fleet Air Arm machines were lost, but another strike went in five days later. This time an armoured-piercing bomb sliced through eight decks of the *Tirpitz*, but failed to explode. Hammy again led his flight on water-level attacks on three destroyers that returned heavy fire. Once again, the Corsairs drew fire away from the Barracudas and Gray was Mentioned in Despatches for his leadership.

Gray underwent another period of enforced boredom as the *Formidable* underwent a refit and spent months being readied for service in the South East Asia Command. The aircraft carrier joined Task Force 57 of the British Pacific Fleet that on May 4, 1945, was attacking an airfield and flak positions on the island of Miyako Jima.

By mid-July the British task force joined the American 3rd Fleet for assaults on the Japanese mainland. On July 28th, Hammy Gray led a low-level strike against the naval base at Maisuru and sank a Japanese destroyer, earning himself a Distinguished Service Cross. His victory came the day after Canada withdrew the HMS *Uganda* from the war.

On August 6th, Col. Paul Tibbets Jr. pulled the *Enola Gay* off the runway at Tinian and flew almost 3,000 kilometres northwest to Hiroshima, a city of 245,000. He was accompanied by two other B-29s that recorded what happened when bombardier Major Thomas Ferebee tripped the release sending "Little Boy" plunging from 31,600 feet. The bombers were 15 miles away when the flash and concussion from the atomic bomb struck.

Three days later, the *Formidable* scheduled three ramrods or fighter sweeps. The first ramrod went out early and Hammy Gray was to lead the second ramrod against airfields on Honshu. Gray waited in his Corsair when a messenger made his way through propellers and shouted up to Gray: "The target's been changed!" The second ramrod would hit shipping in Onagawa Bay.

About an hour and a half later, Hammy Gray led eight Corsairs down from 10,000 feet to water level in an approach that came from inland. Hills surrounded the bay and the pilots had only four seconds for a level bombing run. Gray plunged through the hills to water level and ran into a blast of cannon and machine gun fire from three ships. The pilot behind him saw flames as a bomb was shot off and Hammy dove towards the *Amakusa*. Gray's second bomb penetrated the engine room of the *Amakusa,* blowing up an ammunition magazine. The destroyer quickly capsized and sank. Gray flew towards the exit, but the Corsair suddenly trailed smoke and flame. Then it rolled to the right and hit the water. Hammy Gray died minutes before an atomic bomb destroyed Nagasaki and brought about the Japanese surrender six days later. He was posthumously awarded the Victoria Cross.

That afternoon Gray's stunned squadron flew another ramrod and Lt. G.A. Anderson's aircraft was damaged by flak and lost fuel. The Belleville pilot's engine cut out on the landing approach and he crashed into the stern of the *Formidable* and was killed. He was probably the last Canadian to die in action in WWll.

**ABOVE:** *Typical of the thousands of Canadians who served with RAF squadrons is this group, pictured while on the Arakan coast of Burma. (DND)*

**RIGHT:** *The groundcrew for 413 Squadron was still on the boat from Scotland when Leonard Birchell flew a Catalina out from Ceylon in search of a Japanese fleet. He was shot down, but not before getting off a warning message. (PL-7405)*

**ABOVE:** *Omer Levesque survived prison camp in WWII and later became the first Canadian to bring down a MiG while attached to the USAF in Korea. (DND)*

**OPPOSITE PAGE:** *Sqd/Ldr Andy MacKenzie was shot down twice by the Americans, but his greatest battle became his two years as a Chinese POW of which 18 months were spent in a solitary cell. (DND)*

# 👒 PEACE & POLICE ACTION

*Canadian Sabre pilots close an era born*
*in 1916 and pioneer a new one...*
*The Right Stuff*

*IN 1939 CANADA BEGAN* the Second World War with an air force of some 4,000 personnel and less than 25 remotely competitive aircraft. When peace was won in 1945, the RCAF was the fourth largest air force in the world. With a strength approaching 250,000, it left behind a brilliant legacy at home and around the world. But the real success of Canada's air experience went beyond size or operations flown abroad. It was a unique example of Canadians motivated by a sense of unity, and a determination by the government, the RCAF, and civilians to show the world that we had the right stuff.

Such a quality was not immediately evident in 1939 when Prime Minister Chamberlain originally asked Canada to help with training aircrew. There was a period of stick handling by Prime Minister Mackenzie King who feared such a program might mean disapproval in Quebec. However, once King became committed to the idea, his government, the RCAF and the people of Canada reacted with a sense of unity and determination that made the British Commonwealth Air Training Plan our finest hour.

The bedrock of the plan was civilian. Some 22 flying clubs across Canada volunteered to train pilots and 17 of these became Elementary Flying Schools. Although staffed by civilians, the RCAF provided the aircraft. Then as demand increased, a large number of civilian pilots came forward as instructors. Before being allowed to instruct they were carefully screened and put through a Flying Instructors' Course. There was also a large civilian input in Air Observer Schools. Civilian pilots from firms such as Canadian Pacific Airlines flew aircraft on training flights where RCAF personnel instructed and monitored students.

Although the BCATP accepted some 40,000 women in order to release men for flying duties, it stopped short of assigning licensed female pilots to the same task. Eileen Vollick became the first woman to win a license in 1928 when she flew a ski equipped open-cockpit Jenny to the satisfaction of Jack Elliott at Hamilton. At least five Canadian female pilots later served with the Air Transport Auxiliary in England, flying every type of aircraft through congested skies in deplorable weather.

As any person who ever buckled on a parachute knew, the success of his or her operation depended on a team of experts who remained behind at takeoff. They were the riggers and fitters, the engine mechanics and the armourers, radiomen and radar technicians, and a host of other ground tradesmen who made an operational flight possible. The BCATP was the entry point not only for aircrew, but the indispensable ground crew as well.

The impact of the plan on small communities across Canada was immeasurable and the converse is true. The delights of a Dafoe, Sask., or Chatham, N.B., impressed thousands of 18-year-old trainees with its soda fountains, Tommy Dorsey records, and seductive women in saddle shoes and bobby socks. The community response was often at the soul of the plan that produced 131,533 airmen. Of these 73,825 were Canadians who operated on 43 squadrons around the world, while 28,500 served with the RAF.

Fifteen Canadian squadrons shared in the bombing war while five squadrons flew on Coastal Command. Three squadrons flew with Fighter Command and 17 became very active with the 2nd TAF. One squadron saw service with the Desert Air Force in Italy and two transport squadrons flew in the Far East. An estimated 17,000 Canadians died as a result of the air war, but many survivors went on to productive lives. The federal government responded with generous rehabilitation measures and many former airmen were in university four months after the end of the war. One man who flew his last operation on May 2nd sat in university classrooms that fall listening to a professor delve into the wonders of Beowulf. The professor went to great lengths to explain the author's description of ripples on the ocean as seen from the air. He then made a point of explaining to the class that this was exactly how the ocean appeared from the air. The former pilot choked as he consulted his timetable to see if the next class offered anything better. He was one of thousands who picked up a civilian life, but a few remained in the RCAF and would again see combat in what the politicians called a "police action."

## WINGS OVER THE YALU

Ten North Korean divisions swept into South Korea on June 21,1950, and by the end of the month Prime Minister Louis St. Laurent cautiously told Parliament that Canada would take part in a collective police action under the authority of the newly-created United Nations. St Laurent's words found action one month later as six North Star aircraft from #426 Squadron at Dorval set course for McChord Air Force Base in Tacoma, Wash. The cargo planes soon made the first of some 600 trips to Tokyo where they flew some 13,000 passengers and three million kilograms of freight to what became a distribution zone for the Korean War. In addition to the crews, some 2,000 RCAF personnel were involved in keeping the transports flying. Although #426 Squadron was the only RCAF unit directly involved, 22 fighter pilots with distinguished WWII records were gradu-ally assigned to the American air force as exchange officers.

Sqd/Ldr Omer Levesque was the first. A veteran fighter pilot from the Second World War, Levesque flew with #401 Squadron from Biggin Hill in September 1941. During a sweep over France, they were hit by a gaggle of Me-109s and the new FW 190. Levesque duelled with a 190 from 20,000 feet and became the first Allied pilot to destroy the new fighter. His sketch of the formidable machine was later distributed throughout Fighter Command. In February 1942, he became involved in the Channel Dash. He recalled, "I was leading a section when the German warships *Scharnhorst, Gneisenau* and *Prinz Eugen* slipped out from Brest and made their way up the Channel. We were ordered to orbit over Canterbury for several minutes when we could actually see the Germans dashing at full speed up the Channel."

"I broke off my section and immediately ran into 40 enemy fighters near the battle cruisers. ... After several squirts at 109s and 190s, I was badly hit and being too low to bail out had to ditch in the rough sea ...and was picked up later by a German flagship."

With four victories, Levesque finished the war in Stalag Luft 3 near Berlin, but remained in the RCAF after 1945. He flew with the RCAF's first aerobatic team *The Blue Devils* and became an exchange officer with the USAF two months before the invasion of South Korea. The RCAF program was designed to give its top pilots experience on the most advanced American jets. Levesque soon passed out on the F-16 and by November shipped out to Korea.

By mid-December 1950, he flew the first of 61 missions with American #334 Fighter Interceptor Squadron in support of B-29 heavy bombers. Ironically, the squadron began as the Eagle Squadron, which was formed by Yanks in the RAF during the Battle of Britain. Now a Canadian from Mont-Joli was having right back at them. But the squadron was barely operational at Kimpo airport when the North Koreans broke through to nearby Seoul, forcing an evacuation to Japan. From there Levesque did 26 home defence missions, before the squadron returned to Korea where enemy MiGs had then appeared over the Yalu River. The aerial battleground became the Yalu valley some 200 miles behind the enemy lines.

The MiG pilots had the advantage of climbing to a height, which exceeded the altitude of the F-86 Sabres over friendly territory and then pouncing on the American escorts and bombers. If things became difficult they could then pop over to Manchuria where the Yanks could not venture.

On May 31, 1951, Levesque's squadron rendezvoused with 20 B-29s at 28,000 feet over Pyongang along with 32 F-86s, which climbed higher to provide top cover. The Sabres were flying much faster than the bombers and had to form a protective circuit. As the fighters got closer to the bombers, they encountered not-so-friendly fire from the bombers. Levesque later recalled, "We waggled our wings and the shooting stopped."

"Afterwards," he said, "a couple of MiGs hopped across from Manchuria and took a pass at the B-29s. I tailed one in and followed him in a turn twice. He climbed trying to lose me in the sun, but I was wearing dark glasses ... I hit him with a deflection shot from my six .50 calibre guns and it seemed to damage his hydraulic system because he went into an uncontrollable roll and went down and exploded."

Levesque remained on operations for six months. His victory over the MiG was Canada's introduction to jet combat and six of the Canadians who later moved into the Korean theatre destroyed nine MiGs. Readers may recall that Sqd/Ldr John MacKay of Arbaka, Man., was flying a Spitfire the day he and four other pilots destroyed a German 262 jet in Europe. MacKay must also hold an unofficial record for ammunition economy because on three occasions he downed an enemy without firing a shot. When the Luftwaffe welcomed 1945 by sending over 800 aircraft against Allied bases in Europe, MacKay was scrambled from Heech and vectored to a spot in the Reichwald forest. He destroyed one machine on the ground and as he was returning to base, spotted a FW sliding onto the tail of a Tempest. Shortly after engaging it he ran out of ammunition, but continued to close on the enemy and eventually drove it into the frozen lake where it blew up. MacKay pulled up to engage a Me-109 and once again tried the tactic otherwise known as a bluff. It worked. This time the enemy aircraft flew into trees and blew up. Three days later, MacKay was engaging a FW 190 at low level when the pilot lost control and crashed.

MacKay had 11 victories and one shared in Europe and his victory over a MiG in Korea was the last claimed by a Canadian. However, in between Levesque's first and MacKay's last victory, F/Lt Ernest Glover of Niagara Falls, Ont., accounted for three MiGs and Sqd/Ldr James Lindsay of Arnprior, Ont., scored two. Flight lieutenants Claude Lafrance, Quebec City, and L. Spurr of Middleton, N.S., each claimed one.

Sqd/Ldr Andy MacKenzie went into action in Korea with eight victories from the Second World War, but the Yank jinx caught up with the resident of Oxford Mills, Ont., roughly 20 miles south of the Yalu on December 8, 1952. Trigger-happy Yank gunners had shot him down in Normandy less than a week after D-Day and he was also the victim of friendly fire as he was about to engage 20 MiGs south of the Yalu. An American jet blew his canopy off at 42,000 feet. His Sabre took hits in the right aileron and fuselage, and within a few seconds he was rolling to earth in a dead bird.

He ejected at 40,000 feet and tumbled earthward in the seat at 500 m.p.h. The rush of air was like a knife, slicing off his helmet, oxygen mask, identification card and even his watch. MacKenzie released his seat, kicked his way clear and then pulled the ripcord. He floated down on North Korea, watching two trucks move towards the hill that he hit with a crunch. An old lady looked up from her task of gathering grass for fuel. When MacKenzie touched down, she merely shrugged and went back to work.

Down the hill some 30 enemy soldiers leaped from the trucks, and bullets soon ricocheted off rocks as MacKenzie tried to scramble upwards. Somehow the top of the hill represented freedom, but the strain of falling 40,000 feet without oxygen took its toll, and when he reached the point when he couldn't crawl MacKenzie turned and faced his captors. They stopped firing and surrounded him and took him to the truck. It was the start of a two-year ordeal. Although the war would be over in seven months, Andrew MacKenzie became the victim of two years of mind-bending captivity. During this period, Chinese interpreters would insist that he had been ordered to fly over China, had flown over China and was shot down over China. The Canadian's denial brought 465 days in solitary confinement often in cells with no window, chair or bed. On occasions when his cell would contain a cot, he would be forced to sit at attention throughout the day without being able to stand or walk. It was not until December 5, 1954 when the Canadian government, through the UN, managed to negotiate his release – two years to the hour from the time he was shot down. During most of this time he was engaged in a vicious battle for mind control. "And the only thing that sustained me was thoughts of my wife and four children," he later recalled.

The air war in Korea can be divided into several distinct areas each with varying degrees of success. F-86 patrols over MiG Alley were quite successful, accounting for 792 MiGs destroyed. B-29 crews, meanwhile, were frustrated by primitive conditions in Korea. Few industrial targets existed and transportation targets often consisted of mule trains in mountain passes. Wasteful saturation bombing of questionable targets resulted.

In North Africa and after D-Day in Northern Europe, the rapport between the army and the 2nd Tactical Air Force produced taxi rank efficiency in ground support. A call would bring out a Typhoon flown by a pilot who had full information on the ground situation. This type of co-operation was presumably missing for some time in Korea, but once again the fighter-bomber became a major factor in land action.

Korea was a new frontier in air combat. Height was once the fighter pilot's greatest advantage, but in Korea height above 30,000 left telltale contrails that chalked one's position. Whereas in the Battle of Britain attacking pilots often got so close to an enemy they were hit by debris, in Korea missiles enabled a pilot to score from up to three miles away. Since then smart bombs, stealth bombers and electronics, which can detect what conventional radar cannot, have become tools of the air war. Currently the modern defence industry is at work researching attack "pilots" that will operate from a trailer in some deserted field while directing unmanned aircraft at a target. Perhaps the air war has become an expensive Nintendo game that Canada can no longer afford to play. But from Petawawa to the Yalu and beyond, Canada's personnel both in the air and on the ground have left a proud heritage for this new millennium.

*Some 22 Canadians flew the F-86 Sabre in Korea and downed nine MiGs. As they opened a new era of combat, Sqd/Ldr Omer Levesque remembered the D-Day markings on Allied aircraft. The resultant identification stripes then became the most useful in jet combat. (USAF)*

# ENDNOTES

1 Marching to Armageddon, Desmond Morton & Jack Granatstein, Lester & Orphen Dennys.

2 Starling Burgess' notes.

3 Ibid.

4 Publication on 75th Anniversary of RCAF.

5 Ibid.

6 Flying Fury, J. McCudden, Doubleday

7 The Brave Young Wings, Ron Dodds, Canada's Wing

8 Air Command, Raymond Collishaw, Kimber

9 Ibid

10 German Fighting Machines, Osprey

11 Canadian Airmen and the First World War, S. Wise, U of T Press

12 Air Command, Raymond Collishaw, Kimber

13 Ibid

14 The Red Knight of Germany, F. Gibbons, Bantam

15 Winged Warfare, W. Bishop, McLelland-Stewart

16 Air Command, Raymond Collishaw, Kimber

17 Winged Warfare, W. Bishop, McLelland-Stewart

18 Open Cockpit, A. Gould Lee

19 Words and Music of a Mechanical Man, O. Stewart

20 Ibid

21 Zeppelins, Ernst Lehmann

22 The Great Air War, Aaron Norman, Macmillan

23 The Zeppelin Fighters, Arch Whitehouse, NEL

24 Monsters of the Purple Twilight, E. Dudley

25 The Great Air War, Aaron Norman, Macmillan

26 Canadian Airmen in the First World War, S. Wise

27 Ibid

28 Tommy Williams, interview with the author

29 Ibid

30 Canadian Airmen in the First World War, S. Wise

31 Ibid

32 The Day the Red Baron Died, D. Tiller, Ballantine

33 Flying Minnows, V. Ross

34 The First of the Few, D. Winter, Penguin

35 Ibid

36 War in a Stringbag, Charles Lamb, Arrow Books

37 Airwar, E. Jablonski, Doubleday

38 The Right of the Line, J. Terraine, Wordsworth, p-169

39 Churchill, The 2nd World War, Volume 4

40 The First and The Last, A. Galland, Methune

41 From an interview with Bill Pugh

42 Interview with Harry Smith

43 The First and the Last, A. Galland, Methune

44 Bomber Offensive, Sir Arthur Harris, Stoddart

45 The Nuremberg Raid, M. Middlebrook, Penguin

46 Interview with Jim Kelly

47 Interview with Cal Willis

48 Interview with Richard Bison

49 Bomber Offensive, Sir Arthur Harris, Stoddart

50 The First and The Last, A. Galland, Methune

51 Destruction of Dresden, David Irving, Ballantine

52 Ibid

# Index

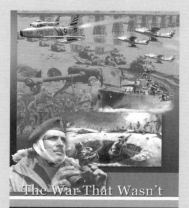